INTRODUCTION TO SCHOOL COUNSELING

Introduction to
School Counseling

Becoming a Leader, Advocate, and Change Agent

Richard D. Parsons, Ph.D., and Karen L. Dickinson, Ph.D.

Bassim Hamadeh, CEO and Publisher
Amy Smith, Senior Project Editor
Casey Hands, Production Editor
Emely Villavicencio, Senior Graphic Designer
Trey Soto, Licensing Specialist
Natalie Piccotti, Director of Marketing
Kassie Graves, Vice President of Editorial
Jamie Giganti, Director of Academic Publishing

Printed in the United States of America.

We dedicate this text to all those who walk alongside of others in times of need, and to our family and friends who are alongside of us in our journeys.

RDP & KLD, 2021

Brief Contents

Detailed Contents

Preface

First Lady Michelle Obama, in her 2014 address to the members of the American School Counseling Association, gave voice to a reality that school counselors have long known.

> You all have one of the hardest, most stressful, most important and most underappreciated jobs of anyone in this country—and I live with the President of the United States. So frankly, when I think about what you all do on an average day, well, quite frankly, I'm amazed.

The 21st-century school counselor is called to assist in the elimination of obstacles to academic success, as well as to provide counseling and respond to problems such as suicide, sudden death, drug and alcohol abuse, and physical and sexual abuse. While research supports the essential value of school counselors in addressing these and other challenges to our students' well-being and academic achievement, for many their value remains underappreciated.

Perhaps one of the greatest struggles or challenges facing the school counselor, one potentially contributing to this underappreciation, is the failure to articulate a clear professional identity. Professional identity for school counselors has been fluid, shifting, and somewhat elusive. The failure of achieving recognition and clear consensus among those we serve in regard to the role, function, and value of school counselors and counseling has contributed to this experience of being underappreciated.

But it is not simply the failure of our stakeholders to understand the what and why of school counseling. For too long those within the profession have lacked a clear professional identity and consistent definition of the role of the school counselor and thus have failed to advocate for that role. The advent of the ASCA national model (American School Counselor Association [ASCA], 2003, 2012, 2019) has solidified the school counselor's professional identity as one serving a "crucial educational function that is integral to academic achievement and overall student success" (ASCA, 2012, p. xi).

It is essential for students beginning their journey in formation of their professional identities as school counselors to understand that which makes school counseling and school counselors uniquely valuable to the development of our school-aged population. The current text introduces the reader to the evolution of the role and function of the school counselor and our emergence as leaders, advocates, and collaborators in the provision of quality education for all students.

Beyond the presentation of material highlighting the role and function of ethical, effective school counselors, a major focus of the text is on fostering the development of the reader's professional identity as a school counselor. With this as a goal, the book employs case illustrations and guided exercise to not only inform but to arouse and excite the reader about the profession they are entering.

FORMAT AND CHAPTER STRUCTURE

You will notice that each chapter opens with a reflection of a school counselor. These reflections provide valuable insight into the actual lived experience of the school counselor. As you read the content of each chapter, consider what is implied or beneath each opening reflection. The principles, values, and constructs discussed within each chapter are not merely words on a page, they are the matter that gives form to the role and function of today's school counselor.

The primary goal for this text is to provide not only information but inspiration in service of the reader's developing professional identity as a school counselor. As such, each chapter will use case illustrations and guided personalized exercises to foster greater understanding of the profession they are embracing.

You are entering a noble profession—one that requires the highest level of competence and commitment. We hope this text provides you with the overview and inspiration needed to continue your professional journey.

RDP/KLD 2021

REFERENCES

American School Counselor Association. (2019). *The ASCA national model: A framework for school counseling programs* (4th ed.). Author.

American School Counselor Association. (2012). *The ASCA national model: A framework for school counseling programs* (3rd ed.). Author.

American School Counselor Association. (2003). *The ASCA national model: A framework for school counseling programs* (2nd ed.). Author.

Acknowledgments

We continue to enjoy a professional relationship with the highly talented and dedicated people at Cognella. They are attentive and always ready to support us, as authors, in any way. It is a pleasure to work with them. Of special mention are Amy Smith, Senior Project Editor, and Casey Hands, Production Editor, for their work in making the production of this text seamless. A special thanks to Vice President of Editorial, Kassie Graves, for her gifts of creativity and insight.

In addition, we thank Jared Heins, graduate assistant, for his careful reading and insightful suggestions.

PART 1

SCHOOL COUNSELING: THE EVOLUTION OF A PROFESSION

CHAPTER 1

MORE THAN A JOB

I can't think of a better way to spend my life.

—Elizabeth, Elementary school counselor

The quote that opens this chapter came from an elementary school counselor who has worked in the same school for 24 years. During her time as a school counselor, she continued her education gaining a certificate in trauma work, gained her license as a professional counselor, and at the age of 47 is finishing her doctoral degree. While she has a husband and two young adult children whom she loves, the central joy in her life (outside of her family) is that of being a school counselor. According to her, that joy "has only increased over the years."

Those choosing to venture down the path of becoming a school counselor often start that journey by gathering the "essential" information needed to guide their decision. They may, for example, investigate the U.S. Bureau of Labor Statistics or review the Occupational Handbook as portals into the "what" of school counseling as well as the outlook for employment. In their due diligence, they may seek those in the field or those experienced with the counseling process and may even read one of the many scholarly texts that describe the what, the why, and even the how of school counseling.

Such a process is one that should be of value for any individual seeking to identify a job or even a pathway to a career. Each of these steps can provide very needed information, information that can guide rational decision-making. However, the data accrued from such a search, while providing information about a career as a school counselor, fail to reflect the full nature of school counseling.

Serving in the role of school counselor is more than stepping into a job or even a career. Those fortunate to serve as school counselors understand their choice was (is) in response to a vocational calling. These school counselors know that *being a school counselor is not simply what they do; it is truly who they are.*

The current chapter presents school counseling as a profession and for those engaged, a vocational calling. Upon completing the chapter, the reader will be able to do the following:

1. Describe the differences between job, career, and vocation.
2. Identify the unique payoffs and costs of serving in the role of school counselors.
3. Describe the value and impact of the school counselor on those served.

MORE THAN A JOB OR CAREER

You have likely had a job, most likely multiple jobs. As you start your journey it is important to understand that for school counselors, those who are effective in their practice, school counseling is *not*, nor can it be, simply a job.

School counselors understand that both the demands of their position and the deep personal satisfaction that can be gained in serving as a school counselor gives evidence to the fact that it is neither a job nor simply a career, but a vocation. As you begin your studies it is important to understand the distinction between the nature of a job, a career, and a vocational calling, as these set the stage for what one is required to give, and in turn what one can be expected to receive, in performing their duties.

A Job

Whether it was your earliest paid position, perhaps as a baby sitter, cashier, or delivery person, the job you held was most likely chosen out of some form of necessity. Jobs are generally viewed as those work-related activities that we perform to earn money and to support our basic needs. Jobs vary in terms of skills needed and responsibilities required. But as a general rule, jobs are defined by the tasks to be performed, and most often the person performing these tasks, while having the needed knowledge and skill, is not personally invested in the job (beyond doing what is required and doing it well). For those serving in a job, the opportunity to move on to a better -paying job is viewed as desirable. As such, any one job may be short-lived, and over several years an individual may have engaged in numerous jobs under various employers.

A Career

Unlike a job, careers are long-term professional journeys. A career might last for one's entire life. Typically, an individual's career involves a series of connected, evolving employment opportunities, where knowledge and skill are increased, as is responsibility and compensation.

In a career, since the goal is advancement, and not merely getting a task done and collecting a check, the individual will often exhibit a desire and need to learn new skills, gain experiences, and build connections. Perhaps your experience with your school counselor has motivated you to go into the counseling profession and do as much or more for your students. Often an individual on a career path will extend themself beyond the strict requirements of the position, to learn and do more than initially expected. This desire to "go the extra mile" is in response, not to an anticipation of extra compensation but as a reflection of the person's investment in their eventual advancement.

SCHOOL COUNSELING: A VOCATION

Perhaps the central difference between a job, a career, and a vocation rests in the individual's perspective and motivation while engaging in each. For those in a job, the perspective is most often focused on the task to be completed, with the motivation being the reception of some form of compensation. For those in a career, the perspective broadens to include not just the task or responsibilities at hand but also the evolution of any one position to some ultimate career destination. The added motive experienced by those in careers often takes form as an internal payoff such as a feeling of competency, a recognition of success, a sense of achievement, and perhaps the realization of movement up their career ladder to some ultimate career goal and position.

For those engaged in a vocation, the perspective and motivation are quite different. Vocation comes from the Latin *vocare* or *vocationem*—which means "to call" or "a calling." A vocation touches a person's dreams, passions, and very sense of life purpose. The fulfillment experienced when engaged in one's vocation is not terminal nor easily satiated. The fulfillment doesn't come from gaining more money, more power, more prestige or some higher position. The fulfillment experienced by one in a vocation reflects the ongoing realization that they are doing not only what they are called to do, but doing something that continually rewards them with a sense of living a life of meaning and value.

School Counseling: A Job, a Career, or a Vocation?

An individual can jump through the various educational hoops to gain the credentials needed to take up a position as a school counselor simply because such a position affords a good salary, a nice working environment, and summers off. With this as a perspective and motive, this person would be engaging in the job of school counseling. For these individuals, it will soon become clear that the demands of this job far exceed these tangible and extrinsic payoffs.

For others, stepping into the role of a school counselor is but the first of many steps on their path toward a position in educational administration or higher education. For these individuals, school counseling is part of a career path to some other destination in the field of education. And while it is hoped that each of these individuals serve their stakeholders, having an eye on the next rung can remove them from the real sense of joy and personal satisfaction that can be experienced with each encounter and each moment serving as school counselor.

As you will soon discover, the duties, the responsibilities, and the challenges experienced by those embracing the profession of school counseling will demand more than such a job or career perspective. For those truly embodying that which is school counseling, theirs is a calling. For these professionals, school counseling is what they feel compelled to do because it gives them a deeper meaning to life. For these individuals, school counseling is not simply what they do, it is *who they are.*

Before someone invests the time and energy in becoming a school counselor it is important to consider the fit of this role and function with the person they are and will become. Job satisfaction is often related to finding one's *fit*, the phenomenon of congruence between an individual and the work they do (Cable & DeRue, 2002). Being able to find a fit contributes to overall job satisfaction and a sense of self (Cable & DeRue, 2002; Erdogan & Bauer, 2005; Resick et al., 2007). Case Illustration 1.1 highlights the value of having a realistic picture of the job demands as they reflect your interests, talents, and professional aspirations. If there is a disconnect, then perhaps school counseling is not your calling?

CASE ILLUSTRATION 1.1: THE RIGHT FIT

Jules and Victor started their graduate work in a school counseling program at the same time. They sat near each other at their new student orientation and during one of the small-group discussions talked about why they were going into school counseling. Victor excitedly shared that he always liked listening to people when they had a concern and helping them come up with solutions. "I think it's so awesome that as a school counselor you can help students, parents, and teachers," Victor continued, "and did you hear them talk about going to conferences and actually continuing to grow in our counselor identity?!"

"That seems a bit much," Jules replied. "Why would you want to keep spending money on more counselor events after getting your degree? This is enough time and money out of my life. I'm sure we'll learn what we need to know, and besides, that one conference is in the summer and having the summers off is a top reason I'm going for this job. I see myself as being available in my office and helping students when they come to me, and I'm sure I'll be great because I love kids!"

"Wow," Victor said softly, "Given what we just heard I can't imagine anyone taking a position in school counseling without committing to continuing their education and ongoing professional development. It doesn't appear to me that a school counselor really has a summer off."

Victor continued to reflect on whether he was going into the right field and thought about how it would be to help students learn skills so they could be successful and explain strategies to teachers so their classrooms are more manageable. It seemed like school counselors had a lot to do, and he was a bit in awe of the responsibility, but more than that, he was even more excited to learn, and keep learning, how to journey together with all students. Yep, this was the right fit for him!

As you begin your journey toward credentialing as a school counselor, it might be helpful to see how such a position will reflect your gifts, your talents, and your calling. Exercise 1.1 provides several questions that may help you to identify patterns that reflect your vocational pathway. As you learn more about the profession of school counseling, you may want to match what school counseling offers, what it requires, and the special challenges and rewards it provides and contrast these factors with those elements that appear to reflect your vocational calling.

Exercise 1.1: Passions and Vocations

Directions: Identifying and selecting a vocational path is important to reflect on the challenges and opportunities of that vocation and how they match your own gifts and talents. Review each of the following and compare your responses to what you know about being a school counselor.

- *Check your earliest memories.* Are there passions or talents that you have exhibited and enjoyed ever since you were a child? For example, are you curious? Do you enjoy problem-solving? Do you like and seek out others?
- *Review your recent engagement.* Look over your recent past, your last couple of years: What activities or experiences truly aroused your excitement, your joy of life? What are the common elements in these experiences that contributed to your joy?
- *Be a difference-maker.* In what way can you make or have you made a difference in someone else's life? When, where, and how have you left your mark? It may be something you did, or simply the way you were.
- *Dream.* If you allow yourself the freedom to dream—free of world constraints and demands—what is your life ambition, that thing or things you would most love to do? With this in mind, what does it say about the nature of your joy, your sense of satisfaction, and the factors that contribute to achieving these?
- *Reflect on interactions.* When reflecting on your interactions with people, while it is likely that not all have been positive, what characterizes those that have been growth-inducing for you? What was it about you, your form of engagement, or the nature of the interaction and relationship that made it so growth-inducing?

THE GIFT OF BEING A SCHOOL COUNSELOR

School counselors are truly gifted by the profession they represent and the work in which they engage. Each student's invitation to the school counselor to join in the journey with them from their place of discomfort to their desired state of well-being is a deep, personal, and valuable gift.

School counselors are invited to move beyond the secular process of helping, a process that directs the gathering of information about another as a prelude to providing some sage advice. School counselors are not advice givers and certainly not sages. They are called to relate first and then perhaps to help resolve.

School counselors are given the opportunity to engage in a deeply authentic, genuine human encounter. They are invited to experience each student at a very deep, authentic, and emotional level so that as counselors they can serve as support for students as they move toward their desired outcomes.

Each student with whom a school counselor works will provide evidence of not only the resiliency of the human condition but also the value of the relationship and the processes experienced in school counseling. There will be times when the counselor may feel lost or less than totally effective, but even in those times, if the counselor can share a moment of trust and genuine acceptance and value of the student with whom they are engaging, then the gift of counseling has been received by both the student and the school counselor.

School counselors are truly privileged. The invitation into a student's life at a time of their vulnerability, while being entrusted with that student's well-being, is an awesome gift, and a responsibility of great magnitude. School counselors know this and should never forget this. The chapters that follow review theory and research, which details the nature of the school counseling profession, the roles and functions served by school counselors, and the unique contributions provided by school counselors to the school's stakeholders (i.e., students, teachers, parents, and administrators). This research, these theories, the scripted word, however, will fall short in characterizing the true wonder of being a school counselor. This wonder is best conveyed by the words of those who embrace it daily.

Table 1.1 provides a sampling of responses provided by school counselors working in elementary, middle, and high schools when asked, "Why would one wish to be a school counselor?"

Table 1.1 The Gift of Being a School Counselor

- To be invited not only in a student's dream, but in their journey toward that dream, makes what I do a gift—something that often takes my breath away.
- There are times when I am simply there with a student in need, being available, showing concern and care. Perhaps this sounds too simple, yet it is so powerful both for my students and myself.
- To experience the trust that this vulnerable, often hurting student places in my hands is both an unbelievable gift and quite a responsibility.
- Where else could I experience an "aha" moment, one that truly leads a student out of their darkness and back to a path of growth?

(Continued)

Table 1.1 *(Continued)*

- When it is working, engaging with a student in counseling is, for me, the purest of human encounters, one that reminds me of the gift of being human and our need to connect.
- Whether it is the tearful expression of the anxious elementary student, or the sense of desperation being shared by a teen, being invited into the heart, the lived experience of one hurting so deeply, is life-altering for me, and I hope it can be for them.
- Hearing from a parent that the memory book their child created with me was instrumental in encouraging that child to talk about feelings.
- It is not only those significant moments or truly life-affecting counseling encounters that remind me of how fortunate I am to be a school counselor; it is also those drop-ins who come to show me the improved test grade, or observing two students sitting at lunch who were so angry at each other yesterday, and who now literally share bread, or even that student bursting with excitement and waving her letter of acceptance—these are the things that make me thankful for each day of my professional life.
- Watching a student succeed in class, especially the student who has struggled so much in the past, makes me smile almost as broadly as they do.
- Seeing a teacher more confidently try a new classroom management strategy after our consultation.
- How could one not like being a school counselor—how could one not celebrate the many opportunities to assist a student during a time of challenge, to be inspired by their resilience and placed in awe at the magic of their development?
- Think about it: Each day I come to school and have the privilege of traveling with students as they navigate life challenges, experience excitement and hope, and begin to become the persons they can be. I can't think of a better way to spend my life.

MAKING A DIFFERENCE

School counselors operate from the premise that all students can learn and succeed. It is in service of this belief that counselors not only work with individual students, but also, acting as leaders within the school, address systemic barriers that impede student growth and success. School counselors are called to serve as advocates, collaborators, visionaries, and leaders (Brenner, 2020).

The voices from the field (see Table 1.1) provide anecdotal evidence of the value and power of school counseling, both for the counselor and those they serve. But the power, the value, and the impact school counselors have is further evidenced by the increasing demands for service and the research supporting the efficacy of that service.

Increasing academic demands, normative developmental challenges, and 21st-century emotional-social pressures can and do take their toll on many of our students. Our students need and seek support. School counselors are an invaluable source of that support. The competency to engage the science of counseling and best practice to guide students in times of struggle makes school counselors a valuable resource in support of student educational achievement. Whether the challenge comes in the form of victimization, disability, low self-esteem, problematic relationships, or substance abuse, it is in the school counselor that our students will find a valued ally.

In the roles of interventionist, serving those who are struggling, and preventionist, engaging proactive strategies such as small-group counseling and classroom presentations, school counselors facilitate the healthy and productive development of students. Research (e.g., Carey & Dimmit, 2012) highlights the significant impact school counselors have on our students' social, emotional, and academic development. When it comes to social and emotional development, counselors can play a significant role in everything from reducing negative student behaviors (Curtis et al., 2010) to reducing the spread of gossip among students (Cross & Peisner, 2009), or increasing awareness of depression and suicide risk (Erickson & Abel, 2013). As for the school counselor's role and impact on student achievement, the research (e.g., Malott et al., 2010; Wyatt, 2009) highlights the significant role school counselors play in not only assisting individual students who are underachieving but also providing programs that help to close the achievement gap between student groups.

The vast and deeply significant impact school counselors have on their students, an impact across academic, behavioral, and socioemotional domains, can be seen by reviewing a sampling of research pointing to the effectiveness of counseling programs and counselors within schools (see Table 1.2).

Table 1.2 School Counselors—Making A Difference (a Sampling of Research Supporting the Value of School Counselors)

TARGET DOMAIN	FINDINGS	SAMPLE RESEARCH
Academic achievement	Support for elementary schools with comprehensive data-driven school counseling programs as displaying higher academic outcomes compared to schools without such programs.	Wilkerson et al. (2013).
Underachievement	School counselors can effectively assist underachieving students using a small group intervention.	Berger (2013).
College interest and admissions	Highly qualified first-generation students are more likely to enroll in four-year colleges if they have greater access to high school counselors (i.e., lower student–school counselor ratios).	Pham and Keenan (2011).
Transitioning students on the autism spectrum	School counselors assisting those on the autism spectrum to transition to college.	Krell and Perusse (2012).
Student self-efficacy	School counselors increasing a student's belief in their ability to succeed and be self-efficacious.	Bardhoshi et al. (2018).

(Continued)

Table 1.2 *(Continued)*

Destructive rumors	School counselors changing school climate and the social norms that fuel destructive rumor spreading by junior high students.	Cross and Peisner (2009).
Depression and suicidal thoughts	School counselors can provide leadership in the early identification and prevention of high school students with depression and suicidal thoughts.	Erickson and Abel (2013).
Bullying and aggression	Reducing bullying by increasing bystander invention.	Midgett et al. (2016).
Schoolwide positive behavior	School counselors can positively impact student learning and behavior in elementary schools by taking key roles in schoolwide behavior support systems.	Goodman-Scott (2013).
Stress reduction	Using mindfulness training to assist students in managing stress.	Sibinga et al. (2016).
Social anxiety and isolation	Use of "buddy bench."	Griffin et al. (2017).
Social anxiety disorder (SAD)	Successfully employing a group model to deliver a cognitive behavioral-based program, called Skills for Academic and Social Success (SASS), to effectively reduce the negative impact of social anxiety of identified teens with social anxiety disorder.	Warner et al. (2016).

A ROLE WITH HEAVY RESPONSIBILITY

School counseling is a valued profession and a needed service. It is also clear that for those who embrace this as their vocation, the rewards are numerous. But school counseling is not without its challenges, both professional and personal.

School counselors are invited to experience life through the perspective, and the experience, of their students. School counselors are invited to connect with the students' view of self and the world in which they are attempting to function. It is this ability to experience deep empathy that is the hallmark of an ethical, effective school counselor. And while the opportunity to encounter another at this level is truly a wondrous gift, it is a gift that can come at a price. Studies have found that school counselors have exceptional levels of job stress, often reporting higher than average burnout scores when compared to other mental health professionals (Wilkerson, 2009).

Think about it! School counselors are invited to journey with a student at a time of their struggle and often at points when they are most vulnerable. The student will meet with the counselor willing to enter a very deep relationship, and in that process the student will share parts of their story that perhaps they have not shared with anyone else. As receivers of this information and trusted keepers of these stories, school counselors are charged with using this information in ways that support the well-being of these students.

Such a charge places the school counselor in a truly challenging and highly responsible position. It is a position that demands the knowledge, skills, and disposition necessary to provide the ethical, effective support and service required. Whether the story being told is one of reflecting a normative developmental challenge or something darker and damaging, the school counselor is called to be totally and completely present for that student. School counselors cannot simply call in their job. As described by Skovholt (2012), counseling requires bringing "so much of our self to the meeting with our client: our emotional self, our intellectual self, our energetic self, our hopeful self, our ethical self, our knowledgeable and competent self, our sensitive self, our emotionally courageous self, our trusting self, our confident self and more and more" (p. 38). Counselors must understand what they are committing to in their role as a counselor. For those without such awareness, their well-being may be in jeopardy. For those unwilling or unable, the well-being of their students may be at risk. Exercise 1.2 invites you to gather firsthand knowledge of what you may encounter in the world of school counseling.

Exercise 1.2: Challenges and Rewards

Directions: Ask for an interview with a practicing school counselor. Consider interviewing more than one school counselor at varying levels (elementary, middle, high school), or different geographic settings, such as urban and suburban schools. The following questions will get you started with your interview. You may want to share your information with classmates to discover similarities and differences in your findings.

1. What do you find rewarding about being a school counselor in this school?
2. What are the challenges you find in this role?
3. What was something that surprised you when you first started as a school counselor?
4. What is something you think is helpful for first-year school counselors to know?

Understanding the nature of the responsibility demanded of school counselors and intentionally embracing that responsibility starts not with the first encounter with a student, but with the first day of graduate school. Unlike some other educational experiences that require retention of material to pass a test, counselor education goes beyond the installation of facts, or the understanding of theory. Counselor education requires the assimilation of these facts, these theories, even certain skills, in such a way that they begin to reform the person of the graduate student. The process of counselor education is not merely one of gaining in knowledge and skill. The process, as you will discover, is truly one of personal formation and the evolution of your identity into a professional school counselor. Consider the reflection of the school counselor following the completion of her first year in the job (see Case Illustration 1.2).

CASE ILLUSTRATION 1.2: SO MUCH TO DO—AND I LOVE IT!

As I think about my first year as an elementary school counselor, I didn't realize there was so much to do. I'm not sitting in my office talking to students all day, although I love when I'm able to meet one-on-one with them. My schedule varies each day, and I have to be so flexible when something pops up, like a kindergartener refusing to come into the building or a fifth grader crying because she didn't get into the group she wanted to be in for the talent show. Some days are busier than others and some are just downright exhausting.

We learned a lot of theory and skill in our counseling program, but the field is where that knowledge starts to become an art. Oh, I made mistakes and will tweak my class lessons, and I learned that I will need to and want to keep learning. I'm beginning to realize what it's like to really "be" with another person when they need help, and it may be emotionally tiring, but my empathy, my acceptance of who they are, leads us to find another way to solve an issue, and we do it together.

I may not hear many comments like "Thank you for listening" or "That was a cool group activity," or even "Thanks for showing us a new strategy," but I know I made a difference in the lives of many by being there, being invested, and bringing my passion into my school counseling position. It's not easy, and there's so much to do, and I love it!

A TAKE-AWAY

You are beginning a journey that will not only increase your knowledge of the human condition, your skills to interact and intervene, but also your view of the world and your view of self. The path to becoming a school counselor is truly *transformational*. It is a path that will merge your sense of what it means to be a school counselor with your sense of what it means to be you.

The remaining chapters will serve as essential inputs to this formational process. The more you know about the profession you are about to enter the more you will appreciate the observation made by First Lady Michelle Obama in her 2014 address to the members of the American School Counseling Association:

> "You all have one of the hardest, most stressful, most important and most underappreciated jobs of anyone in this country."

KEYSTONES

- A job is typically defined by the tasks to be performed and compensation to be received.
- A career involves a series of connected, evolving employment opportunities, where knowledge and skill are increased as are responsibilities and compensation.
- A vocation is that which is pursued, not for extrinsic payoffs such as a paycheck or even an internal sense of advancement, but in response to an internal drive, an almost internal required-ness to engage in that vocation.
- The invitation into a student's life, at a time of their vulnerability, while being entrusted with that student's well-being, is an awesome gift and a responsibility of great magnitude.
- Research (e.g., Carey & Dimmit, 2012; León et al., 2011) highlights the significant impact school counselors have on students' social, emotional, and academic development.
- School counseling demands the knowledge, skills, and disposition necessary to provide the ethical, effective support and service required.
- Research has highlighted the exceptional levels of job stress and the often -reported higher -than -average burnout scores of school counselors when compared to other mental health professionals (Wilkerson, 2009).
- Given the demands, as well as the levels of personal and professional satisfaction to be experienced, school counseling is perhaps best embraced by those who see it as their vocation.

ADDITIONAL RESOURCES

Print

Parsons, R., Dickinson, K. & Asempapa, B. (2020). *Counselor wellness: Caring for self to care for others*. Cognella.

Sumerlin, T., & Littrell, J. (2011). The heart of the school counselor: Understanding passion over the span of a career. *Professional School Counseling, 14*(4), 278–285.

Skovholt, T. M., & Trotter-Mathison, M. (2016). *The resilient practitioner: Burnout and compassion, fatigue prevention and self-care strategies for the helping professions* (3rd ed.). Routledge.

Web

ACA's taskforce on counselor wellness and impairment: http://www.counseling.org/wellness_taskforce/index.htm

American School Counseling Association, "Careers and Roles": https://www.schoolcounselor.org/school-counselors-members/careers-roles

Careers in Psychology (school counseling): https://careersinpsychology.org/starting-a-career-as-a-school-counselor/

Phi Delta Kappan: https://kappanonline.org/oconnor-school-counselors-make-world-difference/

REFERENCES

Bardhoshi, G., Duncan, K., Erford, B. (2018). Effect of a specialized classroom counseling intervention on increasing self-efficacy among first-grade rural students. *Professional School Counseling*, 21(1), 12–25. https://doi.org/10.5330/1096-2409-21.1.12

Berger, C. (2013). Bringing out the brilliance: A counseling intervention for underachieving students. Professional School Counseling, 17(1), 86–96. https://doi.org/10.1177/2156759X000170012

Brenner, P. (2020). *Authentic leadership: A mixed method inquiry of practicum in school counselling student and supervisor experiences* [Unpublished Doctoral Dissertation, Alvernia University, Reading, Pennsylvania].

Cable, D., & DeRue, D. S. (2002). The convergent and discriminant validity of subjective fit perceptions. *Journal of Applied Psychology*, *87*(5), 875–884. https://doi.org/10.1037/0021- 9010.87.5.875

Carey, J., & Dimmitt, C. (2012). School Counseling and Student Outcomes: Summary of Six Statewide Studies. Professional School Counselling, 16(2), 146–153.

Cross, J. E., & Peisner, W. (2009). RECOGNIZE: A social norms campaign to reduce rumor spreading in a junior high school. *Professional School Counseling*, *12*(5), 365–377.

Curtis, R., Van Horne, J.W., Robertson, P., & Karvonen, M. (2010). Outcomes of a schoolwide positive behavioral support program. *Professional School Counseling*, *13*(3), 159–164.

Erdogan, B., & Bauer, T. N. (2005). Enhancing career benefits of employee proactive personality: The role of fit with jobs and organizations. *Personnel Psychology*, *58*, 859–891. https://doi.org/10.1111/j.1744-6570.2005.00772

Erickson, A., & Abel, N.R. (2013). A high school counselor's leadership in providing school-wide screenings for depression and enhancing suicide awareness. *Professional School Counseling*, *16*(5), 283–289.

Goodman-Scott, E. (2013). Maximizing school counselors' efforts by implementing school-wide positive behavioral interventions and supports: A case study from the field. *Professional School Counseling*, *17*(1), 111–119.

Griffin, A. A., Caldarella, P., Sabey, C. V., & Heath, M. A. (2017). The effects of buddy bench on elementary students' solitary behavior during recess. *International Electronic Journal of Elementary Education*, *10*(1), 27–36.

Krell, M., & Perusse, R. (2012). Providing college readiness counseling for students with autism spectrum disorders: A Delphi study to guide school counselors. *Professional School Counseling*, *16*(1), 29–39.

Malott, K. M., Paone, T. R., Humphreys, K., & Martinez, T. (2010). Use of group counseling to address ethnic identity development: Application with adolescents of Mexican descent. *Professional School Counseling, 13*(5), 257–267.

Midgett, A., Doumas, D., & Trull, R. (2016). Evaluation of a brief, school-based bullying bystander intervention for elementary school students. *Professional School Counseling, 20*(1), 172–183. https://doi.org/10.5330/1096-2409-20.1.172

Parsons, R., Dickinson, K. & Asempapa, B. (2020). *Counselor wellness: Caring for self to care for others.* Cognella.

Pham, C., & Keenan, T. (2011). Counseling and college matriculation: Does the availability of counseling affect college-going decisions among highly qualified first-generation college-bound high school graduates? *Journal of Applied Economics and Business Research, 1*(1), 12–24.

Resick, C. J., Baltes, B. B., & Shantz, C. W. (2007). Person-organization fit and work-related attitudes and decisions: Examining interactive effects with job fit and conscientiousness. *Journal of Applied Psychology, 92,* 1446–1455. https://doi.org/10.1037/0021- 9010.92.5.1446

Skovholt, T. M. (2012). The counselor's resilient self. *Turkish Psychological Counseling and Guidance Journal, 4*(38), 137–146.

Sibinga, E. M., Webb, L., Ghazarian, S. R., & Ellen, J. M. (2016). School-based mindfulness instruction: An RCT. *Pediatrics, 137*(1), e20152532.

Warner, M., Colognori, C., Brice, D., Herzig, C., Mufson, K., Lynchn, L., Reis P.T., Petkova, E., Fox, J., Moceri, D., Ryan, J., & Klein, R. G. (2016). Can school counselors deliver cognitive-behavioral treatment for social anxiety effectively? A randomized controlled trial. *Journal of Child Psychology & Psychiatry, 57*(11), 1229–1238.

Wilkerson, K. (2009). An examination of burnout among counselors guided by stress-strain-coping theory. *Journal of Counseling and Development, 84,* 440–450.

Wyatt, S. (2009). The brotherhood: Empowering adolescent African-American males toward excellence. *Professional School Counseling, 12*(6), 463–470.

CHAPTER 2

THE EMERGENCE OF OUR PROFESSION

I can remember when we belonged to the American Personnel and Guidance Association (APGA), we've come a long way … baby!

—Alex, High school counselor of 40 years

Alex started his school counseling career in 1975 and has certainly experienced a lot of changes. The students with whom he works are confronted with issues he could not have imagined when he started. Crack cocaine, school shootings, world ecological crises, and increasing stress on test scores have taken their toll on many of the students and has made his work all the more challenging. It is not, however, just the severity and complexity of the issues encountered that has changed. Over the past 40-plus years those in counseling have seen the emergence of their profession as one rooted in scientific inquiry and engaging in evidence-based practice. The profession of school counseling has come a long way—and it is an evolutionary path that will continue to unfold.

As part of this profession, it is important to understand the seeds of our past, as they serve as the foundation for the hopes for our future. The role, position, and duties of school counselors have historically been muddied by the many influences that have shaped the very profession itself over the last century. According to Dahir (2004), "The history of school counseling has depicted a profession in search of an identity" (p. 345), and it is a search that is reaping many rewards. There is much in which to take pride. The movement from a time of service randomly provided by caring individuals to the collation of specially trained, credentialled professionals abiding by a common sense of professional identity and ethics has made school counseling its own unique and valued profession.

After completing this chapter, the reader will be able to do the following:

1. Describe the characteristics that define a profession.
2. Explain the impact of immigration on the emergence of school counseling.

3. Describe the factors that moved vocational counseling to a more expansive mental health focus.
4. Explain the significance of the development of a programmatic, comprehensive school counseling approach.

THE BEGINNING

While it could be argued that the principles of guidance and counseling existed as early as the 10th century BC in Ancient Greece and Rome (Krumbultz & Koblin, 2003), the evolution and emergence of modern-day school counseling might more accurately be placed with the early 1900s influx of immigrants to our shores and into our schools. As is true with most if not all movements, the emergence of school counseling as a practice occurred in response to a crisis within our schools. The public schools during this expansion of the population were simply ill-equipped to address the needs of students, and as a result students were leaving school unprepared for the workforce, the life, they were about to enter (Wright, 2012).

Frank Parsons, who is often referred to as the father of vocational guidance, developed an approach that encouraged educators to utilize vocational and career counseling models as a means of fostering students' personal and vocational development (Herr, 2001). Parsons had a career that crossed multiple disciplines. He served as a lawyer, an engineer, a college teacher, and a social worker before ultimately becoming a social reformer and working with youth (Hartung & Blustein, 2002; Pope & Sweinsdottir, 2005). However, he is best known for founding Boston's Vocational Bureau in 1908, a major step in the institutionalization of vocational guidance.

Contemporaneously with the work of Parsons, Jesse B. Davis, an educator in Detroit, Michigan, introduced the first systematized guidance program in the public schools (Aubrey, 1977). Davis suggested in 1907 that classroom teachers of English composition teach their students a lesson in guidance once a week to accomplish the goal of building character and preventing problems. Davis's Grand Rapids plan promoted respect for students' differences in abilities, interests, ideas, and cultural identity.

Working separately, these two individuals together spurred increased awareness of the need for and value of focusing on the whole child, an awareness that took form in the creation of the National Vocational Guidance Association (1913) in Grand Rapids, Michigan (Smith et al., 1985), and the provision of federal funding for vocational education and guidance via the passage of the Smith-Hughes Vocational Education Act in 1917 (Hillison, 1995).

What was advocated was not counseling in the modern sense but a forerunner of counseling: school guidance (a preventive educational means of teaching students how to deal effectively with life events). As noted, the programs were initially provided by classroom teachers, with very few "personnel specialists" being employed. These teachers, without training or additional pay, provided a rigid, career-centric plan to move students from school to factory. As this practice continued to develop, it was soon recognized as "a specialized educational function requiring special natural qualifications and special training" (Myers, 1924, p. 139).

ADDRESSING SOCIAL/EMOTIONAL NEEDS

While the early focus was on meeting the vocational needs of students, the 1920s and 30s saw an expansion of school counseling initiatives to include a focus on the mental health of the students and included services such as assessment and direct counseling. The inclusion of such a mental health focus resulted in a fundamental change in "guidance" counselors' approach and services. Facilitating students' adjustment to the social and economic demands of the times remained a goal of guidance services, but now an interest in the child's mental health and ways to facilitate healthy development began to emerge (Tang & Erford, 2010).

The popularity of humanistic psychology and the work of psychologist Carl Rogers helped shift the focus of school counseling to a more student-centered approach, in the 1940s and 50s. Before Rogers, "guidance" focused on the practice of dealing with testing, cumulative records, vocation, and placements. The emphasis began to shift to the importance of the counseling relationship and goals of promoting student personal and social development and well-being. The profession moved away from being one of information- providing and problem-solving, to emphasizing "a growth-oriented counseling relationship" (Schmidt, 1999, p. 11).

With increasing professional recognition of the value of counseling and the school counselor's role in facilitating learning, government funding increased (see the George-Barden Act of 1946; National Defense Education Act of 1958), and a singular voice for the profession took shape in the form of the creation of the American Personnel and Guidance Association (1952) as well as the 1952 charting of the American School Counselor Association (ASCA).

ROLE AS ADVOCATE: EXPANDING TARGETS AND SERVICES

The inclusion of a mental health focus to the services provided for school counselors underwent a reevaluation, with the outcome being a shift from a focus on remediation of those in emotional crisis to providing "developmental rather than remedial goals" (Baker, 2000, p. 8). The decades of 1960 and 1970 saw an expansion of the populations served and services provided by the school counselor. Counselors were expanding their roles and functions to include prevention as well as intervention. School counseling expanded focus on providing educational activities that promote healthy adjustment, social awareness, interpersonal problem solving, and vocational development (Wittmer, 2000).

Through the passage of the National Defense Education Act (NDEA), Title V, in 1964, school counselors took up their professional roles within elementary schools. The passage, one year later, of the Elementary and Secondary Education Act (ESEA), directed counselors' attention to students and families in underserved communities and those struggling with issues of poverty, personal disability challenges, and civil injustice (Tang & Erford, 2010).

The road toward professional identity and recognition was not without its challenges, as the 1970s were a decade of decreasing student enrollment and budgetary reductions, which led to cutbacks in counselor positions (Lambie & Williamson, 2004). Three pieces of legislation, however, help to reinvigorate the role and value of the profession. The Family Education Rights and Privacy Act (1974), the Education of All Handicapped Children Act (1975), and the Career Education Incentive Act (1978) each in different ways cemented the role of counselor in the planning and delivering of direct services and curricula aimed at the facilitation of learning and achievement for all students.

FROM ROLE TO PROGRAMS: COMPREHENSIVE SCHOOL COUNSELING

The pupil personnel service models that guided counselor services through the 60s and 70s positioned counselors to be vulnerable to constant assignment of duties outside the domain of counseling (e.g., administrative and disciplinary functions). The pupil personnel service model focused on the position or role of the counselor without a clear, systemic approach to service.

During the 1970s, the role of school counselor was reconsidered to focus less on its position (a list of duties and goals) to instead focus on the program of school counseling, a coordinated group of structured activities that would expose students to opportunities for personal, social, and educational development (Gysbers & Henderson, 2006). It was also in the late 60s and early 1970s that Norm Gysbers began the work to shift from seeing school counselors as solitary professionals into a more strategic and systemic goal of having a comprehensive developmental school counseling program for all students in K–12 (Aubrey, 1977).

Gysbers (1988) provided a comprehensive, programmatic approach to school counseling that brought together guidance and counseling. The comprehensive school counseling program continued to be refined through the 1990s with school guidance programs being restructured to utilize a team approach (Gysbers, 1990). This comprehensive approach included the setting of goals and objectives, identification of activities or interventions to address them, as well as planning and implementation strategies and evaluative measures. It was the first time that school counseling was defined in terms of developmentally appropriate, measurable student outcomes (Gysbers & Henderson, 2006). Comprehensive school guidance and counseling programs (a) de-emphasize administrative and clerical tasks as well as crisis-centered modes of intervention, and (b) promote guidance activities and structured group experiences designed to support students in developing the personal, social, educational, and career skills needed to function as responsible and productive citizens (Galassi & Akos, 2004).

Delivery of a comprehensive developmental school counseling program is frequently cited as the foundation for the current role of the school counselor. School counselors are engaged in programs and services that not only facilitate student growth and learning but also foster resiliency and psychological wellness.

With the continued emphasis on school improvement, ASCA integrated the work of Gysbers and Henderson (2001), Johnson and Johnson (2002), and Myrick (2003), and connected these approaches to the national standards (ASCA, 1997) and the Transforming School Counseling Initiative (Education Trust, 1997), the result of which took form in the publication of the ASCA (2003) national model. This was a significant step in the development of school counseling as a profession articulating the purpose of school counseling and the roles of the school counselor to include social advocacy, leadership, collaboration, and systemic change (Burnham et al., 2008; Campbell & Dahir, 1997; Dollarhide & Saginak, 2008). The national model (ASCA, 2019a), now in its fourth edition, is the most widely accepted conceptualization of a comprehensive school counseling program (Burnham et al., 2008).

The charge and role of school counselors have changed quite a bit over many decades. Although counselor training and expectations are now very different, the changes may not be as well known and understood in schools. As we can see in Case Illustration 2.1, not everyone may be aware of how the role of the school counselor has changed.

CASE ILLUSTRATION 2.1: LUNCH DUTY, TEST PROCTOR, AND SUB, OH MY!

"Mr. Stuckey, I remember discussing how having to be in the cafeteria for lunch duty and proctoring the AP exams means I have less time to see students in small group counseling and I'm not available for student drop-ins during those periods, yet I see I'm still on the schedule to do these duties next month."

"Oh, yes, well Ms. Lane, as the high school guidance counselor, those AP exams are important and can be considered career development and that is what you do, correct, career guidance?"

"Well, yes, Mr. Stuckey; however, I believe I can be much more impactful with career development by working with students individually or in groups with interest surveys and ..."

"And the lunch duty," Mr. Stuckey interrupts, "why, someone has to do it, and I don't know who else to ask. In fact, we need someone to cover geometry this afternoon, and I would do it but I have a principal's meeting, so would you please report to Ms. Shapely's class next period? Thank you!"

"But, Mr. Stuckey, I have my grief group session next period ..."

"Oh," Mr Stuckey interrupts again, "I guess that will have to wait–thanks. I have to go!"

We need the support of our administrators, particularly our principals, in order to institute change where needed, thus it is very important to know how much advocacy we need to do to educate others as to the role of the school counselor. Exercise 2.1 invites you to explore what others think of the role of the school counselor.

Exercise 2.1: A School Counselor Is ...

Directions: Interview a principal to gather information regarding the understanding the role of the school counselor. You may want to consider talking with principals at different levels (elementary, middle, high school) and different settings such as rural and urban schools.

Take note of the language used, for example *guidance counselor* versus *school counselor*. If the school does not have a school counselor, you may want to explore what the principal would expect or want a school counselor to do. Following are questions you may wish to use in your interview:

1. What is the role of the school counselor in your school?
2. Who do you expect the school counselor to support?
3. What is something you would like the school counselor to do that isn't done presently?
4. What does the school counselor need in order to fulfill their role effectively?
5. If the school does not have a school counselor on staff, why not?

SCHOOL COUNSELING: A UNIQUE PROFESSION

Throughout the early history of school counseling, the roles, the responsibilities, and the unique contributions made by those serving in the role of school counselor were not clearly defined nor universally accepted and applied. Often, the position was seen as an ancillary support service to teachers and administrators, and thus the counselor's duties and identities were often aligned with that of educators. Exercise 2.2 invites you to reach out to a school counselor who has been in the field for over 15 years and gather a firsthand account of the evolution and transformation of school counseling.

Exercise 2.2: Over the Course of Years

Directions: You are invited to reach out to a school counselor, perhaps one you had when you were in school, and ask them to share their experience with the changing nature of school counseling. To gain a sense of the evolution, it would be useful to interview a counselor who has been in the field for at least 15 years. The questions posed are meant to serve as triggers for questions that you may have. The goal is to be enriched by the experience of others.

Sample questions:

- Have the students, and their concerns, changed over the course of your career?
- Has your role, your duties, changed over the course of your career?
- How has the most rewarding aspect of your career changed?
- How has the most frustrating, challenging part of being a school counselor changed?
- Are you a member of ASCA? If so, what have you found to be a benefit of membership? If not, why not? Do you belong to other professional organizations?
- If you had a crystal ball, how would you predict school counseling will change in the next 15 years?

It can be argued that the identity of school counseling as a unique profession, distinct from that of educational administrator or classroom teacher, was marked with emergence of the ASCA in the 1990s and the acceptance of the term *professional school counselor* as the preferred title for those working in that position (Lambie & Williams, 2004). However, the emergence of school counseling as a profession was not the result of a singular event nor at a single point in time. The emergence of school counseling as a profession is a reflection of its evolution, its history, an evolution that will continue into the 21st century.

To understand this evolution along with the importance of professional status, one needs to consider that which defines a profession. The original meaning of *professional* derived from the Middle English *profes*, an adjective meaning "having professed one's vows." The implication of this term, *professional*, is that those holding such a title make a public commitment to a high standard of performance, one that is marked with integrity. For a professional, the goal is in providing quality work rather than mere economic gain (Freidson, 2001). Also, it is generally agreed that a profession is a disciplined group of individuals who possess special knowledge and skills and adhere to ethical standards. There is, of course, much more to a profession and the elements that typically characterize those endeavors that are viewed as professions. Table 2.1 provides a listing of such elements or markers. As reflected in the table, each of these elements, which are typically employed to define a profession, find their existence in the rich history and evolution of school counseling.

Table 2.1 Markers in the Emergence of School Counseling as a Profession

DEFINING CHARACTERISTIC	DESCRIPTION	HISTORICAL MARKERS
A specific body of knowledge	The profession collectively, and the professional individually, possesses a body of knowledge and a repertoire of behaviors and skills (professional culture) needed in the practice of the profession; such knowledge, behavior, and skills normally are not possessed by the nonprofessional.	• Early 1900s: The founding of the National Vocational Guidance Association (NVGA) and the publication of *National Vocational Guidance* magazine (to become the *Journal of Counseling and Development*) to encourage the pursuit of scholarly information related to vocational guidance. • 1960s: Provided the inclusion of psychological theories, particularly humanistic theories to provide a theoretical framework for providing mental health services to students. • 2000s: Highlighted the need and value for engaging in research-based or empirically supported practice, and ASCA provides empirical research studies supporting the value of school counseling.
Accredited training programs	The profession has agreed-on performance standards for admission to the profession and continuance within it. University programs are accredited by oversight bodies that determine whether the programs provide adequate education. Accreditation assures that graduates from accredited programs start their professional lives with the knowledge they need to perform effectively.	• The George Barden Act of 1946 was passed, which allocated vocational education funds for counselor training programs. • In 1981 the Council for Accreditation of Counseling and Related Education Programs (CACREP) was formed and provided for standardized counselor training (counselor education) programs for both master's and doctoral students in the areas of school, community, mental health, marriage and family counseling, and personnel services. • In the late 1990s the American School Counselor Association (ASCA, 1997) published *National Standards for School Counseling Programs.*
A professional organization of peers	Professionals see themselves as part of a community of like-minded individuals who put their professional standards above the individual self-interest or their employer's self-interest.	• In 1952, the American Personnel and Guidance Association was created to provide counselors, who were already in the field providing mental health services, with a professional association. • Also founded in 1952, the ASCA was created to support school counselors' efforts to help students. The Association also provides professional development, publications, and other resources, research, and advocacy.

(*Continued*)

Table 2.1 (*Continued*)

Credentialing of practitioners such as licensure	After completion of education and skills development, a professional is required to pass one or more exams that assure the person has attained a minimum level of knowledge.	• The APGA started a task force to address licensure for counselors, and a benchmark for its success was the passing of successful licensure legislation in Virginia in 1976. Two additional states, Alabama and Arkansas, also had licensure legislation by the end of the decade. • In 1990 the ASCA (revised in 1993, 1999, 2003, and 2015) adopted a position strongly supporting professional credentialing or the licensing of school counselors.
A code of ethics	Professionals are bound to a code of conduct or ethics specific to the distinct profession. Professionals also aspire toward a general body of core values, which are centered on an uncompromising and unconflicted regard for the client's benefit and best interests.	• 1960s: Specifically, the APGA published its first code of ethics, providing guidelines for ethical practice and ultimately protecting the public and increasing professionalism. Also during this time, an APGA report was edited that defined the role of and training standards for school counselors. • 1984: ASCA published ethical standards for school counselors (revised in 1992, 1998, 2004, 2010, and 2016).
Legal recognition		• The Smith Hughes Act of 1917 was passed by Congress, providing funding for public schools to provide vocational guidance programs and allowing schools to separate their vocational guidance programs from standard curriculum courses. • In 1936, the George-Deen Act was approved by Congress, allowing for the creation of the Vocational Education Division of the U.S. Office of Education, representing the first time funds were directly allocated for vocational guidance counseling. • In the 1940s the certification of school counselors was established. • In 1995 the Elementary School Demonstration Act was signed into law. • In 1997 the national standards for school counseling programs were created to define the role of U.S. school counseling programs. • Currently, all states specify educational requirements for certification (see https://www.schoolcounselor.org/school-counselors-members/careers-roles/state-certification-requirements).

It must be highlighted, however, that the advent of the American school counseling model (ASCA, 2003) can be seen as the moment of clarity, increasing unity and and providing a definition of school counseling as a profession. The publication of the ASCA standards ushered in a unique period of professionalization, strengthening school counseling identity, roles, and programs and showing school counseling to be "a crucial educational function that is integral to the academic achievement and overall student success" (ASCA, 2012, p. xi).

The significance of the establishment of the ASCA and the documentation of ASCA national standards for school counseling (2004) cannot be overestimated. As such ASCA and the ASCA national model will serve as the topic of the next chapter.

A TAKE-AWAY

While it could be argued that school counseling has been around perhaps as long as public education, it is clear that the emergence of school counseling as a profession is a relatively recent occurrence. School counseling has a rich history, one shaped by many talented people, both those recognized as historical contributors and the many, many more who have quietly impacted the lives of so many students.

The emergence of the ASCA and the dissemination of the national model and standards for comprehensive school counseling programs has truly served to both unite those identified as school counselors and announce to school administrators, teachers, parents, and community stakeholders that school counselors are professionals who provide an invaluable service to our education community.

KEYSTONES

- The seeds of school counseling were planted in response to the vocational needs of a society experiencing an influx of immigrants and the opportunities of the industrial age.
- Frank Parsons, often referred to as the father of vocational guidance, developed an approach that encouraged educators to utilize vocational and career counseling models as a means of fostering student personal and vocational development.
- Jesse B. Davis, an educator in Detroit, Michigan, introduced the first systematized guidance program in public schools, which saw classroom teachers of English composition teach their students a lesson in guidance once a week to accomplish the goal of building character and preventing problems.
- In the late 40s and early 50s, the popularity of the humanistic psychology movement and the work of Carl Rogers helped shift the focus of school counseling to a more student-centered approach in which interest in the child's development and mental health became a focus of counseling efforts.

- During the 1960s and 70s school counselors expanded their focus on providing educational activities that promote healthy adjustment, social awareness, interpersonal problem solving, and vocational development.
- The 1970s also marked a shift to comprehensive programming that included the setting of goals and objectives, identification of activities or interventions to address them, as well as planning and implementation strategies and evaluative measures. It was the first time that school counseling was defined in terms of developmentally appropriate, measurable student outcomes.
- With the continued emphasis on school improvement, ASCA integrated the work of Gysbers and Henderson (2001), Johnson and Johnson (2002), and Myrick (2003), and connected these approaches to the national standards (ASCA, 1997) and the Transforming School Counseling Initiative (Education Trust, 1997), the result of which took form in the publication of the ASCA (2003) national model.
- The publication of the ASCA (2012) standards ushered in a unique period of professionalization, strengthening school counseling identity, roles, and programs and showing school counseling to be "a crucial educational function that is integral to the academic achievement and overall student success" (ASCA, 2012, p. xi).

ADDITIONAL RESOURCES

Print

Dahir, C. A. (2004). Supporting a nation of learners: The role of school counseling in educational reform. *Journal of Counseling and Development*, *82*(3), 344–353.

Gysbers, N. C. (2010). *School counseling principles: Remembering the past, shaping the future. A history of school counseling.* American School Counseling Association.

Holcomb-McCoy, C. (2007). *School counseling to close the achievement gap: A social justice framework for success.* Corwin.

Web

The ASCA national model: https://www.schoolcounselor.org/school-counselors-members/asca-national-model

DeKruyf, L., Auger, R.W., & Trice-Black, S. (n.d.). The role of school counselors in meeting students' mental health needs: Examining issues of professional identity. *Professional School Counseling*, *16*(5), 271–282. https://digitalcommons.georgefox.edu/cgi/viewcontent.cgi?referer=https://www.google.com/&httpsredir=1&article=1008&context=gsc

The Education Trust: https://edtrust.org

REFERENCES

American School Counselor Association. (1997). *The national standards for school counseling programs.* Author.

American School Counselor Association. (2003). *The American School Counselor Association national model: A framework for school counseling programs.* Author.

American School Counselor Association. (2004). *ASCA national standards for students.* Author.

American School Counselor Association. (2012). *The American School Counselor Association national model: A framework for school counseling programs* (3rd ed.). Author.

American School Counselor Association. (2019a). *The American School Counselor Association national model: A framework for school counseling programs* (4th ed.). Author.

American School Counselor Association. (2019b). *ASCA school counselor professional standards and competencies.* Author.

Aubrey, R. (1977). Historical development of guidance and counseling and implications for the future. *Personnel and Guidance Journal, 55*(6), 288–295.

Baker, S. B. (2000). Middle school counseling in the new millennium: A practitioner's perspective. In J. Wittmer (Ed.), *Managing your school counseling program: K–12 developmental strategies* (2nd ed.) (pp. 49–55). Educational Media.

Burnham, J. J., Dahir, C. A., Stone, C. B., & Hooper, L. M. (2008). The development and exploration of the psychometric properties of the assessment of school counselor needs for professional development survey. *Research in the Schools, 15,* 51–63.

Campbell, C. A., & Dahir, C. A. (1997). *Sharing the vision: The national standards for school counseling programs.* American School Counselor Association.

Dahir, C. A. (2004). Supporting a nation of learners: The role of school counseling in educational reform. *Journal of Counseling & Development, 82*(3), 344–353.

Dollarhide, C. T., & Saginak, K. A. (2008). *Comprehensive school counseling programs: K–12 delivery systems in action.* Pearson.

Education Trust. (1997). *Working definition of school counseling.* Author.

Freidson, E. (2001). *Professionalism, the Third Logic: On the Practice of Knowledge.* Chicago, IL: The University of Chicago Press.

Galassi, J. P., & Akos, P. (2004). Developmental advocacy: Twenty-first-century school counseling. *Journal of Counseling and Development, 82*(2). https://www.researchgate.net/publication/263106588_Developmental_Advocacy_Twenty-First_Century_School_Counseling

Gysbers, N. C. (1988). *Developing and managing your school guidance and counseling program.* American Association for Counseling and Development.

Gysbers, N. C. (1990). *Comprehensive guidance programs that work.* ERIC Counseling and Personnel Services Clearinghouse.

Gysbers, N. C., & Henderson, P. (2001). Comprehensive guidance and counseling programs: A rich history and a bright future. *Professional School Counseling, 4,* 246–256.

Gysbers, N. C., & Henderson, P. (2006). *Developing and managing your school guidance and counseling program* (4th ed.). American Counseling Association.

Hartung, P. J., & Blustein, D. L. (2002). Reason, intuition, and social justice: Elaborating on Parson's career decision-making model. *Journal of Counseling & Development*, *80*(1), 41–47. https://doi.org/10.1002/j.1556-6678.2002.tb00164.x

Herr, E. L. (2001). The impact of national policies, economics, and school reform on comprehensive guidance programs. *Professional School Counseling*, *4*(4), 236–245.

Hillison, J. (1995). The coalition that supported the Smith-Hughes act or a case for strange bedfellows. *Journal of Vocational and Technical Education*, *11*(2), 4–11.

Johnson, C. D., & Johnson, S. K. (2002). *Building stronger school counseling programs: Bringing futuristic approaches into the present.* CAPS.

Krumbultz, J. D., & Kolpin, T. G. (2003). *A brief history of school guidance and counseling in the United States.* http://education.stateuniversity.com/pages/2023/Guidance-Counseling-School.html">Guidance

Lambie, G. W., & Williamson, L. L. (2004). The challenge to change from guidance counseling to professional school counseling: A historical proposition. *Professional School Counseling*, *8*, 124–131.

Myers, G. E. (1924). A critical review of present developments in vocational guidance with special reference to future prospects. *The Vocational Guidance Magazine*, *2*(6), 139–142. https://doi.org/10.1002/j.2164-5884.1924.tb00721.x

Myrick, R. D. (2003). *Developmental guidance and counseling: A practical handbook.* Educational Media.

Pope, M. (2009). Jesse Buttrick Davis (1871–1955): Pioneer of vocational guidance in the schools. *The Career Development Quarterly*, *57*, 248–258. https://doi.org/10.1002/j.2161-0045.2009.tb00110.x

Pope, M., & Sweinsdottir, M. (2005). Frank, we hardly knew ye: The very personal side of Frank Parsons. *Journal of Counseling & Development*, *83*(1), 105–115.

Schmidt, J. J. (1999). *Counseling schools: Essential services and comprehensive programs* (3rd ed.). Allyn & Bacon.

Smith, R. L., Engels, D. W., & Bonk, E. C. (1985). The past and future: The national vocational guidance association. *Journal of Counseling and Development*, *63*(7), 420–423.

Tang, M., & Erford, B.T. (2010). The history of school counseling. In B.T. Erford (Ed.), *Professional school counseling: A handbook of theories, programs, and practices* (2nd ed.) (pp. 9–22). Pro-ED.

Wittmer, J. (Ed.). (2000). *Managing your school counseling program: K–12 developmental strategies* (2nd ed.). Educational Media.

Wright, R. J. (2012). *Introduction to school counseling.* SAGE.

CHAPTER 3

THE PROFESSIONALIZATION OF SCHOOL COUNSELING

Wow, that was mind-blowing!

—Drew, Graduate student

Mind-blowing” is one way to describe a first experience at the American School Counselor Association’s annual conference.

The annual conference often finds more than 3,500 enthusiastic counselors, college professors, site supervisors and graduate students in attendance. The conference schedule is full of multiple days of research presentations, round-robin discussions, new product exhibitions, and so much more. For those attending an ASCA national conference, it becomes quite clear that school counseling is a viable, exciting, and growing profession. The ASCA conference provides updates to the profession and is a wonderful way to network with like-minded counselors; however, there are many ways in which the national organization continually supports school counselors.

The ASCA represents the interests of school counselors and provides a strong foundation in support of the continued development of school counseling as a profession. ASCA’s (2020) stated mission is to “represent professional school counselors and to promote professionalism and ethical practices. Through many means of professional development, standards, and competencies, school counselors can learn and exhibit how to be a professional school counselor.

The current chapter provides an overview of the factors contributing to the professionalization of school counseling and the unifying definition of what it means to be a school counselor. The chapter discusses the significance of the ASCA and the ASCA national model in this march to professionalism.

Upon completing the chapter, the reader will be able to do the following:

1. Describe the elements central to defining a profession.
2. Describe roles and functions that are appropriate for school counselors.

3. Explain each of the four themes articulated by the ASCA national model as they give form to the role and function of school counselors.
4. Describe the four components of the ASCA national model and how they are interrelated.

ASCA: ONE VOICE

As noted in Chapter 2, two of the pillars of any profession are (a) the existence of a professional organization of peers and (b) a code of conduct or ethics that is specific to this distinct profession. Clearly, the creation of the ASCA and the 2002 publication of the ASCA (2003) national model (Bowers & Hatch, 2002) announced the full professionalization of school counseling.

An Organization of Peers

A national association for all counselors was not founded until 1952. It was originally the American Personnel and Guidance Association (APGA). This new counselor organization was founded during a joint meeting of the four dominant organizations related to counseling, including the National Vocational Guidance Association (NVGA, now the National Career Development Association [NCDA]), National Association of Guidance and Counselor Trainers (AGCT, now the Association for Counselor Education and Supervision [ACES]), Student Personnel Association for Teacher Education (SPATE), and the National Association of Appointment Secretaries (now the American College Personnel Association [NCPA] and the American Counseling Association [ACA]). These organizations became the first four divisions in the larger organization. The following year a fifth division was added, the American School Counselor Association (ASCA).

Since its inception, the ASCA has continued to etch out its identity as representing a singularly unique profession, that of school counseling. The identity of school counseling as a unique profession was solidified with the 2018 announcement that the ASCA would now stand independent and autonomous from the American Counseling Association. While both organizations remain committed to work collaboratively "on common advocacy issues that strengthen the work of school counselors to support children and adolescents" (ACA, 2018), they recognized that they had evolved to the point where a more independent relationship made sense.

Although all those trained in counseling programs are taught counseling skills and theory with the end goal of guiding another through a helping relationship, the school is a very different setting than a clinical mental health setting. Likewise, the role of the counselor in a school varies greatly from the role of the counselor in a clinical setting. As an ethical and practicing school counselor, it is important to understand these differences.

Driven by the desire to engage all who served in the role of school counselor, ASCA has believed in one voice—the voice of the professional school counselor. Today, ASCA is self-identified as the leading association of its kind, empowering approximately 40,000 school counselors with the "...knowledge, skills, linkages, and resources needed to promote student success in the school, the home, and the community" (ASCA, n.d., "About ASCA").

Role Defined

The role, position, duties, and even title of school counselors have historically been muddied. "The history of school counseling has depicted a profession in search of an identity" (Dahir, 2004, p. 345). The further school counselors move from the mainstream of counseling and counseling associations, and the less they define themselves by their professional training and expertise, the more they will look and act like educators, administrators, and teachers, rather than counselors. This point is reflected in the fact that in 1989 ASCA recognized that the term *guidance counselor* failed to accurately reflect the school counselor's role and changed the title to school counselor (Beale, 2004).

Professional school counselors are certified/licensed educators with a minimum of a master's degree in school counseling, making them uniquely qualified to address all students' academic, personal/social, and career development needs by designing, implementing, evaluating, and enhancing a comprehensive school counseling program (Sandhu, 2000). As the profession continues to define that which is within the role of the professional school counselor, it continues to set boundaries around those duties that are appropriate for school counselor enactment and those that are not. ASCA's articulation of these various activities helps all school counselors to educate administrators and faculty as they continue to articulate their professional identity and their unique contribution to our school community. Table 3.1 describes that which ASCA identifies as appropriate for one serving as a professional school counselor.

Table 3.1 Appropriate and Inappropriate Duties for School Counselors

Appropriate Activities
■ Individual student academic program -planning ■ Interpreting cognitive, aptitude, and achievement tests ■ Providing counseling to students who are tardy or absent ■ Providing counseling to students who have disciplinary problems ■ Providing counseling to students as to appropriate school dress ■ Collaborating with teachers to present school counseling core curriculum lessons ■ Analyzing grade-point averages in relationship to achievement ■ Interpreting student records ■ Providing teachers with suggestions for effective classroom management ■ Ensuring student records are maintained as per state and federal regulations ■ Helping the school principal identify and resolve student issues, needs, and problems ■ Providing individual and small group counseling services to students ■ Advocating for students at individual education plan meetings, student study teams, and school attendance review boards ■ Analyzing disaggregated data

(*Continued*)

Table 3.1 (*Continued*)

Inappropriate
■ Coordinating paperwork and data entry of all new students ■ Coordinating cognitive, aptitude, and achievement testing programs ■ Signing excuses for students who are tardy or absent ■ Performing disciplinary actions or assigning discipline consequences ■ Sending students home who are not appropriately dressed ■ Teaching classes when teachers are absent ■ Computing grade-point averages ■ Maintaining student records ■ Supervising classrooms or common areas ■ Keeping clerical records ■ Assisting with duties in the principal's office ■ Providing therapy or long-term counseling in schools to address psychological disorders ■ Coordinating schoolwide individual education plans, student study teams, and school attendance review boards ■ Serving as a data entry clerk

Adapted from American School Counselor Association, "Appropriate and Inappropriate Duties for School Counselors."

While counseling is central to the role, function, and identity of school counselors, school counselors are called to do much more than individual and small group counseling. The call is for school counselors to design and deliver school counseling programs that are "comprehensive in scope, preventive in design and developmental in nature" (ASCA, 2017, p. 64). The programs developed by school counselors are not only remedial, intervening with a single student or small group, but they are also preventive and schoolwide in scope. Think about that for a minute. You will be making a difference not only in the lives of a few students, but for all students. You will be able to support students in crisis and teach prevention skills to all. The breadth of service provided by school counselors reflects the expanded nature of their role beyond that of direct-service provider to one who also programs for systemic change (see Table 3.2).

Table 3.2 The School Counselor's Role

School counselors ...

1. Create counseling programs based on defined student standards, detailed professional standards of ethical practice, and counselor competencies.
2. Employ program focus and planning tools to guide both the design and implementation of school counseling programs. As such, programs reflect the beliefs, mission, and vision of the school and the counseling department, as well as data about the school and student outcomes.
3. Create and deliver ethical and effective programs using developmentally appropriate activities and services that help students develop the ASCA mind sets and behaviors for student success, thus improving achievement, attendance, and discipline.
4. Provide effective, data-driven services, regularly assess their programs and services in hopes of improving them, and engage in self-assessment to maintain competencies to employ best practice.

Adapted from ASCA's "The Role of the School Counselor": https://www.schoolcounselor.org/asca/media/asca/Careers-Roles/RoleStatement.pdf

As noted in the preamble of the ASCA (2016) ethical standards for school counselors, "School counselors are advocates, leaders, collaborators and consultants who create systemic change by providing equitable educational access and success by connecting their school counseling programs to the district's mission and school improvement plans." It is clear, given the essential comprehensive nature of the service provided by school counselors, that school counselors must possess the knowledge, skill, and even attitudes and beliefs necessary to perform ethically and effectively.

The professional school counselor is expected to hold the belief that every student not only has the right but has the ability to achieve and that school counselors, as school leaders, can collaboratively employ programs that ensure this success. In addition to such core beliefs, the professional school counselor possesses both the knowledge of human development, theories of change, understanding of cultural and systemic influences that shape student behavior and achievement, and the skills necessary to develop and implement programs and services that support the healthy development and academic achievement of all students. ASCA provides clear direction as to the specific nature of the mind-set required of the professional counselor, along with the specific behaviors (skills) necessary to design, implement, and assess a comprehensive school counseling program (ASCA, 2019b). Table 3.3 provides a summary of these mind sets and behaviors and provides the references for a more detailed description.

Table 3.3 ASCA School Counselor Professional Standards and Competencies

Mind-sets: School counselors believe ...
M.1 Every student can learn, and every student can succeed.
M.2 Every student should have access to and opportunity for a high-quality education.
M.3 Every student should graduate from high school prepared for postsecondary opportunities.
M.4 Every student should have access to a school counseling program.
M.5 Effective school counseling is a collaborative process involving school counselors, students, families, teachers, administrators, other school staff, and education stakeholders.
M.6 School counselors are leaders in the school, district, state, and nation.
M.7 School counseling programs promote and enhance student academic, career, and social/emotional outcomes.
Behaviors
Professional Foundation
B-PF 1. Apply developmental, learning, counseling, and education theories.
B-PF 2. Demonstrate understanding of educational systems, legal issues, policies, research, and trends in education.
B-PF 3. Apply legal and ethical principles of the school counseling profession.
B-PF 4. Apply school counseling professional standards and competencies.
B-PF 5. Use ASCA mind-sets and behaviors for student success standards to inform the implementation of a school counseling program.
B-PF 6. Demonstrate understanding of the impact of cultural, social, and environmental influences on student success and opportunities.
B-PF 7. Demonstrate leadership through the development and implementation of a school counseling program.

(Continued)

Table 3.3 *(Continued)*

B-PF 8. Demonstrate advocacy for a school counseling program.
B-PF 9. Create systemic change through the implementation of a school counseling program.

Direct and Indirect Student Services
B-SS 1. Design and implement instruction aligned to ASCA mind-sets and behaviors for student success in large group, classroom, small group, and individual settings.
B-SS 2. Provide appraisal and advisement in large group, classroom, small group, and individual settings.
B-SS 3. Provide short-term counseling in small group and individual settings.
B-SS 4. Make referrals to appropriate school and community resources.
B-SS 5. Consult to support student achievement and success.
B-SS 6. Collaborate with families, teachers, administrators, and other school staff and education stakeholders for student achievement and success.

Planning and Assessment

B-PA 1. Create school counseling program beliefs, vision, and mission statements aligned with the school and district.
B-PA 2. Identify gaps in achievement, attendance, discipline, opportunity, and resources.
B-PA 3. Develop annual student outcome goals based on student data.
B-PA 4. Develop and implement action plans aligned with annual student outcome goals and student data.
B-PA 5. Assess and report program results to the school community.
B-PA 6. Use time appropriately according to national recommendations and student/school data.
B-PA 7. Establish an agreement with the principal and other administrators about the school counseling program.
B-PA 8. Establish and convene an advisory council for the school counseling program.
B-PA 9. Use appropriate school counselor performance appraisal process.

After looking over the mind-sets and behaviors school counselors are expected to embrace and exhibit, reflect on your own values and ideas about student development and behavior. Do you believe all students should have the resources needed to be successful in the areas or domains of academic, career and socioemotional skills? Exercise 3.1 will help you broaden this reflection and enhance your own development as a professional school counselor.

Exercise 3.1: Where Do I Stand?

Directions: Look at the statements in the far-left column and consider the scope of your awareness and understanding of the statement. Afterward, you may want to consult with your instructor or supervisor to explore resources for further development as a professional school counselor.

MIND-SET STATEMENT	DO I BELIEVE THIS?	WHAT BARRIERS MAY GET IN THE WAY?	DO I NEED MORE INFORMATION?
Every student can learn, and every student can succeed.			

Every student should have access to and opportunity for a high-quality education.			
Every student should graduate from high school prepared for postsecondary opportunities.			
Effective school counseling is a collaborative process involving school counselors, students, families, teachers, administrators, and other school staff and education stakeholders.			
School counselors are leaders in the school, district, state, and nation.			
Comprehensive school counseling programs promote and enhance student academic, career, and social/emotional outcomes.			

ONE VISION: THE NATIONAL MODEL

In 2002, the world was given a clear and unified vision of the school counseling profession. Dr. Judy Bowers and Dr. Trish Hatch expanded on then -existing positions of what school counselors should and could do (see Campbell & Dahir, 1997; Education Trust, 1997; Gysbers, 2001) and integrated these into a singular model. The publication of this seminal work (ASCA, 2003) announced to the world the existence of the profession of school counseling. This new presentation of a national model not only provided clarity for the role of the professional school counselor but also provided school counselors with the tools and materials necessary to craft a comprehensive school counseling program suited to their schools' and their students' needs. The introduction of the national model marked school counseling as unique in education with its more comprehensive and systematic approach to service.

Evolving With the Times

As should be true for all guiding documents, the ASCA national model is a living, changing document and has responded to the changing needs of our students, our schools, and our society. The ASCA national model, which is now in its fourth edition (ASCA, 2019a), is the most widely accepted conceptualization of a comprehensive school counseling program (Burnham et al., 2008). Central to this model is the call for school counselors to use data as both the basis for decision-making and program development but also as an essential element of accountability.

Themes

Even at its inception, the ASCA (2003) national model emphasized the school counselor's role in assisting all students to achieve academically, through the implementation of a systematic and developmentally appropriate set of interventions. The model has consistently promoted the use of data and research to guide the development of programs and practices and has emphasized the role of the school counselor and a comprehensive school program as an integral component serving the school's mission.

By its second edition in 2005, the model highlighted this valuable role of the school counselor, depicting that role as that of leader, advocate, and collaborator whose comprehensive program focuses on systemic change in service of the development and achievement of all students. Table 3.4 describes each of these facets to the counselor's role and function.

Table 3.4 The Comprehensive Model and the Counselor's Role

THEME	COUNSELOR FUNCTION (ILLUSTRATIVE EXAMPLES)
Leadership: Leadership, when viewed from the perspective of the school counselor, is a process of social influence that maximizes efforts of others toward the achievement of the school's mission.	School counselors provide leadership by: 1. defining programs and program focus; 2. analyzing data that inform modification of programs offered; 3. publicizing mission and vision that serve as beacons for services provided; 4. participating in school- and districtwide committees to advocate for student programs and resources; and 5. delivering programs that are aligned with student needs and promote achievement for all students.
Advocacy: School counselors advocate for the health, well-being, and academic achievement of every student.	School counselors serve as advocates by: 1. providing direct services to students through one-on-one counseling, group activities, crisis response, and core curriculum; 2. providing indirect student services and program management; 3. engaging in needs assessment and establishing program goals; 4. identifying systemic problems and implementing advocacy for those most affected; and 5. promoting policies at the district and state levels when student problems reflect a needed change to existing policies.

Collaboration: School counselors take an ecological/systemic perspective and thus collaborate with all stakeholders in the development and management of a comprehensive program.	School counselors collaborate in many ways and with many stakeholders by: 1. teaming and co-equally partnering with teachers, parents, and administrators; 2. organizing advisory committees composed of those within and outside of the school system; 3. sharing data about students and student programs and outcomes to those with a need to know; and 4. employing open communications to all stakeholders and actively seeking their input into program development, implementation, and maintenance.
Agents of systemic change: A school counselor can, with data-driven designed programs, have a positive impact on all students as well as the systemic operation of a school.	A school counselor can act as an agent of systemic change by: 1. identifying and removing barriers to student access to educational opportunities; 2. addressing and changing cultural elements that are antithetical to the mission of the school, as would be the case when addressing bullying; and 3. developing programs that are preventive and address entire populations or segments within the school, as would be the case in Tier I MTSS programming.

The third edition of the ASCA (2012) national model, while not modifying the themes or the content of that which preceded it, did include some additional material regarding the themes, such as voices from practicing school counselors and special topics.

The fourth edition of the ASCA (2019a) national model maintained the four themes of leadership, advocacy, collaboration, and systemic change but presented them as integral and woven throughout the model. The fourth edition also introduced changes in language to more accurately reflect that employed within education and moved from the use of nouns as describers of the four components of the model (i.e., foundation, management, delivery, and accountability) to the use of more active descriptors of what counselors do (i.e., define, manage, deliver, and assess).

The ASCA model provides a valuable framework from which school counselors can develop their comprehensive programs. You may find that not all school personnel are aware of the updates to the school counseling professions. As seen in Case Illustration 3.1, you may need to use your skills to help increase awareness of your training and the ASCA model so that you are able to be the most effective school counselor possible.

CASE ILLUSTRATION 3.1: SCHOOL COUNSELOR, NOT GUIDANCE COUNSELOR

"I don't understand why the other counselors in my department are still calling themselves guidance counselors and why my principal thinks it's okay for me to be in charge of all this testing coordination. We learned the do's and don'ts of the ASCA model in our counseling program, and the model has been around for many years, so why do I feel like the only one who knows what a comprehensive counseling program is all about?"

With exasperation, Josey asked her past internship supervisor, Carlos, if it gets any better. "I've been in this position for two years now and I'm not able to make the changes I need to make or see the students who need me because I'm doing paperwork or spending hours on administrative tasks that don't need a counselor."

Carlos responded, "It can be very frustrating to work with people who don't understand the ASCA model and haven't been told all the change you can help implement with your prevention and intervention strategies. For a long time a counselor in a school was there for vocational guidance, and some people haven't been versed in the updates. They think you're there to only help with career goals and administrative activities, but that is nowhere near all you can do. It sounds like you need to put on your leader and advocate hats and educate your administration and faculty on how you can reach and support the entire school community as a school counselor, not a guidance counselor. Provide them with the ideas you have to enhance your program and remember to use your team and others who embrace your vision. It's a powerful message to relay that you can be able to serve all students through a carefully planned and supported program."

Components

As initially developed, the model contained four elements, or quadrants, for creating and maintaining effective comprehensive programs (ASCA, 2012). Initially, these quadrants were identified as *foundation*, *delivery system*, *management*, and *accountability*.

Foundation identified the philosophy and mission on which the program is built. The second component, delivery system, consisted of the proactive and responsive services included in the program. The third quadrant, management, provided a detailing of the way resources are organized and utilized. The final quadrant, accountability, reflected the fact that comprehensive programs use data to drive delivery while providing direction for adjustments to programming (ASCA, 2012; Dollarhide & Saginak, 2008).

While the fourth edition of the ASCA (2019a) national model neither introduced nor eliminated substantive components from the previous editions, it did make changes in the language employed. One significant change in language was that nouns previously employed to describe the four components of the national model (i.e., foundation, management, delivery, and accountability) were replaced by the use of more active descriptors identifying what counselors did. Thus, the identifier *foundation* became *defining*; the label *management* became *managing*; *delivery* became *delivering*; and finally, *accountability* was transformed into *assessing*. The changes were not merely wordplay. The modification reflected both a philosophical shift to focusing on counselor action and provided increased clarity around the specific tasks or activities involved with each component.

Table 3.5 provides a summary of the changes made to these components. It is highly recommended that all counselors review the complete ASCA model and not rely solely on summaries.

Table 3.5 Summary of Changes in the ASCA National Model (3rd to 4th Edition)

COMPONENTS	CHANGES IN 4TH EDITION
Define (previously Foundation)	This component identifies the standards that define the school counseling profession: • ASCA mind-sets and behaviors for student success • ASCA ethical standards for school counselors (2016) • ASCA school counselor professional standards and competencies (2019b)
Manage (previously Management)	This component helps school counselors effectively and efficiently manage the school counseling program and includes two sections: • Program focus highlighting beliefs, vision, and mission statements • Program planning emphasizes the need to review data to inform goals, activities, and interventions. Primary data types in program planning include (a) participation (who participates in what activities); (b) mind-sets and behaviors (what did they learn?); and (c) outcome (how did learning affect achievement, attendance, or discipline?) Managing also includes review of data profiling achievement, attendance, and discipline schoolwide; annual student outcome goals; and closing-the-gap action plans and results.
	Assessments included new school counselor competencies assessment; revised program assessment, and a new use-of-time assessment.
	Tools included an annual agreement, advisory counseling, school data profile, action plans, lesson plans, and calendar templates (annual and weekly).
Deliver (previously Delivery)	This component focuses on the method of implementing the school counseling program directly to students and indirectly for students and includes the following: • Direct student services (e.g., instruction, appraisal, advisement, counseling) • Indirect student services (e.g., referral, consultation, collaboration)

(Continued)

Table 3.5 *(Continued)*

Assess (previously Accountability)	This component has been renamed to emphasize the ongoing formative assessment of the school counseling program to inform improvements to the design and implementation of a school counseling program. This component not only addresses the assessment of programs but also the school counselor's assessment and appraisal. • Program assessment involves formative as well as summative assessments and the reporting of the data. • School counselor performance provides data on the counselor's acquisition of the mind-sets and behaviors needed to provide ethical, competent service.

Adapted from ASCA national model, 4th edition changes: https://videos.schoolcounselor.org/asca-national-model-fourth-edition-changes-intro

What is very clear is that the formation of the ASCA and the development of the ASCA national model have not only solidified school counseling as a profession but have placed school counselors at the center of the education process. This is most evidenced in those schools that have initiated comprehensive school counseling programs that reflect the values and goals of the ASCA national model. Exercise 3.2 invites you to learn about RAMP schools and to investigate those in your community.

Exercise 3.2: RAMPing It

Directions: ASCA has developed a process through which schools who engage exemplary comprehensive school counseling programs can be recognized nationally. These programs have been designated as RAMP (Recognized ASCA Model Programs) schools.

Following you will find a link for a list of RAMP schools across the nation. Your task is to investigate schools in your state or in your immediate location and do the following:

1. Reach out and congratulate those that are RAMP schools.
2. Inquire from those in your location who are not RAMP schools if they have considered applying.

Current RAMP schools state by state can be found at https://www.schoolcounselor.org/school-counselors/recognized-asca-model-program-(ramp)/current-ramp-schools

---

A TAKE-AWAY

While school counselors may still find themselves sitting in their office addressing student schedule change requests, completing college application references, and even dealing with the crisis of the moment, these activities no longer define the role and function of today's school counselor. School counselors now serve vital roles in the overall educational endeavor. School counselors in their roles as leaders, advocates, and coordinators bring the educational community together in service of its mission and in fostering the academic achievement, personal/social, and career development of all students.

KEYSTONES

- School counselors are differentiated from other educators and mental health specialists working within the school by their attention to developmental stages of student growth, the tasks that need to be addressed, and the challenges to overcome to promote wellness and healthy development.
- The school counselor's role is multifaceted. Counselors provide developmental guidance, mentoring, and individual, small group and large group interventions. They are engaged in crisis intervention and conflict resolution and serve as liaisons with parents and community agencies.
- As professionals, school counselors employ skills of leadership, advocacy, and collaboration to provide for equity and access to opportunities that will maximize achievement for all students.
- The ASCA national model, through its various iterations, emphasizes the need for school counselors to take a systematic, empirical approach to the design, implementation, and outcome evaluation of their services.
- The ASCA's national model provides a framework that, when implemented, places professional school counselors in the center of the education process.

ADDITIONAL RESOURCES

Print

American School Counselor Association. (2019a). *The ASCA national model: A framework for school counseling programs* (4th ed.). Author.

American School Counselor Association. (2019b). *ASCA school counselor professional standards and competencies.* Author. https://www.schoolcounselor.org/getmedia/a8d59c2c-51de-4ec3-a565-a3235f3b93c3/SC-Competencies.pdf

Web

ASCA, the role of the school counselor: https://www.schoolcounselor.org/getmedia/ee8b2e1b-d021-4575-982c-c84402cb2cd2/Role-Statement.pdf

ASCA Position Statement (professional statements of position on a wide variety of topics): https://www.schoolcounselor.org/Standards-Positions/Position-Statements/ASCA-Position-Statements

American School Counselor Association. (2019). *ASCA school counselor professional standards and competencies.* Author. https://www.schoolcounselor.org/getmedia/a8d59c2c-51de-4ec3-a565-a3235f3b93c3/SC-Competencies.pdf

REFERENCES

American School Counselor Association. (2003). *The ASCA national model: A framework for school counseling programs.* Author.

American School Counselor Association. (2005). *The ASCA national model: A framework for school counseling programs* (2nd ed.). Author.

American School Counseling Association. (2016). *ASCA ethical standards for school counselors.* https://www.schoolcounselor.org/getmedia/f041cbd0-7004-47a5-ba01-3a5d657c6743/Ethical-Standards.pdf

American School Counselor Association. (2017). *The school counselor and school counseling programs.* https://www.schoolcounselor.org/Standards-Positions/Position-Statements/ASCA-Position-Statements/The-School-Counselor-and-School-Counseling-Program

American Counseling Association. (2018). *American Counseling Association and American School Counselor Association announce new collaborative relationship.* https://www.counseling.org/news/updates/2018/03/21/american-counseling-association-and-the-american-school-counselor-association-announce-new-collaborative-relationship

American School Counselor Association. (2019a). *The ASCA national model: A framework for school counseling programs* (4th ed.). Author.

American School Counselor Association. (2019b). *ASCA school counselor professional standards and competencies.* Author. https://www.schoolcounselor.org/getmedia/a8d59c2c-51de-4ec3-a565-a3235f3b93c3/SC-Competencies.pdf

American School Counseling Association. (n.d.). About ASCA. https://www.schoolcounselor.org/About-ASCA/Vision,-Mission-Goals

American School Counselor Association. (2020). About ASCA. https://www.schoolcounselor.org/About-ASCA

Beale, A.V. (2004). Questioning whether you have a contemporary school counseling program. *The Clearing House, 78*(2), 73–76.

Bowers, J. L., & Hatch, P. A. (2002). *The national model for school counseling programs.* American School Counselor Association.

Burnham, J. J., Dahir, C. A., Stone, C. B., & Hooper, L. M. (2008). The development and exploration of the psychometric properties of the assessment of school counselor needs for professional development survey. *Research in the Schools, 15,* 51–63.

Campbell, C. A., & Dahir, C. A. (1997). *Sharing the vision: The national standards for school counseling programs.* American School Counselor Association.

Dahir, C. A. (2004). Supporting a nation of learners: The role of school counseling in educational reform. *Journal of Counseling & Development, 82*(3), 344–353.

Dollarhide, C.T., & Saginak, K.A. (2008). *Comprehensive school counseling programs: K-12 delivery systems in action.* Boston: Allyn and Bacon.

Education Trust. (1997). *Working definition of school counseling.* Author.

Gysbers, N.C. (2001). School guidance and counseling in the 21st century: Remember the past into the future. *Professional School Counseling, 5*(2), 96–105.

Sandhu, D. S. (2000). Alienated students: Counseling strategies to curb school violence. *Professional School Counseling, 4,* 81–85.

PART 2

THE SCHOOL COUNSELOR: SERVING THE SCHOOL COMMUNITY

CHAPTER 4

SERVING THE SCHOOL AND ITS MISSION

How do we know if we are making progress ... if we don't know where we are going?
—Dr. J.P., Counselor

While the question posed by Dr. J.P. could certainly apply to a variety of activities in which we engage, it becomes especially poignant and valuable when applied to decision-making, especially when all the stakeholders have different ideas about where to go. Schools have limited resources. These resources will need to be allocated across numerous programs, services, and activities. Because of the very limited nature of resources available, some programs, and thus some stakeholders, may find that their request for support is reduced or even denied. The question is, how should these decisions be made? Upon what criteria should a school's resources be allocated?

It is clear that with each stakeholder's investment in their programs and their services they will most likely answer these questions with a resounding "mine." But, as will be discussed in this chapter, resource allocation, be that materials, personnel, or money, should not be based on what one constituency or stakeholder values, but rather on the criteria of what will best serve and support the enactment of the school mission, and movement toward its vision.

Upon completion of this chapter, the reader will be able to do the following:

1. Explain the difference between a mission and a vision statement.
2. Describe the value of a school's mission statement.
3. Describe the domains of a counselor's work as identified by ASCA.
4. Explain how a counselor in the role of leader and advocate can affect systemic change.

A MISSION, A VISION: MORE THAN MERE STATEMENTS ON THE WALL

Developing the school's vision and mission are two of the most important steps toward creating a successful program. Done well, a school's mission and vision statements provide clarity and direction for a school.

Mission

Lots of different organizations have mission statements—nonprofit organizations, government departments, small businesses, and big corporations. A mission statement defines what an organization is, why it exists, its reason for being.

Schools, like other systems, have developed in service of some identified needs. The specifics of the needs to be addressed and the uniqueness with which a school intends to meet those needs are the ingredients for a school's mission statement. Sadly, a mission statement is too often created and then placed on a plaque and positioned on a wall, or filed in a cabinet, never to be reviewed or used.

Mission statements are not meant to be passive reflections of some committee work. Mission statements are not simple pro forma documents or reflections of some generic template. A school's mission statement should be the public announcement of the commitment and purpose of all employed within the school and be central to all the school's efforts, energies, resource allocations, and decision-making.

A school's mission statement reflects the needs of those being served. As such, each school's mission statement should reflect the uniqueness of the stakeholders and constituent groups that serve as the population for whom the school was created. A school's mission will identify the uniqueness of the population they serve, the specific needs that will be addressed, as well as the means (e.g., curricula and extracurricular services and activities) for satisfying those needs. Generally speaking, a school's mission should provide (a) a statement of core values; (b) identification of goals and objectives; and (c) a reflection of its uniqueness.

An articulation and acceptance of a school's mission, with its clarity about the reason for existence as well as the uniqueness of the population served, provides decision-makers with a framework from which to not only establish goals and objectives but also prioritize these along with the allocation of resources. For example, how might an administration decide on the allocation of limited funds when some are calling for a new artificial turf for the football field, while others are seeking to expand the counseling program? Perhaps as you read this you felt as if the choice was obvious. It is not.

If a particular school exists for the primary purpose of preparing its students for entry into roles as athletic trainers, coaches, or even professional athletes, both a new field and counseling resources may be of value. However, if resources are limited, administrators may decide that maintaining the training necessary as preparation for these careers, while ensuring student health and safety is a priority, and that thus resources should be allocated to the upgrading of the current athletic facilities. This could be contrasted to another school, where the mission is clear that value and emphasis is placed on the fostering the socioemotional development of their students. In this setting, while improved athletic facilities may be desirable, funding the resources necessary to promote an antibullying program or the development of resilience may be seen as a higher priority and more in line with the school mission.

The point being made is that the school's mission statement is not merely words on a page; it is intended to be a cornerstone for decision-making. The articulation of the reason for the school's existence and the identification of the uniqueness of both the services provided and the market served provide the criteria against which to judge goals and plan resource allocation.

As you may have anticipated, understanding a school's mission and strategically placing a comprehensive school counseling program as central to that mission should be a primary concern and responsibility for the school counselor. Understanding the needs of the students and the expectations of the parents, administration, and community is important. Participating in Exercise 4.1 will help you to learn more about these needs.

Exercise 4.1: Who Are Our Constituents?

The school population and surrounding community are not only different in every state; they may be varied among districts and counties within a state. It is important to identify who the consumers are in the school in which you are serving as school counselor. The school exists to meet the needs of these constituents; that is the school's mission.

The school's mission, as well as the mission statement for the school counseling department, should exist not only to identify the specific consumer being served and the needs of that consumer but to give direction to the type of services to be provided. As you research placements for your field experience, and most certainly as you begin to search for job opportunities, it is important to review the school's mission and the degree to which the school constituents' needs and school counseling services parallel your interests and vision of the role of school counselor.

Your task for this exercise is to research a school's mission statement and information on the demographics of their student body. You may also find it valuable to interview each of the following regarding their thoughts regarding the needs of their students' families and community:

Students
Faculty/staff
Parents
Community businesses
Community services

Compare your findings with a classmate. What do the data suggest about the types of services counselors from varying schools should be offering?

Vision

Whereas the mission statement summarizes what, how, and why a school exists, a vision statement presents an image of what success will look like as a result of a school achieving all the goals that reflect that mission. A vision statement addresses the question, "Assuming that we are extremely successful in enacting our mission, how will people (parents, students, taxpayers, etc.) describe our school?" The answer to this question highlights the school's long-term goals and highest priorities. A vision statement, like a mission statement, needs to be more than a broad, flowery statement of wishful thinking. For a vision statement to be of value, it needs to provide a concrete description of the anticipated services to be rendered and the impact those services will have on the school's stakeholders.

The concretizing of goals and priorities in a vision statement can serve as a valuable navigation tool when thinking about those decisions that will move the school into the future. A vision statement will not only inform planning and priorities but will also help focus all aspects of school life and provide a means of articulating shared beliefs. Exercise 4.2 highlights the impact of a school's vision on its priorities and allocation of resources; it also invites you to consider the role a school counselor could play in programming for such an envisioned future.

Exercise 4.2: Impact of Vision

Directions: In completing this exercise, it may be helpful to consult with a colleague or classmate. Read each of the vision statements listed and describe (a) what you feel would be a primary target for resource allocation and (b) what program, activity, or service could be offered by a counselor in support of this vision.

VISION STATEMENT	SCHOOL PRIORITY FOR RESOURCE ALLOCATION	COUNSELOR PROGRAMMING IN SUPPORT OF ENVISIONED FUTURE
In five years we will have produced more national merit scholars than any other school in the state.	Development of advanced placement courses	Providing stress management programs, both as intervention (individual and small-group) and prevention (classroom lessons)
By the year 2026, we will be known for developing students who actively contribute to their community and the society at large.		
Five years from today our graduates will be actively pursued by top-tiered Division I athletic programs.		

By the year 2026 we will be recognized as the premier school for art and music in the tri-state area		
In five years we will have expanded the vocational choices and interests of our graduates beyond the current interests in agriculture to include those of trades and associate degrees.		

For a vision or mission statement to be of true value to decision-making it needs to avoid gimmicky, catchy phrases or any clichés that reflect current fads or trends. A school's vision and mission statements need to be a reflection of the identified needs of that school's constituents and be crafted as authentic, honest statements of how the school intends to address those needs. Both the mission and vision statements need to specific enough to serve as guides to decision-making while being be broad enough to cover the diversity of constituencies served and responsive to rapidly changing needs and priorities. More than any of this, however, those within the school need to embrace the values expressed in the school's mission and vision statements and be challenged to enact those values in the performance of their roles and functions. The school counselor in the role of leader and advocate can serve to keep a school's mission at the forefront of all decision-making.

THE SCHOOL COUNSELOR'S LEADERSHIP: VITAL TO MISSION FULFILLMENT

A quick sampling of the mission statements posted by schools across the nation (see Table 4.1) reveals both the uniqueness and the commonality of these mission statements.

Table 4.1 A Sampling of School Mission Statements

Philadelphia, PA	The School District of Philadelphia will deliver on the civil right of every child in Philadelphia to an excellent public school education and ensure all children graduate from high school ready to succeed, fully engaged as a citizen of our world.
Des Moines, IA	Working in partnership with each family and the community, it is the mission of the district to educate responsible lifelong learners so that each student possesses the skills, knowledge, creativity, sense of self-worth, and values necessary to thrive in and contribute to a diverse and changing world.
Pine Ridge, SD	The mission of Red Cloud Indian School is to develop and grow as a vibrant church, through an education of the mind and spirit that promotes Lakota and Catholic values.

Lancaster, PA	The Lancaster Central School District's purpose is to provide our students with a comprehensive educational program that will allow them to develop fully the necessary academic and social skills to become responsible and productive members of a democratic society.
Fairbanks, AK	The mission of the Fairbanks North Star Borough School District is to provide an excellent and equitable education in a safe, supportive environment so all students can become productive members of a diverse and changing society.
St. Petersburg, FL	Admiral Farragut Academy provides a college preparatory environment that promotes academic excellence, leadership skills, and social development within a diverse community of young men and women.

In each of these mission statements, carefully chosen words were employed to reflect the uniqueness of the populations served and the outcome desired. While colored with uniqueness, each mission implies the desire to foster the development and growth of the students served. Viewing these statements of purpose (i.e., mission) or similarly, considering the hoped-for outcomes (i.e., vision) can be inspiring. However, the fulfillment of these aspirations can be, and in many situations is, thwarted by various factors that interfere with student learning and healthy development and thus impede mission fulfillment.

School counselors recognize that many students encounter idiosyncratic factors that impede their learning and achievement. Consider, for example, the impact on a student's ability to achieve when their life, their personal experience, is affected by persistent health problems, difficult family circumstances, anxiety, depression, community violence, and drugs. These are but a few of the conditions that many of the students within our schools encounter. These are conditions that not only block their ability to achieve but can interfere with their healthy, normative development. These are conditions the school counselor is uniquely qualified to address.

The reality that schools fail some of our students and thus don't fulfill their mission is not limited to those students presenting with individual learning challenges. There is abundant evidence that highlights the reality that not all students are achieving their personal best nor developing to their fullest. The evidence is clear that even today there is a significant and persistent disparity in academic performance or educational attainment between different groups of students. While the degree and severity of this gap can vary from group to group or even place to place, achievement gaps exist and are observable across our educational systems. The existence of an achievement gap is evidence that a school is falling short of its mission. The specific causes for any particular achievement gap remain elusive since they are often complex and overlapping. Several studies have identified a wide variety of factors contributing to this achievement gap, many within the school's control and others outside of that control. Table 4.2 provides a listing of some of those factors gleaned from the research (Abramson, 2018; Banks et al., 2001; Fergus, 2016; Hattie, 2009; Howard, 2002; Saphier, 2016).

Table 4.2 Factors That Contribute to Achievement Gaps

WITHIN SCHOOLS' CONTROL	OUTSIDE SCHOOLS' CONTROL
Low expectations for student achievement	Economic opportunity for students' families and limited family support for students' education
Lack of rigor in the curriculum	Access to health and social services
Large class size	Community safety
Tracking groups of students into a less demanding curriculum	Access to libraries, museums, and other institutions that support students, development
Unsafe schools	Access to childcare and after-school programs and facilities.
Culturally unfriendly environments	English as second language
Poor, or no, instructional leadership	Inequities in funding among school districts
	Societal bias (racial, ethnic, social class)

School counselors are not only a valuable resource in supporting a school's mission to help children and adolescents develop into healthy, well-functioning, contributing members of society (Holman et al., 2019), but in their roles as advocate, leader, and coordinator they can facilitate systemic changes that reduce both the achievement and access gaps existing in our schools (Chen-Hayes et al., 2011).

SCHOOL COUNSELORS REMOVING BARRIERS TO EDUCATIONAL SUCCESS

School counselors develop, implement, assess, and adjust data-driven practices that remove barriers impeding student learning, thus helping to promote student success and achievement. It is the school counselor who serves a vital role in maximizing success for all students (Lapan et al., 2007; Stone & Dahir, 2006).

According to ASCA (2012), school counselors are responsible for activities that foster the academic, career, and personal/social development of students. Students will often experience idiosyncratic and systemic factors that interfere with their successful growth in these three domains, and it is the calling of the school counselor to remove those barriers.

Academic Development

While academic issues and concerns, such as failing classes, losing interest or motivation, or experiencing a disconnect between teaching and learning styles often serve as the impetus for a student to engage a school counselor, the work of the school counselor, in supporting academic development, extends beyond addressing such personal or individual issues and concerns. School counselors not only assist students at times of academic crisis but also assist students in exploring interests, goals, and aptitudes as a foundation for developing their pathway to maximum academic success. School counselors provide programs and activities to support and maximize each student's ability to learn and thus place them within the role of a viable contributor to the educational mission of their school.

Career Development

Historically, one of the primary responsibilities for the school counselor was helping students prepare for post-high school life and transitioning to continuing education and/or careers. School counselors help students (a) understand the connection between school and the world of work, and (b) plan for and make a successful transition from school to postsecondary education and/or the world of work.

This role is especially important given the ever- expanding directions available to students upon graduation and the rapidly changing demands of our workforce. With so many options and yet a rapidly changing career landscape, students will often present with anxiety and concern about making a "mistake" in career selection. It is the skills and knowledge that school counselors can bring to their interaction with students that will help students understand that a balance of focus and commitment with flexibility and adaptability will serve them well, not just with career choices, but life in general (Gellatt, 1996). Beyond providing direct service to their students, counselors may also engage in a way to affect the system in which the student is attempting to navigate their future. For example, a student seeking a pathway to the trades may need the counselor to advocate for them and their career choice with administrators who value post-high school college and/or parents who have had other expectations regarding their child's career path.

Social and Emotional Development

Central to the role of the school counselor is the process of counseling. In addition to providing direct service to students encountering personal social/emotional challenges, school counselors will provide preventive programs and foster development of personal and social skills. Depending on the setting and the developmental levels of the students, school counselors may offer a program that addresses issues of identity, relationships, conflict resolution, stress management, resiliency, and wellness. In the process, the school counselor may effectuate systemic change, one impacting the entire school's curriculum, as would be the case with the introduction of a schoolwide antibullying program.

While varying in degree and emphasis, all schools, as evidenced by their mission and vision statements, seek to promote student academic achievement, socioemotional development, and post-high school transition. However, students may encounter many challenges, both personal and systemic, that can interfere with this development. The school counselor is charged with helping students at times of personal challenge, as seen in Case Illustration 4.1. Through one-on-one direct service to individuals and small groups of students, school counselors provide interventions and support when needed. However, this is not the only role, function, or focus for a school counselor, especially when system factors are serving as a barrier to student development and mission fulfillment.

CASE ILLUSTRATION 4.1: CAN I CONSIDER COLLEGE?

Pablo has stopped in to see Mr. Fernandez every week during lunch over the past few weeks. His visits started as he was contemplating whether he should bother applying to college next year when he would be a senior. As a first-generation student, Pablo did not know where to start in the application process, where he should apply, or even if he would be able to receive financial aid. Mr. Fernandez was instrumental in providing information to Pablo and furthered the discussion to include what Pablo might be interested in studying.

Over the course of the month, Pablo and Mr. Fernandez explored career interest surveys, and Mr. Fernandez was able to guide Pablo toward a more informed course selection for senior year. When Pablo mentioned that he wasn't sure if his parents would agree with his decision to go to college, Mr. Fernandez worked with Pablo on a pro and con list and role-played how the discussion with his parents might sound.

Pablo and Mr. Fernandez were able to work together on academic, career, and personal/social goals in just a few weeks, yet their goals will have long-term effects!

A BROADER, SYSTEMIC FOCUS

While providing service to those students in need, the school counselor also possesses the knowledge and skills necessary to challenge those within school to stay true to their mission and vision, and in the process inspire all involved to hold to their stated goals and values. In this role, the school counselor performs as a leader, advocate, and agent of systemic change. It is in these roles that the school counselor can ensure that equity and access to meaningful and growth-filled educational experiences will be provided for all students.

An Ecological Systemic Perspective

The Education Trust (2009) invited school counselors to expand their perspective and their services to be more systemic and more ecological: "School counseling is a profession that focuses on the relations and interactions between students and their school environment to reduce the effects of environmental and institutional barriers that impede student academic success" (para. 3).

Embracing a systemic perspective positions the counselor to provide programs and services that not only assist a student with their challenges but also address systemic, ecological factors that may be, or soon will be, impeding the successful development and academic achievement of many other students. The counselor engaging such an ecological perspective will employ multilevel assessments and incorporate multilevel interventions to impact the various systems in which the student is performing (McMahon et al., 2014). For example, a school counselor may be engaged with a student who, now starting a new semester with new classes, is exhibiting a drop in their previous levels of enthusiasm, engagement, and performance. The counselor, in providing direct service, will certainly meet with the student to ascertain what, if any, personal, psychosocial issues are inhibiting their performance. The counselor with a systemic view, however, will expand the nature of his search for answers and consider the possibility of a mismatch between the student's learning style with that of the teacher's instructional approach. From this perspective, the counselor will not only work with the individual student but will collaborate with the teacher to investigate and perhaps institute modification to the class and the pedagogical approach. Further, investigation into the cultural inclusiveness of the curriculum may show that there is bias in the curricula being used and there is a need for updating curriculum. Such a systemic, ecological approach will not only expand the levels of intervention and support provided to this one student but may also assist other students at risk of a similar fate.

School Counselor as Leader

While schools have organizational charts that show positions of authority and implied leadership, leadership can be viewed as a function rather than a role or title. School counselors have been taught principles of group dynamics, how to build consensus and facilitate communication within and between groups, and how to move groups to win-win decision-making outcomes. This knowledge, these skills, position the school counselor to *function* as a leader, even when not ascribed that position or role.

School counselors should step forward in those circumstances that call for advocating for student success, fostering the development of healthy school and classroom environments, and employing data as a means of assessing the effectiveness of the programs and services offered. School counselors also should take a leadership role, working to assist in building a climate of diversity appreciation and maintaining strong home/school collaborations (Amatea & West-Olatunji, 2007). School counselor leadership has been called for in the design and advocacy for specific programs in support of student development (Dollarhide, 2003; Hatch & Bowers, 2002), in efforts in stimulate school reform (Adelman & Taylor, 2002; Bemak, 2000; Dollarhide, 2003), and to play proactive, catalytic roles in defining the future for programs that augment the education of all students (Adelman & Taylor, 2002).

School counselor leadership incorporates a proactive approach grounded in program assessment and collaboration with all educational stakeholders, including families and the community (Young & Bryan, 2015). For the counselor to provide such proactive, broad-based support services and interventions, as well as serve in preventive roles effecting system change, they will need to engage with the other significant players in the school and community to improve student functioning and achievement (Bryan & Holcomb-McCoy, 2010; Epstein & Van Voorhis, 2010; Stone & Clark, 2001). It is in this role as collaborators and coordinators that school counselors move from interventionists to preventionists, from direct service providers to advocates and agents of system change.

School Counselors as Advocates

Most individuals, even with limited knowledge of the role of the school counselor, might assume that school counselors advocate on behalf of individual students who may fail to thrive in the school setting. In any one day, a school counselor may be called to advocate for a student in response to unfair discipline practices or seek an adjustment of a policy (e.g., homework) given a personal circumstance that interferes with the student's ability to adhere to that policy, or even advocate for the student seeking to pursue a career or college choice that is currently resisted by their parents.

Advocating for students is what school counselors are trained to do. Counselors engage an advocacy role when it is clear that external factors are acting as barriers to a student's development. This role as advocate extends beyond direct service to any one student or groups of students. As one of the themes found within the ASCA (2019) national model, school counselors are charged with stepping up in the face of social justice issues, school climate issues, and any time there is an abuse of power. The ASCA (2003) national model states, "Advocating for the academic success of every student is a key role of school counselors and places them as leaders in promoting social reform" (pp. 24–25). School counselors advocate for individual students, underrepresented student groups, campus practices, district policy evaluation, even legislative changes. According to the national model, school counselors' advocacy efforts are aimed at (a) eliminating barriers impeding students development; (b) creating opportunities to learn for all students; (c) ensuring access to a quality school curriculum; (d) collaborating with others within and outside the school to help students meet their needs; and (e) promoting positive systemic change in schools.

School counselors step up as advocates when identifying systemic factors that are antithetical to a school's mission fulfillment and contribute to a culture and environment that presents barriers to student development. The school counselor serves as a voice to change the status quo when the status quo is standing in the way of student development and school mission achievement. In their role as agents of system change, school counselors will do the following:

- Assist in education reform that targets reducing the achievement gap among low-income and minority students.
- Gather data on school climate in terms of inclusion/exclusion elements.
- Help the school confront injustice in policy and practice.
- Provide solutions to reduce rates of failure and dropout.
- Provide curriculum and programs that promote healthy, normative development.
- Lead in efforts to collaborate and coordinate resources of school and community stakeholders in programming for the personal, social, academic, and career needs of all students.

Counselor as Collaborator and Coordinator

Identifying the school counselor as a leader and advocate is not meant to suggest that they must, or for that matter should, do it alone. While the adage that "it takes a village" applies to many settings, it certainly has applications within the school. Schools are systems composed of many interrelated parts, and coordination of all those parts and resources is essential if a school's mission and vision will be realized.

In their role as leaders and agents of systemic change, school counselors employ skills to organize and manage a comprehensive counseling program that is integrated within and across all aspects of the school's educational process. In forming such a comprehensive counseling program, the school counselor engages and collaborates with teachers, administrators, parents, and other interested stakeholders. They engage processes of coordinating ideas, resources, materials, and even personnel in the development and implementation of their programs.

This role of coordination can be seen in the counselor's efforts to (a) schedule meetings (e.g., teacher or parent consults, advisory board meeting, etc.); (b) compile and analyze data (e.g., test results, classroom grades, discipline referrals, etc.); (c) facilitate teams to address the systemic issues of underachieving students; and (d) even coordinate the work with special educators and other school professionals serving students, whether employed by the school or part of a community resource. Following up with Pablo from Case Illustration 4.1, we see how the school counselor can be a leader, advocate, and systemic change agent in Case Illustration 4.2.

CASE ILLUSTRATION 4.2: I CAN GO TO COLLEGE!

As Pablo explored the idea of going to college he felt like he kept coming up against barriers: barriers from his parents, barriers for finances, barriers in writing essays, barriers in filling out applications. He felt like it was not meant to be for him to go to college, even though he had high grades and a strong desire to earn a degree in information technology, a field in which he had exceptional skills.

As Pablo was deciding to give it up, Mr. Fernandez checked in with him to see how things were going. When Pablo relayed all the issues he was having and thought college would not work for him, Mr. Fernandez thanked him for letting him know, asked him to "hang in" and come back the following week.

When Pablo returned the next week, Mr. Fernandez laid out the following plan:

1. Parent information session regarding financial aid, with interpreters and childcare available
2. An elective course for first-generation students to review how to fill out applications, write essays, and search for colleges with specific programs
3. Mentorships for students and families with alumni who were first generation
4. Work internship opportunities with community businesses during senior year and college breaks

Mr. Fernandez asked Pablo if he thought these ideas would help him and other potential first generation students. Pablo excitedly affirmed the ideas and offered to help, which Mr. Fernandez gladly accepted. When Pablo stated that he didn't know how to thank Mr. Fernandez, Mr. Fernandez replied, "It's me that is thanking you for helping me see these issues and working to move these barriers to make some positive change!"

A TAKE-AWAY

Highlighted throughout this chapter is the role of school counselors as leaders, collaborators, advocates, and agents of systemic change. It is important when considering each of these roles to remember that none of these roles or counselors' actions is to be employed solely in service of the likes or dislikes of any one constituent (i.e., student, teacher, parent, or administrator). Rather, school counselors employ their knowledge and skills in service of the mission and vision of the school in which they are employed.

Given the fundamental charge of our schools as that being to provide for student opportunities to learn and to develop, the counselor's role and the value of a comprehensive school counseling program is that it addresses and removes individual and systemic barriers to student academic achievement and development and as a result facilitates the successful fulfillment of a school primary mission.

KEYSTONES

- A school's mission is a statement of the reason it exists and typically describes (a) its core values, (b) its goals and objectives, and (c) its uniqueness.
- A school's vision statement presents an image of what success will look like as a result of a school achieving all the goals that reflect that mission.
- The mission and vision statements and the values implied provide the criteria against which to judge goals and plan resource allocation.
- Successful satisfaction of a school's mission can be thwarted by various factors that interfere with student learning and healthy development and thus impede mission fulfillment.
- School counselors are valuable resources in supporting a school's mission to help children and adolescents develop into healthy, well-functioning, contributing members of society.
- School counselors develop, implement, assess, and adjust data-driven practices that remove barriers impeding student learning, thus helping to promote student success and achievement.
- In their roles as advocates, leaders, and coordinators, school counselors can ensure that equity and access to meaningful and growth-filled educational experiences will be provided for all students.
- In their roles as advocates, leaders, and coordinators, they can facilitate systemic changes that reduce both the achievement and access gaps existing in our schools.

ADDITIONAL RESOURCES

Print

Dickinson, K., & Parsons, R. (2019). *The school counselor as consultant: Expanding impact from intervention to prevention.* Cognella.

Dollarhide, C. T., & Saginakm K. A (2018). *Comprehensive school counselling programs* (3rd ed.). Pearson.

Stemler, S. E., & Bebell, D. J. (2012). *The school mission statement: Values, goals, and identities in American education.* Eye on Education.

Young, A., & Miller-Kneale, M. (2013). *School counselor leadership: The essential practice.* American School Counselor Association.

Web

American School Counseling Association. (2014). *The role of the school counselor.* https://www.schoolcounselor.org/getmedia/ee8b2e1b-d021-4575-982c-c84402cb2cd2/Role-Statement.pdf

American School Counseling Association. (n.d.a.). ASCA national model. https://www.schoolcounselor.org/school-counselors-members/asca-national-model

American School Counseling Association. (n.d.b.). Recognized ASCA model program (RAMP). https://www.schoolcounselor.org/school-counselors/recognized-asca-model-program-(ramp)

REFERENCES

Abramson, A. (2018, February 21). *What is the achievement gap and what can educators do about it?* https://www.rasmussen.edu/degrees/education/blog/what-is-the-achievement-gap/

Adelman, H. S., & Taylor, L. (2002). School counselors and school reform: New directions. *Professional School Counseling, 5*, 235–248.

Amatea, E. S., & West-Olatunji, C. A. (2007). Joining the conversation about educating our poorest children: Emerging leadership roles for school counselors in high-poverty schools. *Professional School Counseling, 11*(2), 81–89. https://doi.org/10.5330/PSC.n.2010-11.81

American School Counselor Association. (2003). *The ASCA national model: A framework for school counseling programs.* Author.

American School Counselor Association. (2005). *The ASCA national model for school counseling programs* (2nd ed.). Author.

American School Counselor Association. (2012). *The ASCA national model: A framework for school counseling programs* (3rd ed.). Author.

American School Counseling Association. (2014). *The role of the school counselor.* https://www.schoolcounselor.org/getmedia/ee8b2e1b-d021-4575-982c-c84402cb2cd2/Role-Statement.pdf

American School Counselor Association. (2019). *The ASCA national model: A framework for school counseling programs* (4th ed.). Author.

Banks, J., Cookson, P., Gay, G., Hawley, W. D., Irvine, J. J., Nieto, S., Schofield, J. W., & Stephan, W. G. (2001). *Diversity within unity: Essential principles for teaching and learning in a multicultural society.* Center for Multicultural Education, University of Washington.

Bemak, F. (2000). Transforming the role of the counselor to provide leadership in educational reform through collaboration. *Professional School Counseling, 3*, 323–331.

Bryan, J., & Holcomb-McCoy, C. (2010). Collaboration and partnerships with families and communities. *Professional School Counseling, 14*, ii–v.

Chen-Hayes, S. F., Miller, E. M., Bailey, D. F., Getch, Y. Q., & Erford, B. T. (2011). Leadership and achievement advocacy for every student. In B. T. Erford (Ed.), *Transforming the school counseling profession* (3rd ed.) (pp. 110–128): Pearson.

Dollarhide, C. T. (2003). School counselors as program leaders: Applying leadership contexts to school counseling. *Professional School Counseling*, 6, 304–308.

Education Trust. (2009). *The new vision for school counseling.* https://edtrust.org/resource/the-new-vision-for-school-counselors-scope-of-the-work/

Epstein, J. L., & Van Voorhis, F. L. (2010). School counselors' roles in developing partnerships with families and communities for student success. *Professional School Counseling, 14*, 1–14.

Fergus, E. (2016). *Solving disproportionality and achieving equity: A leader's guide to using data to change hearts and minds.* Corwin.

Gellatt, H. B. (1966). Developing a future sense. In R. Feller & G. Walz (Eds.), *Career transitions in turbulent times: Exploring work, learning, and Careers* (pp. 387–394). ERIC Counseling and Student Services Clearinghouse.

Hatch, T., & Bowers, J. (2002). The block to build on. *ASCA School Counselor, 39*, 12–21.

Hattie, J. (2009). *Visible learning: A synthesis of over 800 meta-analyses relating to achievement.* Routledge.

Holman, L. F., Nelson, J., & Watts, R. (2019). Organizational variables contributing to school counselor burnout: An opportunity for leadership, advocacy, collaboration, and systemic change. *The Professional Counselor, 9*(2), 126–141.

Howard, G. (2002). School improvement for all: Reflections on the achievement gap. *Journal of School Improvement, 3*(1), 11–17.

Lapan, R. T., Gysbers, N. C., & Kayson, M. A. (2007). *Missouri school counselors benefit all students.* Missouri Department of Elementary and Secondary Education.

McMahon G. H., Mason, E. C.M., Daluga-Guenther, N., & Ruiz, A. (2014). An ecological model for school counseling. *Journal of Counseling and Development, 92*, 459–471.

Saphier, J. (2016). *High expectations teaching: How we persuade students to believe and act on "smart is something you can get."* Corwin.

Stone, C. B., & Clark, M. A. (2001). School counselors and principal: Partners in support of academic achievement. *NASSP Bulletin, 85*, 46–53. https://doi.org/10.1177/019263650108562407

Stone, C., & Dahir, C. (2006). *The transformed school counselor.* Lahaska.

Young, A., & Bryan, J. (2015). The school counselor leadership survey: Instrument development and exploratory factor analysis. *Professional School Counseling, 19*(1), 1–15.

CHAPTER 5

PROVIDING ETHICAL AND EFFECTIVE SERVICE

It is a lot to learn, a whole lot.

—Ernest, First-year graduate student in school counseling

As suggested by Ernest, our first-year graduate student, there is much to be learned if one is to become an ethical and effective school counselor. There is knowledge to gain, skills to develop, and values to embrace. Further, this formation does not stop once an individual gains a degree or a certificate. The call to ethical practice demands that all school counselors remain lifelong learners.

The current chapter presents the core ingredients to ethical, effective practice. At the completion of the chapter readers will be able to do the following:

1. Describe what is meant by a code of ethics and the core values underlying the codes.
2. Describe the standards and competencies expected of school counselors.
3. Explain what is meant by the term *evidence-based practice.*
4. Describe the value of self-care to ethical professional practice.

ETHICAL STANDARDS AND BEHAVIOR

A defining characteristic of a professional organization is the formulation of standards of practice (Gorman & Sandefur, 2011). The establishment of a code of ethics or standards of conduct signifies the maturation of a profession (Mabe & Rollin, 1986). The ASCA (2016) ethical standards for school counselors are more than a public pronouncement of professional identity; they are guidelines for practice.

While the code of ethics is prescriptive in terms of the professional behavior expected, the true hope of our profession is that each school counselor will internalize the profession's collective values and articulated principles. School counselors understand that professional ethics is not something one merely steps into at the time of employment, but rather the principles outlined in our professional code that reflect values that are fundamental to the personal and professional identity of the school counselor.

Knowing the code of conduct and the ethical values it reflects is necessary but not sufficient. All counselors are called to live out these principles. Although there are some differences in school counseling and clinical counseling, school counselors may use both the ASCA's code of ethics and the ACA's code of ethics for guidance. As noted in the preamble of the ACA's (2014) code of ethics, the core values are "an important way of living out an ethical commitment." Specifically, counselors value the following:

1. Enhancing human development throughout the life span
2. Honoring diversity and embracing a multicultural approach in support of the worth, dignity, potential, and uniqueness of people within their social and cultural contexts
3. Promoting social justice
4. Safeguarding the integrity of the counselor–client relationship
5. Practicing in a competent and ethical manner

As applied to school counseling (see ASCA, 2016), these values give form to the school counselor's beliefs that all students have the right to the following:

1. *Be respected, be treated with dignity,* and have access to a comprehensive school counseling program that advocates for and affirms all students from diverse populations.
2. School counselors serving as *social-justice advocates* who support students from all backgrounds and circumstances and consult when their competence level requires additional support.
3. Receive the information and support needed to move toward *self-determination,* self-development, and affirmation within one's group identities.
4. Receive *critical, timely information* on college, career, and postsecondary options and understand the full magnitude and meaning of how college and career readiness can have an impact on their educational choices and future opportunities.
5. *Privacy that should be honored* to the greatest extent possible, while balancing other competing interests (e.g. best interests of students, safety of others, parental rights) and adhering to laws, policies, and ethical standards pertaining to confidentiality and disclosure in the school setting.
6. A *safe school environment promoting autonomy and justice* and free from abuse, bullying, harassment, and other forms of violence.

In its statement of purpose, the ACA (2014) code of ethics states that counselors are expected to use a credible decision-making approach to resolve dilemmas:

> When counselors are faced with ethical dilemmas that are difficult to resolve, they are expected to engage in a carefully considered ethical decision-making process.

The "what" is clear: Counselors must engage in ethical decision-making. The "how," however, is less clear. According to Cottone and Clause (2000), there are over 30 ethical decision-making models available. It is beyond the scope of this chapter to review all the existing models. However, Parsons and Boccone (2021) reviewed several models available and created a practical, culturally sensitive eight-step model for ethical decision-making (see Table 5.1).

Table 5.1 Questions Guiding Ethical Decision-Making

Pre-decision preparation: • Am I knowledgeable of the latest code of ethics? • Is the latest version of the code of ethics available? • Am I familiar with some of the contemporary challenges to ethical practice? • Am I aware of my values, prejudices, bias, and view of self and others? • Am I aware of those areas of need or self-interest that may come under challenge in an ethical dilemma?
Problem identification: • What are the facts of the situation? • Is this a personal problem? • Is this a clinical problem? • Is this a legal problem? • Is this an ethical problem? • Is it more than one of the above? • Is legal advice needed? • How might the problem be viewed by one having a different worldview?
Formulate ethical concern: • How might the dilemma relate to specific principles listed in the professional code of ethics? • How might the dilemma relate to the institutional policies of the context in which you experienced the dilemma? • How might the dilemma relate to your own values? • How might the dilemma relate to your worldview? • Does the dilemma tap into your own personal needs, biases, or prejudices?

Determine the nature and dimension of the dilemma:

- What implications might this have for the principle of autonomy?
- What implications might this have for the principle of nonmaleficence?
- What implications might this have for the principle of beneficence?
- What implications might this have for the principle of justice?
- What implications might this have for the principle of fidelity?
- What are the possible impacts of this dilemma on all stakeholders?

Generate potential courses of action:

- Have you brainstormed possible courses of action (being nonjudgmental as to feasibility)?
- Have you engaged a colleague in the process?

Assess each option:

- What is the possible impact (both positive and negative) of each course of action on the client (physical, psychological, social realms)?
- What is the possible impact on the principles of doing no harm and promoting the welfare of the client?
- What is the possible impact (both positive and negative) of each course of action on other stakeholders (family, friends, coworkers)?
- What is the possible impact (both positive and negative) of each course of action on the client's community?
- What is the possible impact (both positive and negative) of each course of action on the public view of the counseling profession?
- How will the option look to others once it is known?
- Would this option be applied to others in similar circumstances?
- Would this option be recommended to a colleague in a similar situation?

Selection and implementation:

- Are the needed resources available for the implementation of the selected course of action?
- Is there a set plan or steps in place to support implementation?

Documentation:

- Have I recorded not only the decisions I have made but the resources I may have employed in making those decisions?
- Does my documentation adequately convey my desire to tend to the welfare of my client while adhering to laws and regulations governing my practice?
- Is the confidentiality of my client maintained even in the process of documenting the issues and the dilemmas I encountered?

Adapted from Richard D. Parsons and Peter J. Boccone, "Questions—Guiding Ethical Decision Making," Ethical Decision Making: A Guide for Counselors in the 21st Century, *pp. 36-37.*

Through training and practice experience, school counselors will discover that these principles will become amplified and assimilated as personal values and standards that will guide all practice decisions. The goal is not simply to know ethics, but rather to be ethical. Exercise 5.1 invites you to explore the codes of ethics for situations you may encounter as a school counselor.

Exercise 5.1: Using the Ethical Codes

Directions: Using the ASCA ethical standards for school counselors and the ACA code of ethics, how might you proceed with the following scenarios?

1. A new student who is identified with a learning disability is being required to take the state assessment exams and your school team hasn't reviewed the individualized education plan yet.
2. A teacher comes to you to ask if you would please counsel her because she is having difficulties with her partner at home and she thinks you are such a good listener.
3. A special education teacher in your school has arranged a meeting with parents who do not speak English and has not asked an interpreter to attend, saying it's a short meeting just to change one goal and an interpreter isn't necessary.
4. At your monthly district school counselor meeting, you hear the counselor in the middle school talking to a high school counselor about "fixing" some grades so that some deserving students can take advanced classes in the high school.
5. A parent approaches you to ask if you would see his son in your private practice because you have such a wonderful relationship with him as his school counselor.

COMPETENCE

Identifying oneself as a school counselor and taking up the role and function assigned that title implies that one not only accepts the responsibilities of that position but also possesses the necessary qualifications and competence to perform the duties assigned. It perhaps seems obvious that one should not engage in practices that require knowledge or skills beyond those they currently possess. The implications are, of course, that not everyone with an educational credential is competent to serve in the role of school counselor. Ethically, competence means that a counselor has both the knowledge of the treatment in use and the ability to implement it at an acceptable standard (Fairburn & Cooper, 2011). The ACA (2014) is very clear about this matter, directing its members to "practice only within the boundaries of their competence based on their education, training, supervised experience, state and national professional credentials, and appropriate professional experience" (C.2.a).

Pursuit and maintenance of competence does not cease upon graduation. In addition to initial academic training, a key element to the development of competency, both during the initial formation stage of one's professional life and as ongoing support and development even when one is in the field, is the use of supervision. Orlinsky et al. (2001) identified supervision as only second to working directly with clients as a factor contributing to the professional development of counselors. This point is highlighted by the ACA (2014) by informing its members that "counselors recognize the need for continuing education to acquire and maintain a reasonable level of awareness of current scientific and professional information in their fields of activity" (C.2.f), and by the ASCA (2016), which states that school counselors "seek consultation and supervision from school counselors and other professionals who are knowledgeable of school counselors' ethical practices when ethical and professional questions arise" (B.3.h). Reflect on the possible harm that could occur if we don't follow our ethical guidelines, as in Case Illustration 5.1.

CASE ILLUSTRATION 5.1: I READ ABOUT THAT IN A BOOK!

Mr. Clifton knocked on the door of the school counselor's suite. One of the counselors, Ms. Waltman, called out to come in. Mr. Clifton, the principal, started explaining the reason for his visit to the office. He explained that a new student was coming to the school who was diagnosed with Tourette's syndrome. He wondered if the school multidisciplinary team needed to meet or if the teacher should be informed of anything.

"Oh, Mr. Clifton, I know exactly what to do because I read a book last summer that had a character who had Tourette syndrome," Ms. Waltman said.

Mr. Clifton started to ask more questions about how the teacher and other staff members might prepare themselves since there had never been a student with Tourette's syndrome in attendance in the school. Once again, a very excited Ms. Waltman exclaimed it was all good and she would take care of everything.

Just then, the other middle school counselor, Ms. Geiger, came out of her office and said that she was sorry to interrupt, but Ms. Waltman may be too hasty in her offer to take care of the new student.

"Mr. Clifton, as counselors we are ethically obligated to not practice in areas in which we aren't competent, and we are charged to seek professional development in order to effectively support all our students. I know not all people with Tourette's syndrome have the same symptoms, and we wouldn't want to inadvertently hurt someone. Would you be able to send us to a training to learn about Tourette's syndrome so that we can appropriately support the student and give strategies to the school faculty and staff?"

Being competent in the performance of one's professional duties is an ethical mandate, but what constitutes competence? What knowledge and skills are fundamental to professional practice as a school counselor?

Skills and Knowledge

While there is no single definitive answer to the question of what fundamental skills and knowledge defines competency, guidelines have been provided by the Council for Accreditation of Counseling and Related Educational Programs (CACREP) in terms of the core areas of education and resulting competencies that a counselor should have. In addition to these core competencies, CACREP (2016) set forth a listing of knowledge and skills needed by those with a school counseling specialty (see Table 5.2).

Table 5.2 CACREP (2016, 5.G) Statement of Knowledge and Skills for School Counseling

Students who are preparing to specialize as school counselors will demonstrate the professional knowledge and skills necessary to promote the academic, career, and personal/social development of all P–12 students through data-informed school counseling programs. Counselor education programs with a specialty area in school counseling must document where each of the lettered standards listed below is covered in the curriculum.

1. FOUNDATIONS
   a. history and development of school counseling
   b. models of school counseling programs
   c. models of P-12 comprehensive career development
   d. models of school-based collaboration and consultation
   e. assessments specific to P-12 education
2. CONTEXTUAL DIMENSIONS
   a. school counselor roles as leaders, advocates, and systems change agents in P-12 schools
   b. school counselor roles in consultation with families, P-12 and postsecondary school personnel, and community agencies
   c. school counselor roles in relation to college and career readiness
   d. school counselor roles in school leadership and multidisciplinary teams
   e. school counselor roles and responsibilities in relation to school emergency management plans, and crises, disasters, and trauma
   f. competencies to advocate for school counseling roles
   g. characteristics, risk factors, and warning signs of students at risk for mental health and behavioral disorders
   h. common medications that affect learning, behavior, and mood in children and adolescents
   i. signs and symptoms of substance abuse in children and adolescents as well as the signs and symptoms of living in a home where substance use occurs
   j. qualities and styles of effective leadership in schools
   k. community resources and referral sources
   l. professional organizations, preparation standards, and credentials relevant to the practice of school counseling
   m. legislation and government policy relevant to school counseling
   n. legal and ethical considerations specific to school counseling

3. PRACTICE
   a. development of school counseling program mission statements and objectives
   b. design and evaluation of school counseling programs
   c. core curriculum design, lesson plan development, classroom management strategies, and differentiated instructional strategies
   d. interventions to promote academic development
   e. use of developmentally appropriate career counseling interventions and assessments
   f. techniques of personal/social counseling in school settings
   g. strategies to facilitate school and postsecondary transitions
   h. skills to critically examine the connections between social, familial, emotional, and behavior problems and academic achievement
   i. approaches to increase promotion and graduation rates
   j. interventions to promote college and career readiness
   k. strategies to promote equity in student achievement and college access
   l. techniques to foster collaboration and teamwork within schools
   m. strategies for implementing and coordinating peer intervention programs
   n. use of accountability data to inform decision making
   o. use of data to advocate for programs and students

A further articulation of the knowledge, skills, and mind-sets to be exhibited by ethical and competent school counselors has been provided by the ASCA (2017) (see Table 5.3).

Table 5.3 ASCA (2017) School Counselor Professional Standards and Competencies

MINDSETS School counselors believe ...
• Every student can learn, and every student can succeed. • Every student should have access to and opportunity for a high-quality education. • Every student should graduate from high school prepared for postsecondary opportunities. • Every student should have access to a school counseling program. • Effective school counseling is a collaborative process involving school counselors, students, families, teachers, administrators, other school staff and education stakeholders. • School counselors are leaders in the school, district, state, and nation. • School counseling programs promote and enhance student academic, career, and social/emotional outcomes.

(*Continued*)

BEHAVIORS School counselors demonstrate the following standards in the design, implementation, and assessment of a school counseling program.		
Professional Foundation	**Direct and Indirect Student Services**	**Planning and Assessment**
B-PF 1. Apply developmental, learning, counseling, and education theories.	**B-SS 1.** Design and implement instruction aligned to ASCA mind-sets and behaviors for student success in large group, classroom, small group and individual settings.	**B-PA 1.** Create school counseling program beliefs, and vision and mission statements aligned with the school and district.
B-PF 2. Demonstrate understanding of educational systems, legal issues, policies, research, and trends in education.	**B-SS 2.** Provide appraisal and advisement in large group, classroom, small group, and individual settings.	**B-PA 2.** Identify gaps in achievement, attendance, discipline, opportunity, and resources.
B-PF 3. Apply legal and ethical principles of the school counseling profession.	**B-SS 3.** Provide short-term counseling in small group and individual settings.	**B-PA 3.** Develop annual student outcome goals based on student data.
B-PF 4. Apply school counseling professional standards and competencies.	**B-SS 4.** Make referrals to appropriate school and community resources.	**B-PA 4.** Develop and implement action plans aligned with annual student outcome goals and student data.
B-PF 5. Use ASCA mind-sets and behaviors for student success to inform the implementation of a school counseling program.	**B-SS 5.** Consult to support student achievement and success.	**B-PA 5.** Assess and report program results to the school community.
B-PF 6. Demonstrate understanding of the impact of cultural, social, and environmental influences on student success and opportunities.	**B-SS 6.** Collaborate with families, teachers, administrators, other school staff and education stakeholders for student achievement and success.	**B-PA 6.** Use time appropriately according to national recommendations and student/ school data.
B-PF 7. Demonstrate leadership through the development and implementation of a school counseling program.		**B-PA 7.** Establish agreement with the principal and other administrators about the school counseling program.
B-PF 8. Demonstrate advocacy for a school counseling program.		**B-PA 8.** Establish and convene an advisory council for the school counseling program.
B-PF 9. Create systemic change through the implementation of a school counseling program.		**B-PA 9.** Use an appropriate school counselor performance appraisal process.

BEST PRACTICE: COUNSELING PRACTICE BASED IN SCIENCE

While there are fundamental skills expected to be mastered by all professional counselors, these tried and true fundamentals of the counseling relationship and counseling process are essential yet insufficient for effective, ethical practice. The science of our practice is continually finding strategies of intervention and prevention that have demonstrated effectiveness. It is therefore important that counselors maintain an awareness and a proficiency in employing the latest empirically supported techniques. The ACA's code of ethics, for example, notes that "counselors have a responsibility to the public to engage in counseling practices that are based on rigorous research methodologies" (Section C, Introduction). Or even more specifically, "when providing services, counselors use techniques/procedures/modalities that are grounded in theory and/or have an empirical or scientific foundation" (C.7.a).

Efforts put forth by the ACA (Morkides, 2009) and the American Counseling Association Practice Research Network (Bradley et al., 2005) have revealed that evidence-based interventions are critical to the optimal functioning of counselors. It has been suggested that counselors who do not employ research and empirical findings to inform diagnosis, assessment, and treatment decisions may be doing their clients a disservice (Shimokawa et al., 2010).

Although there is no similar, direct statement found in the American school counselors ethical standards (ASCA, 2016), the school counselor's standards note that school counselors "provide effective, responsive interventions to address student needs" (A.1.h.). It is clear that to provide such effective and responsive interventions school counselors must engage in the intentional use of the empirically supported evidence in planning, implementing, and evaluating school counseling interventions and programs (Dimmitt et al., 2007; Zyromski & Mariani, 2016).

The employment of evidence-based principles as the foundation for services provided by school counselors ensures that school counselors use the best existing evidence as a starting framework for the development of an approach that is flexible and responsive to the needs of the individual student (Parsons et al., 2021). Support for a data-driven, evidence-based school counseling practice is provided by the National Panel for School Counseling Evidence-Based Practice, which provides unbiased information about school counseling practices that are supported by scientific information. In addition, school counselors now hold an annual Evidence-Based School Counseling Conference (EBSCC) that provides school counselors with a venue to share effective strategies especially related to evidence-based practices, as well as opportunities to develop effective innovative school counseling program components and interventions.

SELF-CARE

In their book *Field Experience: Transitioning from Student to Professional*, Zhang and Parsons (2016) introduced the concept of self-care with a quote attributed to Viktor Frankl

(1963): "What is to give light must endure burning." While not a reference to the work of a school counselor, Frankl's quote speaks volumes to those who live the experience of the school counselor. As noted by Parsons and Zhang (2014), "One cannot foster health and well-being in another if such is lacking in oneself" (p. 284).

Given the nature of our work it is not unexpected to find that many counselors find it difficult to maintain their own health and well-being. Counselors have reported experiencing emotional exhaustion and at times loss of concern or feelings for their clients. These "symptoms" are potential indications of counselor burnout or compassion fatigue (Figley, 1995; Gladding, 2011; Parsons et al., 2020).

The reality of counselor burnout and compassion fatigue moved the ACA to develop a task force for the sole purpose of decreasing impairment and enhancing wellness among its members. Similarly, the need and ethical responsibility for counselor self-care is highlighted in the ACA's (2014) code of ethics, which directs its members to: "engage in self-care activities to maintain and promote their emotional, physical, mental and spiritual well-being to best meet their professional responsibilities" (Section C, Professional Responsibility). Similarly, ASCA (2016) directs its members to "monitor their emotional and physical health and practice wellness to ensure optimal professional effectiveness. School counselors seek physical or mental health support when needed to ensure professional competence" (B.3.f). Without being intentional about our wellness plan, the effects of our demanding job can take a toll on us and our work in the school, making us less than effective, and possibly unethical, as we see in Case Illustration 5.2.

CASE ILLUSTRATION 5.2: I CARE FOR OTHERS, NOT ME!

Julia was going to be late again, and she'd forgotten to pack a lunch. Getting her son out the door and to school on time wasn't easy; single parenting was hard. As a new school counselor she didn't want to make waves, but these team meetings before school were impossible to make on time. She hoped they changed the time for the second half of the year. Darn. She'd left her protein shake on the table, so no breakfast today.

Julia ran into the school and just made it as the meeting started. As she listened to the teacher drone on about the same issues she heard day in and day out, she could feel her eyes start to droop. Just then the bell rang to start the day and off she went to bus duty. She couldn't even remember what student they were discussing. The schedule for the day was filled with junior planning meetings, so there was no time to get to the cafeteria for lunch. By the end of the day Julia felt tired, cranky, and angry that she'd be spending the night returning emails she didn't get through during the day.

As Julia was leaving school to pick up her son, one of the other counselors stopped her to ask if she was okay. Julia responded that of course she was fine, but the other counselor replied, "You don't look good; you missed a meeting right after school and one of the parents called the principal because you promised to call them to follow up to report on the reentry of their son from his hospitalization and it's been days and they haven't heard from you, not to mention you haven't checked in with the student. You need to take care of you or you can't take care of others!"

Julia sobbed, "I care for others, not me! I don't have time for me!"

Self-care is essential to ethical, competent practice. While there is no absolute means of protecting or insulating oneself from the stress and strain of being a school counselor, there are strategies involving cognitive, emotional, and behavioral self-care measures that serve a preventative function (Baird, 2008). Norcross and Guy (2007) suggest that a good plan starts with self-assessment. Exercise 5.2 invites you to reflect on your own choices as they support care of your mind, body, and spirit.

Exercise 5.2: Wellness Check and Commitment

Directions: Maintaining your health and wellness is not only a practical directive but an ethical mandate if you are to be effective for your students. The table that follows identifies activities that can contribute to your health and wellness. Your task is two-fold:

1. Engage in an honest self-assessment of your current life choices and activities.
2. Identify at least one item in each of the domains listed and make a specific plan for wellness improvement.

It may be beneficial to revisit this plan throughout your training program and adjust as needed.

DOMAIN	SPECIFIC EXAMPLES	I AM COMMITTED TO ...
Physical health	Eat well-balanced meals, including fruits and vegetables.	
	Reduce sugar intake.	
	Monitor caffeine intake.	
	Exercise—in some form for 30 minutes at least three times a week	
	Engage in enjoyable physical activities: danceing, swimming, golfing, bowling. etc.	
	Other (your ideas)	

Social connection	Connect with family member/friend.	
	Smile and say hi to those you encounter in the course of your typical day.	
	Disengage from thoughts of clients when in nonwork social settings.	
	Attend a group educational or recreational experience (lecture, concert, sporting event).	
	Connect with colleagues about professional issues/questions and concerns.	
Psychological domain	Engage in self-reflection.	
	Read for recreation.	
	Contract for personal counseling, coaching, or spiritual direction.	
	Employ stress- and anxiety-reduction techniques.	
	Seek opportunities to learn and expand skill and knowledge outside the professional realm (e.g. learn a foreign language or how to play an instrument).	
	Give yourself permission and take the opportunity to "zone out" as a way of decompressing (e.g. watching television, playing a video game, etc.).	
Affective domain	Engage in activities that make you laugh.	
	Find opportunities to celebrate life with others (e.g. birthday, holidays, anniversaries).	
	Freely express feelings of sadness or loneliness (freedom to cry).	
	Reconnect via review of old pictures or tapping memories of loved ones and loving experiences.	
	Find time to sing/dance.	
	Grant yourself permission to do or attempt to do those activities you always wished you could do.	
	Other (your ideas)	
Inner life	Engage in meditational readings.	
	Engage in personal reflection.	
	Meditate.	
	Commune with nature.	
	Participate in structured spiritual activity (church service, prayer group, retreat, etc.).	
	Find opportunities for expression of gratitude.	

	Celebrate your gifts of life.	
	Seek a moment, or an opportunity, to be in awe.	
	Other (your ideas)	
Professional domain	Set realistic daily task demands.	
	Identify those tasks/activities that are exciting and life- giving and integrate those with those activities that tend to be more draining.	
	Move away from the desk—by way of a simple break or a quick visit to a colleague or a short walk.	
	Close your door to allow for quiet, uninterrupted time to complete a task.	
	Say no to an invitation to do more when you already have enough.	
	Leave work issues and concerns in the office.	
	Engage in peer support regarding client and case issues as well as regarding personal questions and concerns.	
	Engage with a supervisor or mentor.	
	Establish your workspace so that it is both comfortable and comforting.	
	Set boundaries with colleagues, especially when their interactions are intrusions on your limited time or when their requests are overburdening.	
	Take a moment to review your day while identifying one aspect that was professionally satisfying.	
	Other (your ideas)	

Adapted from Naijian Zhang and Richard D. Parsons, Field Experience: Transitioning From Student to Professional, pp. 306-310. Copyright © 2016 by SAGE Publications. Reprinted with permission.

A TAKE-AWAY

For school counselors the provision of ethical services requires the acquisition of professional knowledge and skills. A school counselor's competency begins to take shape on the first day of graduate training and is completed only when one retires from their professional position.

The professional training standards outlined by CACREP serve as beacons to guide counselor-educators in the formation of meaningful curriculum that will form school counselors. Additionally, the professional standards and competencies listed by the ASCA calls all in the profession to not only develop but maintain the mind-sets and behaviors essential to ethical, effective practice.

School counseling is a profession entrusted with the academic achievement and development of our students. As such, it is a profession that demands the highest levels of ethical behavior and professional competency.

KEYSTONES

- Ethical standards signify the maturation of a profession, provide guidelines for practice, and prescribe professional behavior.
- Ethical standards are fundamental to the personal and professional identity of the school counselor.
- Ethical behavior includes honoring diversity and embracing a multicultural approach in counseling.
- School counselors serve as advocates for social justice.
- It is ethical practice to use a decision-making model when faced with an ethical dilemma.
- Being an ethical counselor includes only doing what you are competent to do, which is dependent on training, supervision, continued professional development, and certification in specialty areas.
- Delivering an ethical and effective school counseling program includes using data and evidence-based research.
- Self-care is not only a sound idea, it is an ethical obligation to be intentional about one's self-care as a counselor.

ADDITIONAL RESOURCES

Print

Parsons, R. D., & Dickinson, K. L. (2017). *Ethical practice in the human services.* SAGE.

Parsons, R. D., Dickinson, K. L. & Asempapa, B. (2020). *Counselor wellness: Caring for self to care for others.* Cognella.

Parsons, R. D., & Boccone, P. J. (2021). *Ethical decision making: A guide for counselors in the 21st century.* Cognella.

Sheperis, D. S., Henning, S. L., & Kocet, M. M. (2016). *Ethical decision making for the 21st century counselor.* SAGE.

Web

American Counseling Association. (2019). *Continuing education for counselors.* https://www.counseling.org/continuing-education

American School Counselor Association. (n.d.). *ASCA school counselor competencies.* http://schoolcounselor.org/asca/media/asca/home/SCCompetencies.pdf

American Counseling Association. (2014). *Code of ethics.* http://www.counseling.org/resources/aca-code-of-ethics.pdf

Markkula Center for Applied Ethics: https://www.scu.edu/ethics/ethics-resources/ethical-decision-making/

Ronald H. Fredrickson Center for School Counseling Outcome Research & Evaluation (CSCORE): https://www.umass.edu/schoolcounseling/

REFERENCES

American Counseling Association. (2014). *ACA code of ethics.* Author.

American School Counselor Association. (2016). *ASCA ethical standards for school counselors.* Author. https://www.schoolcounselor.org/asca/media/asca/Ethics/EthicalStandards2016.pdf

American School Counselor Association. (2019). *ASCA school counselor professional standards and competencies.* Author.

Baird, B. N. (2008). *The internship, practicum, and field placement handbook: A guide for the helping professions* (5th ed). Prentice Hall.

Bradley, L. J., Sexton, T. L., & Smith, H. B. (2005). The American Counseling Association Practice Research Network (ACA-PRN): A new research tool. *Journal of Counseling & Development, 83,* 488–491.

Cottone, R. R. & Claus, R. E. (2000). Ethical decision-making models: A review of the literature. *Journal of Counseling & Development, 78,* 275–283.

Council for Accreditation of Counseling & Related Educational Programs. (2016). CACREP 2016 standards. https://www.cacrep.org/for-programs/2016-cacrep-standards/

Dimmitt, C., Carey, J., & Hatch, T. (2007). *Evidence-based school counseling: Making a difference with data-driven practices.* Corwin.

Fairburn, C. G., & Cooper, Z. (2011). Therapist competence, therapy quality, and therapist training. *Behaviour Research & Therapy, 49*(6–7), 373–378.

Figley, R. (Ed.). (1995). *Compassion fatigue: Coping with secondary traumatic stress disorder in those who treat the traumatized.* Brunner/Mazel.

Frankl, V. (1963). *Man's search for meaning.* Simon and Shuster.

Gladding, S. T. (2011). *The counseling dictionary: Concise definitions of frequently used terms.* Pearson.

Gorman, E. H., & Sandefur, R. L. (2011). "Golden Age," quiescence, and revival: How the sociology of profession became the study of knowledge-based work. *Work and Occupations, 38,* 275–302.

Mabe, A., & Rollin, S. (1986). The role of a code of ethical standards in counseling. *Journal of Counseling and Development, 64,* 294–297.

Morkides, C. (2009). Measuring counselor success. *Counseling Today.* http://ct.counseling.org/2009/07/measuring-counselor-success/

Norcross J. C., & Guy, J. D. (2007). *Leaving it at the office: A guide to psychotherapist self-care.* Guilford.

Orlinsky D. E., Botermans, J. F., & Ronnestad, M. H. (2001). Towards an empirically-grounded model of psychotherapy training: Five thousand therapists rate influences on their development. *Australian Psychologist, 36,* 139–148.

Parsons, R., & Boccone, P. (2021). *Ethical decision making.* Cognella.

Parsons, R., Dickinson, K., & Asempapa, B. (2020). *Counselor wellness: Caring for self to care for others.* Cognella.

Parson, R., Dickinson, K., & Asempapa, B. (2021). *Intervention & prevention strategies that work: Empirically supported approaches to multitiered school counseling services.* Cognella.

Shimokawa, K., Lambert, M. J., & Smart, D. W. (2010). Enhancing treatment outcome of patients at risk of treatment failure: Meta-analytic and mega-analytic review of a psychotherapy quality assurance system. *Journal of Consulting and Clinical Psychology, 78,* 298–311.

Zhang, N., & Parsons, R. D. (2016). *Field experience: Transitioning from student to professional.* SAGE.

Zyromski, B., & Mariani, M. A. (2016). *Facilitating evidence-based, data-driven school counseling: A manual for practice.* Corwin.

CHAPTER 6

FROM INTERVENTION TO PREVENTION (MTSS)

School counselors ... promote psychosocial wellness and development for all students.
—ASCA, 2015

When most people think of school counseling the idea of intervention may be first and foremost in their mind. School counselors, after all, respond to those students in crisis as well as those who are struggling to achieve. But school counselors are not only interventionists providing remedial services. As described in Chapter 4, school counselors are truly agents of systemic change who provide comprehensive counseling programs that promote academic achievement, career awareness, and wellness and personal development of all students, not just those who are struggling.

The current chapter presents MTSS, a multitiered system of support, and an evidence-based, systemic approach to providing comprehensive and schoolwide services to improve student learning and socioemotional-behavioral function for all students. Upon completion of this chapter readers will be able to do the following:

1. Describe what is meant by a multitiered system of support (MTSS).
2. Distinguish between MTSS Tiers I, II, and III.
3. Describe what is involved with a program of positive behavioral interventions and supports.

MULTITIERED SYSTEM OF SUPPORT

Educators have been called to revise their assessment strategies curriculum, pedagogy, and interventions to best serve the academic, behavioral, and postsecondary education and career goals of all students (Lewis et al., 2016). This call for revisions has taken shape in the implementation of a multitiered system of supports (MTSS), which is the overarching framework for schoolwide approaches to improve student learning and behavior.

MTSS is an evidence-based framework implemented in K–12 schools utilizing data-based problem solving to integrate academic and behavioral instruction and intervention at tiered intensities to improve students' learning, behavioral, and social/emotional functioning (Sink, 2016). The essence of this approach is that it provides tiers of services based on the student's academic benchmark assessments and behavioral data (Sugai & Horner, 2009; Sugai & Simonsen, 2012). MTSS takes a three-tiered approach for providing academic, behavioral, and social supports to all students based on their needs and skills (Cook et al., 2015; Harlacher et al., 2014; Sugai & Simonsen, 2012). Programs targeting academic challenges have often been referred to as *response to intervention* (RTI; Brown-Chidsey & Steege, 2010; Haager et al., 2007), whereas those addressing behavioral needs are often identified as positive behavioral interventions and supports (PBIS).

School Counselor Role

School counselors believe that all students are capable of grade-level learning when provided adequate support. Further, school counselors believe that the degree of support given to each student should be based on their needs and reflect evidence-based, data-driven practices. With these as operating values, and with training in data analysis, program development and evaluation and direct service delivery, school counselors find themselves uniquely positioned to play a critical role in the implementation of MTSS programs (Belser et al., 2016).

MTSS programs align well with the ASCA (2019) national model and can foster the equity of student access to service and result in academic and behavioral success (Daigle et al., 2016). ASCA's position is that school counselors are stakeholders in the development and implementation of MTSS (ASCA, 2018). Within the framework of a data-informed school counseling program, school counselors employ their collaboration, coordination, and leadership skills to meet the needs of all students and identify students who are at risk of not meeting academic and behavioral expectations (Shepard et al., 2013). The implementation of MTSS, as aligned with a comprehensive school counseling program (e.g. ASCA national model) positions school counselors to advance culturally responsive prevention and interventions to serve students more effectively (Goodman-Scott et al., 2016).

According to the ASCA (2018), school counselors can be pivotal in fostering the academic, career, and social-emotional development of students by the following:

- Providing all students with a standards-based school counseling curriculum to address universal academic, career and social/emotional development
- Analyzing academic, career, and social/emotional development data to identify struggling students

- Identifying and collaborating on research-based intervention strategies implemented by school staff
- Evaluating academic and behavioral progress after interventions
- Revising interventions as appropriate
- Referring to school and community services as appropriate
- Collaborating with administrators, other school professionals, community agencies and families in the design and implementation of MTSS
- Advocating for equitable education for all students and working to remove systemic barriers (p. 45)

A Continuum of Support

An MTSS provides a continuum of evidence-based academic and behavioral practices. Typically, MTSS includes three progressive tiers with increasing intensity of supports based on student responses to core instructions and interventions (Prasse et al., 2012). Using universal screening tools, students are screened to establish baselines and to identify behavior and academic challenges. These data serve as the basis on which to make decisions regarding the levels of support needed.

Tier I, or schoolwide systems, are put into place to support all students academically, socially, and behaviorally and thus work as primary preventions. Tier I programs are typically presented as part of the curriculum or special psychoeducational programs and are expected to meet the needs of an estimated 80% of the students in a school.

Some students, often those identified as being a risk for significant academic or behavioral challenges, would receive targeted interventions (i.e., Tier II). While having been identified as showing some signs of struggling, these students are not yet failing or exhibiting significant behavioral difficulties. As such, the programs offered or services rendered are geared to catch the problem early within its stage of development and thus prevent (secondary prevention) it from coming to full fruition. The estimated percentage of students needing such additional services has been placed at about 15%. The services offered at Tier II may be delivered individually or in small group formats.

Finally, for some students, evidence of their academic failure, behavioral disruption, and socioemotional dysfunction is clear and immediate, and for these students previous support programs have been inadequate, thus a more intensive team-based system (Tier III) would be put in place. Tier III represents services needed by an estimated 5% of students who give evidence of requiring intensive individualized interventions (Ockerman et al., 2012). For these students, more intense, direct support in the form of individual and small group counseling, or referral, may be necessary. As an example of how a school counselor may use the three tiers in response to need, see Case Illustration 6.1.

CASE ILLUSTRATION 6.1: MEETING NEEDS AT DIFFERENT LEVELS

As Max, a fifth-grade student, left the office of school counselor Mr. Roesch, thoughts about the needs he'd heard over the last few weeks filled his head. Several teachers had approached him last week to let him know that a few students in each of their classes had expressed concerns with taking the state test coming up in a few weeks. These students were doing well and did not typically show symptoms of anxiety; however, the idea of these state tests seem to put more stress on the students.

And then there was Max. He appeared to have perfectionistic tendencies and was exhibiting signs of increased anxiety, such as a racing heart and negative self-talk. Certainly, something needed to be done. Mr. Roesch was starting to work individually with Max on reframing his thoughts and was having him practice relaxation techniques. Working one-to-one with Max on a Tier III level was showing success. But what about those other students who were at risk of increased test anxiety?

Following the MTSS framework, Mr. Roesch set up small -group counseling time for the students who were referred to him for anxiety. These Tier II intervention/prevention groups will teach the same types of strategies Max was learning, but not at the same level of intensity. Thinking about prevention for this issue, Mr. Roesch approached the principal to ask if he could implement mindfulness minutes at the start of every day for everyone's participation. Over the intercom system, Mr. Roesch would start the school day with a strategy for breathing or stretching for the entire school to do. This Tier I prevention would help all the students and would also contribute to the wellness of the staff and faculty as they modeled the strategies!

Research that has compared schools implementing MTSS to those non-implementing schools shows that MTSS schools had higher scores on academic accountability measures (Marin & Filece, 2013), reduced discipline referrals and suspensions (Benner et al., 2012), and increased student and staff perception of school safety and supportive climate (Horner et al., 2009). Positive effects of MTSS implementation has been reported across grade levels (elementary through high school) and school settings (rural, suburban, and urban) (Farkas et al., 2012).

COUNSELING (TIER III)

For most school counselors, direct one-on-one intervention usually targets short-term issues, most often of a developmental nature, as would be the case for students having difficulty transitioning into a new school, gaining access to a social group, or navigating interpersonal conflicts. Quite often school counselors will engage in short-term, goal-oriented and strengths-based approaches that focus on those skills and dispositions that the student possesses and that can be brought to bear on their current challenges (Gallassi et al., 2008). Such an approach turns the student's attention to their internal strengths and resourcefulness rather than dwelling on weaknesses, failures, and shortcomings (Masten et al., 2008).

It is important to note that even at this level of direct intervention, prevention remains a goal. While intervention is needed and targeted to assist the student to move out of their current crisis, the counselor will employ strategies that not only remediate the situation but hopefully position the students in a way to avoid a similar crisis in the future, thus providing a third-level or tertiary form of prevention.

For some students the challenges presented may require a longer term of engagement, perhaps over the semester or academic year, and involve consulting with teachers and parents. Often in these situations the counselor is assisting the student in developing new coping skills while attempting to mitigate some troublesome or negative element within the student's life. Finally, some students will present a level of struggle that is not only blocking their academic achievement but is placing them in physical and/or psychological harm. When such conditions or issues are chronic or perhaps life- endangering, the school counselor's role shifts from direct service provider to one of support and referral to community health professionals who can best assist the student and their family in their time of need (Smith & Archer, 2000). This would certainly be the case for a counselor, who while working with a student who was initially referred as a result of a significant drop in grades reveals that she has feelings of depression and thoughts of suicide. For this counselor, the call is to provide for immediate crisis intervention, suicide prevention, and the referral to a mental health provider in the community.

Counseling interventions at Tier III include individual counseling, one-on-one mentoring, or referrals to community agencies for more intensive services (Ockerman et al., 2012). Providing service at this level requires counselors to be knowledgeable and competent in providing interventions that reflect evidence-based practice. Given the potential for needing to refer and find support from community-based professionals, counselors also need to have local knowledge of such service and be familiar with various treatment modalities and their effectiveness for the types of student issues presented. Table 6.1 provides a sampling of evidence-based programs and services that have been employed as Tier III interventions.

Table 6.1 Sampling of Tier III Programs

PROGRAM	DESCRIPTION	REFERENCE
Coping Cat/CAT project	Coping Cat is a cognitive behavioral program incorporating the following: • Recognizing and understanding reactions to anxiety • Clarifying thoughts and feelings in anxious situations • Developing plans for effective coping • Evaluating performance and giving self-reinforcement	www.workbookpublishing.com
Incredible Years	A series of evidence-based programs for parents, children, and teachers with the goal of preventing and treating children's behavior problems while promoting socioemotional and academic competence	http://www.incredibleyears.com/

REACHING THOSE AT RISK (TIER II)

Some students provide early indications that they are on a path toward academic and/or socioemotional difficulties. These are students who, while receiving solid academic and behavioral support, exhibit some deficiencies (Horner et al., 2015). On a socioemotional level, a student, while participating within the classroom, may be observed self-isolating at lunch or recess. Or perhaps a teacher begins to notice verbal and nonverbal signs that a student is getting increasingly frustrated with the unit under study or seems to show signs of stress and anxiety during unit tests. While the students in either of these examples are not exhibiting self-harmful behaviors or showing indications of thwarted academic achievement, the behaviors could be indicative of later problems. These early indications that a student is at higher risk for academic or socioemotional difficulties serve as invitations to the school counselor to engage in secondary prevention services. Thus, with these data, a counselor may attempt to intercede in a way that helps the student avoid the development of additional, more challenging problems. The counselor, for example, may invite the student to learn and practice social skills or develop stress and anxiety management techniques either individually or in small groups.

The goal at Tier II, therefore, is to provide services early in the development of the student's struggles to stop the decline in their functioning or prevent the emergence of more significant issues (Parsons et al., 2021). It is this focus on preventing the full development of a problem or shortening the duration and impact of an issue that characterizes Tier II programs as forms of secondary prevention (Dickinson & Parsons, 2019). Counselors engaged with Tier II programming will provide individual and group counseling, work with teachers to develop classroom-based interventions, and often engage the student with check-in, check-out (CICO) contact as a way of ensuring they are prepared for class (check in) and are motivated and prepared for home assignments (check out) (Baker & Ryan, 2014; Maynard et al., 2013). Table 6.2 illustrates Tier II, secondary prevention programs provided by school counselors.

Table 6.2 Sampling of Tier II Programs

PROGRAM	DESCRIPTION	REFERENCE
AVID Advancement via Individual Determination)	AVID is a resource for closing the opportunity gap in college graduation rates among diverse and underrepresented demographic groups.	http://www.avidcenter.org
CASASTART (Striving Together to Achieve Rewarding Tomorrows)	A community-based, intensive case management model that aims to prevent drug use and delinquency among high-risk adolescents, age 11 to 13.	https://www.crimesolutions.gov/ProgramDetails.aspx?ID=284#targetText=CASASTART%20(Striving%20Together%20to%20Achieve,-substance%20abuse%20and%20delinquent%20involvement

SCHOOLWIDE DEVELOPMENTAL PROGRAMMING (TIER I)

It is in Tier I programming that a school counselor can most clearly be seen in the roles of leader, advocate, and agent of systemic change. Counselors operating from the perspective of Tier I programming are mindful of the system factors that can confront all students and may make academic progress and socioemotional development less than optimal.

At the level of Tier I the counselor will implement programs that impact an entire school population, that is an entire class, grade level, or even the school as a whole. These programs take on a primary prevention nature in that they foster the students' development of adaptive knowledge and skills, which will prepare them to address challenges to their normative development and academic achievement. The very nature of Tier I programming as broad -based, schoolwide and preventive aligns these programs with the comprehensive school counseling programs depicted in the ASCA (2019) national model.

Because the focus of Tier I programming is in essence extra-personal, that is, looking at the factors outside of the student that are facilitating or hindering their progress, counselors will engage in consulting and coordinating with others in the school. In this role, counselors may assist teachers with differentiated instruction or work with school teams to address policies or procedures that are detrimental to student development. Programs such as schoolwide bullying prevention programs (see for example Olweus Bullying Prevention Program, www.violencepreventionworks.org/public/olweus_bullying_prevention_program.page) and Positive Behavioral Interventions and Supports (see www.pbis.org) are Tier I programming (Donohue et al., 2016; Goodman-Scott, 2016).

As the school counselor you will hear and see many issues, and as you identify the needs of the students, you may consider what prevention and intervention strategies you can implement at each tier. Use Exercise 6.1 to start your list of possible strategies.

Exercising 6.1: Thinking in Tiers

Directions: Consider the types of strategies that may be needed and implemented for issues that may impact your students. A few examples have been provided. You may wish to speak with a practicing school counselor for input for typical needs at the level (elementary, middle, high school) you would like to work.

POSSIBLE ISSUE	TIER I STRATEGY	TIER II STRATEGY	TIER III STRATEGY
Name- calling	Classroom lesson on respect; participation in No Name- Calling Week	Psychoeducational small-group counseling focusing on empathy and appropriate expression of feelings	Your idea
Failing tests	Learning styles inventory for all students fourth grade and up; strategies provided for each learning modality	Your idea	CICO (check-in/check-out) for homework, books and study outlines; study skills instruction
Excluding others			
Skipping class			
Physical fights			
Other			

POSITIVE BEHAVIORAL INTERVENTIONS AND SUPPORTS

A Multitiered Approach

The description of MTSS has emphasized its tiered nature and the distinction of the focus of each tier. In reality, programs can be designed to cut across tiers and thus offer multiple levels of support. One such program is the Positive Behavioral Interventions and Supports (PBIS).

PBIS is a three-tiered preventative continuum of data-driven and evidence-based practices all focused on the improvement of students' academic and social behaviors (Sugai & Simonsen, 2012). PBIS is grounded in the principles of applied behavior analysis and is implemented schoolwide (Shepard et al., 2013). Student data, including those reflecting suspension and office discipline referrals, grades, and attendance, are gathered and analyzed and serve as the basis for program development and adjustments (Sugai & Horner, 2009). The PBIS programs can operate as a Tier I, primary prevention program, targeting the whole school. Such a program may employ token economy behavioral systems and establish supportive expectations and school cultures that are positive and safe. These behavioral principles can be adjusted so that they can be used as additional forms of support for those students needing Tier II and III services. In this situation, the services may take on the form of behavior modification contracts, social skills training sessions, or tailored wrap-around services.

A SIMPLIFIED ILLUSTRATION OF PBIS-SERVICING ACROSS ALL TIERS

ABC Elementary School

Description: Our goal is to provide a positive focus to encouraging desirable student behaviors resulting in a positive climate that maximizes learning. A set of universal expectations for behavior, positively stated, are established *for all students in all locations of the school.* These expectations generally promote core values such as respect, responsibility, and safety.

The positive approach of PBIS ensures that our students will be taught the behaviors we expect. They will be rewarded when they succeed and corrected when they make mistakes. Our goal is to provide a positive focus to encouraging desirable student behaviors resulting in a positive climate that maximizes learning. The fact that our program is schoolwide means that teachers, administrators, and staff will support appropriate behavior in the classroom and non-classroom (bathrooms, assemblies, hallways).

Our program of support will occur along a continuum of three layers, as described.

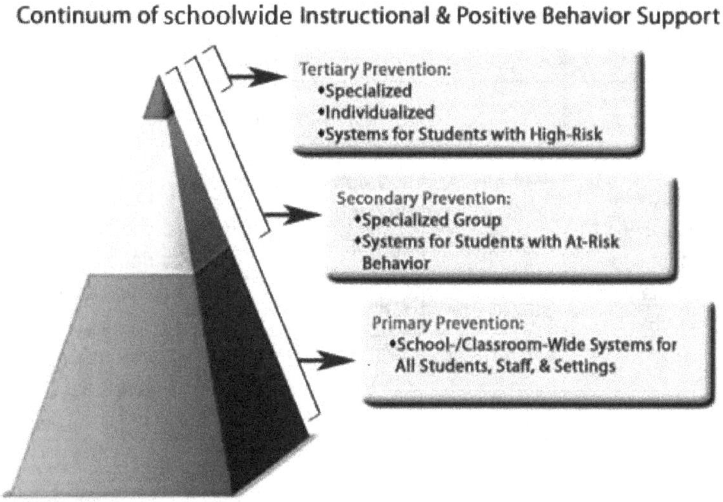

Continuum of schoolwide Instructional & Positive Behavior Support

Tertiary Prevention:
•Specialized
•Individualized
•Systems for Students with High-Risk

Secondary Prevention:
•Specialized Group
•Systems for Students with At-Risk Behavior

Primary Prevention:
•School-/Classroom-Wide Systems for All Students, Staff, & Settings

Tier I: Primary Prevention

Our behavioral expectations: For all members of ABC school community to be safe, respectful, and responsible.

What This Looks Like (Behavior Indicators)

	HALLWAYS	CAFETERIA	RECESS	ASSEMBLIES	BATHROOM	LIBRARY
Be safe	Use rails for support. Walk don't run in the halls. Walk on the right side of the hall. Keep personal space.	Keep hands to yourself. Voice level 1 or 2. Follow lines.	Hands to yourself, unless playing tag. Follow equipment-use instructions.	Enter in a line. Keep hands and feet to self. Follow directions.	Use hand-washing procedure. Flush the toilet.	Keep hands and feet and objects to yourself. Enter and exit in a line.
Be respectful	Voice level 1 or 2. Wave silently to friends. Hats off.	Take turns. Say please and thank you. Follow clean-up directions.	Follow line-up procedure. You can use any voice level. Take turns on equipment. Use appropriate language.	Use polite cheering. (voice level 0, 1, 2, or 3). Quiet feet. Stand during pledge. Say pledge (or be quiet).	Clean up after yourself. Keep hands, feet, and eyes to yourself. Wait patiently.	Voice level 1 or 2. Follow adult directions. Sit in small chairs or on the rug.
Be responsible	Enjoy wall displays with your eyes (no need to touch).	Wait patiently. Pick up trash. Stay in your seat.	Follow snow play procedure. Pick up your trash. Wait patiently for your turn.	Class sits in designated spot. After the class's turn, return to the designated spot.	Go back to class to when you're done. Voice level 1 or 2. Pick up your trash.	Return books on time. Stay in personal space. Use library time to search for or read books.

Teaching to expectations: All students will receive direct instruction in the behavior expectations. Our teachers will teach these behaviors as they would teach academics or any other skill, and as such will do the following:

- Provide frequent trials or lessons. Refresh lessons throughout the school year.
- Keep lessons brief (5–15 minutes typically).
- Take students to various locations in the school for instruction. Plan for this to occur over the first week or so of implementation.
- Model those behaviors at all times.

Tier I Program for Reinforcing Success
For the individual student:

- Smiles and words of praise from adults who acknowledge appropriate student behavior and provide a ROAR (really on a roll) card with a picture of our lion mascot.
- The left half of the card goes to the student for gift or privilege.
- The right half of the card goes to the classroom raffle box.

At the classroom level:

- Each Friday, the teacher draws two ROAR cards from classroom raffle box.
- Students selected receive a ROARING certificate (a certificate acknowledging success), plus go to office to choose one thing from the menu of rewards. They will also take their ROAR cards and place them in the office raffle box for monthly schoolwide PBIS assembly drawings.

At the grade level:

- At the monthly schoolwide PBIS assembly, the grade level with the greatest number of ROAR cards receives the **ROARING LOUD** certificate to be hung in their class.
- The grade also receives a pizza lunch party.

At the school level:

- At the monthly schoolwide PBIS assembly, 10 ROAR cards will be drawn from the office raffle box.

- The 10 students whose ROAR cards are drawn from the box will receive the PRIDE PROUD award (a special award certificate).
- Award winners go to the office to choose one thing from the special menu of rewards.

Examples of the Rewards (Tangibles and Privileges) Included in Menu

PRE-K–GRADE 1	GRADES 2–3	GRADES 4–6
Sparkly pencils	Multicolored pens	Stickers (medium and large)
Sticky hands	Magnifying glass	Playing cards
Pass for first in recess line	Computer time for 15 min	Positive call home from teacher
Teacher to read aloud to the class	Lunch with teacher	Free homework pass
Pick book for teacher to read	Tell a joke	Be teacher's assistant for a lesson
Free recess	Assist the custodian	Lunch with principal
Be teacher's assistant	Bring class outside for lunch	Choose outdoor activity for the whole class

(Items are updated monthly at student suggestions)

Tier II: When Additional Support is Needed

Some of the students may need additional teaching, motivation, and reinforcement. While the number of students should be smaller in percentage, our counselor and the On the Prowl team will meet and identify students who would appear to benefit from additional support. The counselor or team members will meet with the students to do the following:

- Identify locations in the school or times of the day that are especially problematic and then problem-solve simple solutions for those situations.
- Implement targeted interventions, including increased structure, prompts, and feedback for students with instruction on skills needed to be successful.
- Provide small-group instruction and facilitate the development of social skills and replacement behaviors.
- Consider providing stronger incentives (shaping desired behaviors) and expanding reinforcement system to engage parents and family setting.
- Check in with students, monitor behavior, and provide additional encouragement.

Tier III Intervention (For Those Unresponsive to Tier I or II)

Our counselor along with the Prowl team will identify students who have been unresponsive to Tier I and II interventions and supports. These students are those identified as being highly disruptive, chronic/frequent violators of the expected behavior, and experiencing social and educational difficulties.

The counselor in collaboration with the teacher(s) will engage in a functional behavior assessment (FBA) and develop an individual behavioral support program. Counselors employing one-on-one services may provide additional intensive social skills and replacement behavior instructions and consult with the classroom teacher(s) to implement additional classroom management strategies.

A TAKE-AWAY

The unique values, knowledge, and skills possessed by today's school counselor positions them in a critical role in the implementation of MTSS programs. Trained not only as direct service providers and program developers, the school counselor's abilities to collaborate and coordinate across all school personnel is crucial if schools are to provide universal preventive programs as called for by MTSS. The implementation of MTSS, as aligned with a comprehensive school counseling program (e.g. ASCA national model) positions school counselors to advance prevention and intervention programs that will serve all students more effectively.

KEYSTONES

- MTSS programs are evidence-based, holistic, and systemic approaches to providing comprehensive and schoolwide services to improve student learning and socioemotional-behavioral function.
- The main goal of MTSS is to provide an integrated systemic approach to meet the needs of all students and use resources most effectively and efficiently to enable every child to be successful.
- MTSS invites the counselor to engage with all students on a remedial–prevention continuum, modifying the intensity of services as a reflection of the degree of need.
- Services offered within the framework of MTSS are divided into three tiered categories based on the level of risk and need.
- Tier I provides services to all students in support of their academic and behavioral development. The estimate is that approximately 80% of students are successful with such support.

- Tier II addresses students with elevated needs who require more specialized strategies than those offered to the general student body. The estimated percentage of students needing such additional support has been placed at about 15%.
- Tier III represents the estimated 5% of students who need intensive individualized interventions. For these students, direct one-on-one counseling or even referral to outside services may be the approach of choice.
- Counselors need to (a) understand the nature of MTSS, (b) have the ability to engage in risk assessment, and (c) employ evidence-based practices that serve the continuum of need across all tiers.

ADDITIONAL RESOURCES

Print

Baker, B., & Ryan, C. (2014). *The PBIS team handbook: Setting expectations and building positive behavior.* Free Spirit.

Clark, A. G., & Dockweiler, K. A. (2019). *Multi-tiered systems of support in secondary schools.* Routledge.

Goodman-Scott, E., & Betters-Bubon, J. (2019). *The school counselors guide to multi-tiered systems of support.* Routledge.

Web

Hatch, T. (2018). *Multi-tiered, multi-domain system of supports (MTMDSS) video.* https://www.hatchingresults.com/videos/

Madison Metropolitan School District MTSS Toolkit: https://mtss.madison.k12.wi.us/mtss-toolkit

Mississippi Department of Education. *Multi-tiered system of supports documentation packet.* Mississippi Department of Education. *Multi-tiered system of supports documentation packet.*

Panorama 42 MTSS intervention Strategies to Bring Back to Your Support Team: https://www.panoramaed.com/blog/mtss-intervention-strategies

REFERENCES

American School Counselor Association. (2015). *The school counselor and student mental health.* https://schoolcounselor.org/Standards-Positions/Position-Statements/ASCA-Position-Statements/The-School-Counselor-and-Student-Mental-Health

American School Counselor Association. (2018). *The school counselor and multitiered system of supports.* https://www.schoolcounselor.org/Standards-Positions/Position-Statements/ASCA-Position-Statements/The-School-Counselor-and-Multitiered-System-of-Sup

American School Counselor Association. (2019). *The ASCA national model: A framework for school counseling programs* (4th ed.). Author.

Baker, B., & Ryan, C. (2014). *The PBIS team handbook: Setting expectations and building positive behavior.* Free Spirit.

Belser, C. T., Shillingford, M. A., & Joe, J.R. (2016). The ASCA model and a multi-tiered system of supports: A framework to support students of color with problem behavior. *The Professional Counselor,* 6(3), 251–262.

Benner, G. J., Nelson, J. R., Sanders, E. A., & Ralston, N. C. (2012). Behavior intervention for students with externalizing behavior problems: Primary-level standard protocol. *Exceptional Children, 78*(2), 181–198.

Brown-Chidsey, R., & Steege, M. W. (2010). *Response to intervention: Principles and strategies for effective practice.* Guilford.

Cook, C. R., Lyon, A. R., Kubergovic, D., Wright, D. B., & Zhang, Y. (2015). A supportive beliefs intervention to facilitate the implementation of evidence-based practices within a multi-tiered system of supports. *School Mental Health, 7,* 49–60.

Daigle, J. M., Goodman-Scott, E., Cavin, J., & Donohue, P. (2016). *Integrating a multi-tiered system of supports with comprehensive school counseling programs.* http://tpcjournal.nbcc.org/integrating-a-multi-tiered-system-of-supports-with-comprehensive-school-counseling-programs/

Dickinson, K., & Parsons, R. (2019). *The school counselor as consultant.* Cognella.

Donohue, M. D. (2014). *Implementing school-wide positive behavioral supports (SWPBIS): School counselors' perceptions of student outcomes, school climate, and professional effectiveness* [Doctoral dissertation, University of Connecticut]. digitalcommons.uconn.edu/cgi/viewcontent.cgi?article=6616&context=dissertations

Farkas, M. S., Simonsen, B., Migdole, S., Donovan, M. E., Clemens, K., & Cicchese, V. (2012). Schoolwide positive behavior support in an alternative school setting: An evaluation of fidelity, outcomes, and social validity of Tier I implementation. *Journal of Emotional and Behavioral Disorders, 20*(4), 275–288.

Gallassi, J. P., Griffin, D., & Akso, P. (2008). Strengths-based school counseling and the ASCA national model. *Professional School Counseling, 12*(2), 176–181.

Goodman-Scott, E. (2015). School counselors' perceptions of their academic preparedness and job activities. *Counselor Education and Supervision, 54,* 57–67.

Goodman-Scott, E., Betters-Bubon, J., & Donohue, P. (2016). Aligning comprehensive school counseling programs and positive behavioral interventions and supports to maximize school counselors' efforts. *Professional School Counseling, 19,* 57–67.

Haager, D., Klinger, J., & Vaughn, S. (2007). *Evidence-based reading practices for response to intervention.* Brookes.

Harlacher, J. E., Sakelaris, T. L., & Kattelman, N. M. (2014). *Practitioner's guide to curriculum-based evaluation in reading.* Springer.

Horner R. H., Sugai, G., Smolkowski, K., Eber, L., Nakasato, J., Todd, A., & Esperanza, J. (2009). A randomized, waitlist-controlled effectiveness trial assessing school-wide positive behavior support in elementary schools. *Journal of Positive Behavior Interventions, 11*(3), 133–144.

Horner, R. H., Sugai, G., & Anderson, C. M. (2010). Examining the evidence-base for school wide positive behavior support. *Focus on Exceptional Children, 42*, 1–14.

Horner, R. H., Sugai, G. M., & Lewis, T. (2015). Is school-wide positive behavior support an evidence-based practice? https://www.pbis.org/resource/is-school-wide-positive-behavior-support-an-evidence-based-practice

Lewis, T. J., Mitchell, B. S., Bruntmeyer, D. T., & Sugai, G. (2016). School-wide positivebehavior support and response to intervention: System similarities, distinctions, and research to date at the universal level of support. In S. R. Jimerson, M. K. Burns, & A.M. Van Der Heyden (Eds.), *Handbook of response to intervention: The science and practice of multi-tiered systems of support* (2nd ed.) (pp. 703–717). Springer.

Marin, A. M., & Filce, H. G. (2013). The relationship between implementation of school-wide positive behavior intervention and supports and performance on state accountability measures. *SAGE Open, 3*, 1–10.

Masten, A. S., Hebers, J. E., Cutuli, J. J., & Lafavor, T. L. (2008). Promoting competence and resilience in the school context. *Professional School Counseling, 12*, 76–84.

Maynard, B. R., Kjellstrand, E. K., & Thompson, A. M. (2013). Effects of check and connect on attendance, behavior, and academics: A randomized effectiveness trial. *Research on Social Work Practice, 24*, 296–309.

Ockerman, M. S., Mason, E. C., & Feiker-Hollenbeck, A. (2012). Integrating RTI with school counseling programs: Being a proactive professional school counselor. *Journal of School Counseling, 10*(15), 1–37.

Ockerman, M. S., Patrikakou, E., & Feiker-Hollenbeck, A. (2015). Preparation of school counselors and response to intervention: A profession at the crossroads. *The Journal of Counselor Preparation and Supervision, 7*, 161–184.

Olsen, J., Parikh-Foxx, S., Flowers, C. & Algozzine, B. (2016/2017). *Professional School Counseling, 20*(1), 159–171.

Parsons, R. D. Dickinson, K., & Asempapa, B. (2021). *Intervention and prevention strategies that work! Empirically supported approaches to multitiered school counseling services*. Cognella.

Prasse, D. P., Breunlin, R. J., Giroux, D., Hunt, J., Morrison, D., & Their, K. (2012). Embedding multi-tiered system of supports/response to intervention into teacher preparation. *Learning Disabilities: A Contemporary Journal, 10*(2), 75–93.

Shepard, J. M., Shahidullah, J. D., & Carlson, J. S. (2013). *Counseling students in levels 2 and 3: A PBIS/RTI Guide*. Corwin.

Sink, C. (2016). *Incorporating a multi-tiered system of supports into school counselor preparation*. http://tpcjournal.nbcc.org/wp-content/uploads/2016/09/Pages203-219-Sink.pdf

Smith, S. L., & Archer, J. (2000). The developmental school counselor and mental health counseling. In J. Wittmer (Ed.), *Managing your school counseling program: K-12 developmental strategies* (2nd ed.) (pp. 68–74). Educational Media.

Sugai, G., & Horner, R. H. (2009). Responsiveness-to-intervention and school-wide positive behavior supports: Integration of multi-tiered system approaches. *Exceptionality, 17*, 223–237.

Sugai, G., & Simonsen, B. (2012). *Positive behavioral interventions and supports: History, defining features, and misconceptions.* http://idahotc.com/Portals/6/Docs/2015/Tier_1/articles/PBIS_history.features.misconceptions.pdf

IMAGE CREDITS

IMG 6.1: Manitoba, "Continuum of School-Wide Instructional & Positive Behavior Support," Copyright © by Manitoba. Reprinted with permission.

CHAPTER 7

A PROFESSIONAL AMONG PROFESSIONALS

It takes a village, and fortunately we have so many caring and dedicated professionals working with our students.

—Raul, Middle school counselor

The issues and challenges that are facing today's students are complex and multifaceted. Addressing the issues, the needs, and the demands experienced by all our school's stakeholders requires a coordinated effort and collaboration between all concerned.

Today's school counselor is trained to engage as a leader, a collaborator, and a coordinator of all resources necessary to support the academic achievement and the behavioral and socioemotional development of our students. The current chapter presents both the reality of schools as systems with many contributing parts along with the role counselors can and need to play in coordinating these parts in service of a school's mission.

Upon completing this chapter readers will be able to do the following:

1. Explain the implications of knowing that a school is a system.
2. Describe the value of the school counselor in the role of coordinator.
3. Describe the component elements of consultation as a mode of service delivery.
4. Explain the value of a collaborative consultation to a comprehensive school counseling program.

SCHOOLS AS SYSTEMS

When you think about a system, even one of our physiological systems, such as the circulatory system, you can begin to appreciate not only the many parts that are involved in a system but the clear need to coordinate the workings of these parts as they come together in servicing some desired goal. Organizations, be they business, governmental, or educational, are designed and operate as systems and as such are entities that are "made up of interconnected parts, with recognizable relationships that are systematically arranged to serve a perceived purpose" (Kurpius, 1985, p. 368). This definition of systems offered by Kurpius (1985), while succinct, is packed with significant implications for the school counselor.

Entity

The use of the term *entities* implies that systems are viable and organic and thus expected to change over time. That certainly appears reasonable in that schools are serving in a culture that changes over time, as do the needs of the school's stakeholders. Should a school's community demographics change, the impact on the student's educational needs can also change. As policies and procedures imposed by outside forces (e.g. governmental policies) or available resources (e.g. tax base) change, the school as a viable entity will need to adjust. This adjustment, while responsive to the changing realities, does so while restructuring, all in continued service to the mission. The effective school is the one that can adapt in curriculum, in services, in processes and procedures, and in ways that continue to respond to the needs of its stakeholders. The school counselor, as an advocate and agent of system change, must identify the changing nature of the needs and the resources and facilitate the creative adjustment of policies, programs, and procedures in service of the mission.

Interrelated Parts

A second concept that seems to have relevance to understanding schools as systems is that systems are made up of interconnected parts. A quick look at a school's organizational chart can give us a fuller appreciation of the number of parts that are interrelated in the service of our students. The chart presented is truly a simplified or basic illustration of a middle school's hierarchy of departments. In reality, there are many more people involved, and their relationships are much more complicated. Understanding the dynamic relationship between all of the stakeholders in our schools (e.g. administrators, teachers, staff students, parents, community leaders), along with the various resources (e.g. buildings, teaching materials, money) and processes (e.g. curriculum, support programs, decision-making structures, management procedures) as they operate both independently and interdependently in hopes of achieving some common goal (i.e. the mission), is essential. If all these parts fail to work together the system will break down and the mission will not be achieved. Remember the reference to the circulatory system: Consider what happens when a blood clot occurs anywhere within that system. Things come to halt, often with dire outcomes.

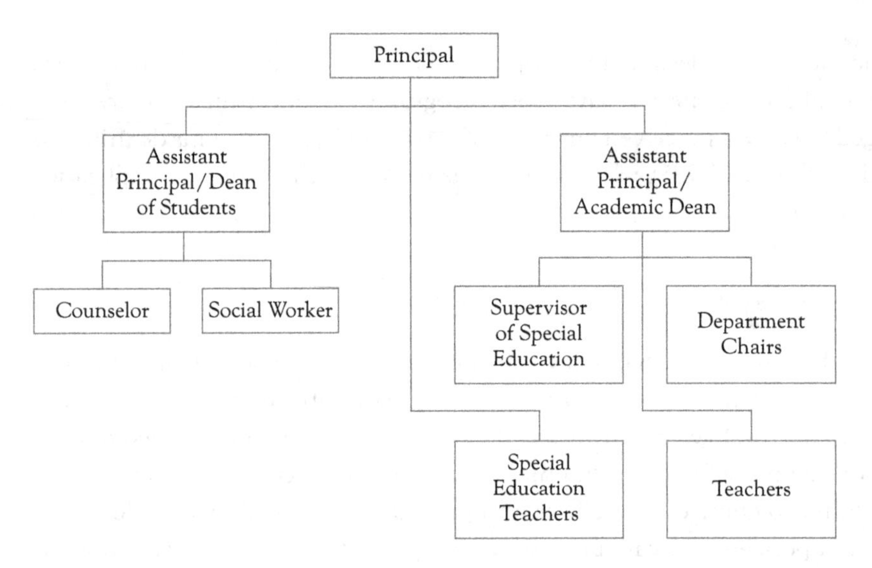

Figure 7.1 Simplified illustration of interrelated parts of a school (a middle school organizational chart)

School counselors, with the understanding that all decisions to add or delete a resource or change a process or procedure will impact not only specific stakeholders (e.g. a specific group of students, teachers) but will affect the degree to which a school stays mission driven, place themselves in a position to advocate. That advocacy will not be just for one student or set of students, or for one program or process, but for decisions that are mission driven and thus serve all.

Serving a Perceived Purpose

Perhaps out of all the characteristics of a system depicted in this definition, the one inviting our attention is the statement that these parts are "systematically arranged to serve a perceived purpose." As noted in Chapter 4, the perceived purpose of any one school is detailed in its mission statement, a statement that explains the reason for the school's existence and announces a set of values guiding all decisions and practices.

With all the significant, and even mundane, decisions that need to be made in any one day within our schools, and the numerous individuals (see Figure 7.1) making those decisions, staying true to a school mission (i.e., *singular perceived purpose*) is essential. It is in support of this coordination of efforts that a counselor's leadership, advocacy, and coordination skills can prove invaluable. The following case illustration (7.1) highlights the need for such coordination and the role a school counselor can play in that process.

CASE ILLUSTRATION 7.1: FACILITATING A BLENDING OF SCHOOLS

Central Middle School was a school with a major challenge: to transition students and families from a neighboring community into Central. The closure of the neighboring middle school presented Central with numerous challenges.

Selena R., Central's middle school counselor and all-around go-to person, gathered a volunteer planning team composed of two teachers from the neighboring school, two from Central, the vice principal, and four parent participants. The team met throughout the summer to identify possible challenges to meeting the needs of this new student population and the types of programs that would be needed. Four issues emerged as essential to the transition and the development of a productive school year: (a) transitioning students to a new system and school culture; (b) forming a unified school identity for all students; (c) revamping course selection processes to facilitate placement and equitable access to courses, and (d) expanding services to students who were English learners (EL).

Teams were established and charged with developing programs and strategies for each of these issues. The school counselor provided leadership and coordination of all program activities, funding, data collection (on impact), and the dissemination of outcome findings.

From need recognition through team formation, to the final reporting of outcomes and impacts, the school counselor demonstrated competence as leader, advocate, and coordinator.

COUNSELORS AS CENTRAL TO COORDINATION

The development, implementation, maintenance, and assessment of a comprehensive school counseling program is a challenging task. Once created and employed such a comprehensive school counseling program will impact all stakeholders in a way that facilitates the achievement of the school's mission. But, as can be seen with the PBIS illustration (see Chapter 6), the services rendered within such a comprehensive counseling program are not always directly delivered by the school counselor. To be effective, counselors need to engage the services of teachers, administrators, and certainly parents in the delivery of programs and services. Such engagement of these others requires the school counselor's knowledge and skills of coordination.

When viewed from the perspective of the ASCA (2019) national model (see Chapter 3), the management system addresses administrative agreements, coordination of the advisory council, action planning, use of time and calendars, and use of data—all requiring the coordination of a school counselor. Additionally, school counseling programs require the collection of data as both formative and summative assessments, and such collection of data in service of the accountability element of the national model will require coordination of various departments to acquire those data (e.g. discipline, attendance, grades, etc.).

Often the counselor in the role of coordinator will engage in advocacy activities. For example, the counselor as coordinator-advocate may involve inviting administration to expand scheduling for teacher–parent meetings so that they are not only during the hours when some parents may be working; or coordinating teams of stakeholders can consider cultural, community, or even school factors that may be interfering with a student's functioning. One arena in which the school counselor's efforts as coordinator and advocate have proven valuable is in the area of coordinating services for those with unique needs. Whether it is coordinating services for those with learning challenges or those living in conditions that place them at risk, school counselors can bring together various professionals—administrators, teachers, school psychologists, school nurses and social workers—and community resources in service to these students. Finally, as illustrated in Chapter 6, school counselors can be central to the coordination and delivery of schoolwide programs (e.g. PBIS), which target the climate of the school and the values the school wishes to instill. You can get an idea of what this coordination may look like in Case Illustration 7.2.

CASE ILLUSTRATION 7.2: TEAM WORK

Ms. Gibson, the school counselor, hung up the phone after speaking to Mrs. Lane, a new parent who was planning on registering her two daughters in the school. Mr. and Mrs. Lane would be returning from Columbia in a few weeks with their newly adopted twin daughters. Although the girls were chronologically old enough to be place in first grade, Ms. Gibson suggested having a team meeting now to talk about what the girls might need and how the school might best support the new students and newly formed family.

Knowing that the girls did not speak English, Ms. Gibson invited the ESL teacher to attend the meeting. Additionally, the ESL teacher gave her the name of a community resource that hosted events for people in the area that were from Brazil, Peru, and Columbia, which she called and invited, as well. The principal, a classroom teacher, the nurse, and the social worker were also on the list of attendees.

At the meeting, the Lanes were thrilled to find so many people who were invested in making their daughters successful. They were impressed that these people would take the time to speak with them in preparation of their girls' first day. Each attendee explained what they could do to make the girls feel welcome and connected. Ms. Gibson assured the Lanes they would follow up after the girls arrived to see what else was needed. Team work makes a difference!

The school counselor's coordination efforts are not always lofty or esoteric. Commonplace activities such as scheduling advisory meetings, compiling data, or orchestrating career days or college rep visits are often the types of coordinating activities essential to effective programming. As with all the services provided by the school counselor, coordination efforts will touch the students in three different domains: academic development, career development, and personal/social development. Table 7.1 provides several examples of these counselor-coordinated programs and services. Exercise 7.1 invites you to use this list as a reference point to interview a school counselor and acquire additional examples of their coordinating efforts.

Table 7.1 Coordinating Programs and Services

ACADEMIC DEVELOPMENT	CAREER DEVELOPMENT	PERSONAL/SOCIAL DEVELOPMENT
Peer tutoring	Career day	Peer mediation
Cross-grade tutoring program	"Shadow a person at work" day	Access to community-based mental health services
Student orientation (new and transition students)	Trip to vocational school	Buddy programs
Community volunteer tutors	Interview those in the field program	Substance abuse prevention presentations
Learning styles testing program	Vocational interest testing programs	Recess bench and share-a-lunch table programs

Exercise 7.1: Coordinating in Service of My Students

Directions: Using the examples of coordination provided in Table 7.1, interview a school counselor (preferably three: one in elementary, middle, and high school) and gather information about the specific programs and services they coordinate in each of the three domains of development. It would be beneficial to share your findings with your classmates and begin to develop your portfolio of possible programs to offer.

In addition to facilitating the coordination of efforts occurring within the school, facilitating the connection and coordination between school and family is essential to student success. School counselors have been identified as a key player in this coordination (Bemak, 2000).

The specifics of parent/family inclusion can range from employing them as parents and family members for academic support or part of a PBIS program to involving them in advisory groups. Beyond employing parents as a resource, the school, through the school counselor, can serve as a resource to the parents and families. Efforts such as providing information about social skill development, stress management, organization and time management, as well as providing directories of community services, are examples of the value and benefit of counselor as coordinator.

COUNSELOR AS COLLABORATIVE CONSULTANT

The provision of one-on-one and small group counseling continues to be a mainstay of the school counselor's role and function. However, school counselors are also quite aware of the value of engaging others in service to the students. School counselors are not only being called on to share their expertise but are also recognizing the value of working with others (teachers, learning specialists, parents, etc.) in a collaborative relationship of shared expertise and resources.

The need and value of such collaboration are clear when viewed from the perspective of providing comprehensive school counseling services that are preventive. This consulting, or collaborating, is a meaningful way to provide responsive and preventive services while advocating for systemic change (Clemens, 2007; Schmidt, 2014). Several professional organizations emphasize the school counselor's role as a consultant, including ASCA (2019a, 2019b) and the Council for Accreditation of Counseling and Related Educational Programs (CACREP, 2015). Teacher consultation is an efficient, systemic strategy for school counselors to impact students' academic and personal success (Stone & Dahir, 2016), enabling school counselors to reach more students than individual or group counseling (Brigman et al., 2005). Consultation, therefore, should be part of a comprehensive school counseling program.

Consultation: An Operational Definition

The forms of service and interaction that have been grouped under the rubric of consultation are many and can look quite different. The term *consultation* has been applied to activities as varied as the informal discussion between friends regarding an issue of importance or a couple "consulting" their calendars to plan a dinner party, to the process of sharing of advice and service by an expert or one with specialized training. As applied to school counselors, consultation can be characterized as a voluntary, problem-solving process involving a help- giver (the counselor-consultant), a help- seeker (the consultee) and another, about whom the consultee has a concern (i.e., the student-client) (Dickinson & Parsons, 2019; Parsons & Kahn, 2005).

In reviewing this very elementary definition of consultation what becomes immediately apparent is that consultation as a mode of service delivery increases the number of roles that are engaged. When contrasted to direct service where the dynamic is dyadic involving the role of helper/counselor and the role of helpee/client, consultation includes a third role, that of consultee.

The consultee, be it an administrator, teacher, parent, or coach, is the individual who has responsibility for the student's work-related behavior and is experiencing some concern or difficulty concerning that student or that student's performance. The inclusion of this third party into the helping process expands the perspective and skill set that can be brought to bear on the concern at hand. Further, the inclusion of this other who is engaged with the student provides for the possibility of expanding the types and frequency of intervention that can be used. Finally, as a result of effective consultation, not only will the immediate issue be resolved but the consultee can develop knowledge and skill that can be used in similar future situations, thus expanding the impact from intervention with one to prevention for many.

Mode and Style of Consultation

The mode or form that consultation can take has been described as (a) provisional, (b) prescriptive, (c) collaborative, and (d) mediational (see Baker et al., 2009; Dickinson & Parsons, 2019; Parsons, 1996; Parsons & Kahn, 2005).

Provisional Mode

In the provisional mode, the school counselor as a consultant becomes the means of implementing the intervention, providing such service directly to the student/client. In the provisional mode, the consultant is expected to apply specialized knowledge (content and process expertise) to implement action plans toward the achievement of goals defined by the consultee. In this form of consulting, the consultant defers to the consultee for the determination of the problem and formulation of the desired outcome, thus two-way communication is limited (consultee initiates, consultant responds) (Dickinson & Parsons, 2019).

An example of such provisional consultation would be if a teacher, expressing a concern about the increasing taunting and verbal bullying occurring within his classroom, asked the school counselor to provide a specific classroom lesson on respect. A counselor who accepts the teacher/consultee's problem definition and intervention plan, thus delivering the desired lesson, would be operating from a provisional mode.

Prescriptive Mode

The school counselor operating from a prescriptive mode is often seen by the consultee, as the expert in the field and thus is called on to provide insight and direction to the consultee. In a prescriptive mode, the school counselor will often gather data, draw conclusions, and offer advice for implementation. Within the school, this mode would be typically initiated by the consultee, usually out of a sense of need. The school counselor would step into the role of problem analyzer and intervention prescriber. The application of the intervention would fall to the consultee.

Mediational Mode

Whereas the provisional and prescriptive modes of consultation were initiated by the consultee, the mediational mode is initiated by the consultant. School counselors who have embraced an ecological approach to comprehensive service delivery are aware of factors that may be impeding student progress or may have a potential for causing future difficulties. Under these conditions, the counselor would go to the party or parties who are responsible for the functioning of this element or factor and invite them into a consult in order to intercede with the potential problem. This mode of consultation has sometimes been referred to as initiation mode (Baker et al., 2009).

Regardless of the title of the mode, in these instances the consultant will undertake the connection before the consultee's recognition or experience of need. The school counselor engaged in a mediational mode of consultation will gather, analyze, and synthesize existing information as a way of defining the problem and develop an intervention plan for implementation. Significant to this mode is that the consultant not only has to address the problem at hand but has to "sell" the need for intervention to the consultee. For example, a school counselor might have overheard middle school students talking about how easy it is to cheat in a particular class, where the teacher, who is in her first year, appears overwhelmed and is having difficulty with classroom management. In this situation, the counselor might initiate contact and approach the teacher with their observations and, without presenting as being judgmental, offer to assist.

Collaborative Mode

In a collaborative mode, the consultant approaches the consultee as a co-equal in the problem-solving dynamic. In this mode, both parties have unique expertise of knowledge and skills that are valuable resources in the problem-solving process. Collaboration engages the consultant and consultee in a mutual and reciprocal attempt to reach a common goal through the process of shared decision-making (Kampwirth & Powers, 2012).

When engaged collaboratively, the counselor-consultant realizes that both the consultant and consultee bring expertise to the relationship—not one more expert than another, simply co-equal with varying perspectives, knowledge bases, and skill sets. The school counselor operating in this mode would attempt to facilitate the blending of the different perspectives, expertise, and skill sets to increase the accuracy of the problem identification and the utility of the intervention. Working from an egalitarian, nonhierarchical relationship, decisions can be derived that are more effective both as intervention and prevention measures. Through such a process strengths and resources are shared and built on, thus providing the most comprehensive and effective services for the student (Baker et al., 2009).

It has been suggested elsewhere that rather than viewing collaboration as a separate mode it be viewed as a style to be employed across modes (Dickinson & Parsons, 2019). From this orientation, even when engaged in a provisional role, the consultant with a collaborative style will seek the consultee's input, provide their perspective, and use communication skills to arrive at common goals and accepted strategies, strategies to be employed by the consultant. Similarly, when engaged in a prescriptive mode of consultation, effectiveness will be enhanced if the counselor-consultant employs a collaborative style to co-equally engage the consultee in problem identification, goal setting, and intervention planning. In this way, the strategies to be prescribed are those the consultee would have embraced and therefore value.

CONSULTING IS NOT PERSONAL COUNSELING FOR THE CONSULTEE

As used in reference to school counselors serving as consultants, consultation is a process that focuses on a work-related issue. The belief is that while the student (as client) is exhibiting difficulty, the individual (e.g. teacher or parent) who is charged with fostering the development of that student is experiencing a problem in performing that function successfully. While the consultee may be experiencing personal issues and frustrations around the student or the inability to achieve the desired outcome, the focus of a consultation needs to remain on the "inability to achieve the desired outcome" and not on the personal issues or experiences of the consultee.

The nature of the consulting relationship requires the counselor to use helping skills; many of the same are employed in counseling. Attending to the consultee, checking for understanding by way of engaging active reflective listening and focusing the exchange with the use of clarification and summarization are both necessary for an effective consulting process and outcome. While these same skills are employed within the counseling dynamic, their use in the consultation is meant to facilitate understanding of the client's (i.e., student's) issues, not those of the consultee. While this may appear clear-cut and relatively simple, the truth is that it is not always easy to walk the fine line between consultative help and providing personal counseling to the consultee.

School counselors are trained to walk that fine line. School counselors use their skills to not only convey genuine interest and concern, nonjudgment, and a sense of empathy, but they use their communication skills to keep the focus on the student–client relationship and the resources the consultant and consultee can bring to bear on assisting that student or group of students. This doesn't preclude the counselor -as -consultant from helping the consultee gain new knowledge and skills that can be used in the situation. Consultee growth and development would be a desirable outcome of a successful consult and position the consultee to be able to engage in preventive activities. The target for such growth, however, is the professional knowledge and skill of the consultee and not the insight and strategies needed to address and remediate any of their issues.

A TAKE-AWAY

School counselors trained in group dynamics, leadership, and advocacy play a central role in coordinating services provided to our nation's students. Not only do counselors utilize coordination in the organization and management of comprehensive counseling programs, but they coordinate the collection, analysis, and dissemination of results reports and program audits to improve the program based on results and help schools maintain focus and progress toward mission accomplishment.

School counselors are not only essential direct services providers, but by way of their engagement in collaborative consultation with the school community, including teachers, administrators, and parents, they expand the impact of their services from intervention to prevention and facilitate needed systemic changes in support of student development.

KEYSTONES

- Schools as a system are entities that are "made up of interconnected parts, with recognizable relationships that are systematically arranged to serve a perceived purpose" (Kurpius, 1985, p. 368).
- As an entity, it can be expected that schools make organization changes in reflection of the changing needs of its stakeholders.
- For schools to successfully achieve their mission all interrelated parts must be systematically arranged in service of that mission.
- School counselors, through their knowledge and skills, can coordinate resources and functions in service of the mission.
- School counselors can expand the impact of their service from intervention to prevention by engaging others in collaborative consultation.
- Whether a school counselor is employing provisional, prescriptive, or mediational modes of consultation, they will be more effective if each is approached from a collaborative, egalitarian relationship.

ADDITIONAL RESOURCES

Print

Dickinson, K., & Parsons, R. (2019). *The school counselor as consultant: Expanding impact from intervention to prevention*. Cognella.

Dougherty, A. M. (2014). *Psychological consultation and collaboration in school and community settings* (6th ed.). Brooks/Cole.

Schmidt, J. J. (2014). *Counseling in schools: Comprehensive programs of responsive services for all students* (6th ed.). Pearson.

Web

Missouri Department of Elementary and Secondary Education. (2015). *Professional school counselor consultation guide: A professional school counselor's guide to consulting and collaborating.* http://www.missouricareereducation.org/doc/consult/CollabConsult.pdf

Pereza-Diltz, D. M., Moe, J. L., & Mason, K. L. (2011). An exploratory study in school counselor consultation engagement. *Journal of School Counseling, 9*(13). https://files.eric.ed.gov/fulltext/EJ933179.pdf

Warren, J. M, & Baker, S. B. (2013). School counselor consultation: Enhancing teacher performance through rational emotive-social behavioral consultation. *VISTAS Online.* https://www.counseling.org/docs/default-source/vistas/school-counselor-consultation-enhancing-teacher-performance.pdf?sfvrsn=2debf64c_11

REFERENCES

American School Counselor Association. (2019a). *The ASCA national model: A framework for school counseling programs* (4th ed.). Author.

American School Counselor Association. (2019b). *ASCA school counselor professional standards and competencies.* Author.

Baker, S., Robichaud, T., Westforth-Dietrich, V., Wells, S. & Schreck, R. (2009). School counselor consultation: A pathway to advocacy, collaboration, and leadership. *Professional School Counseling, 12*(3), 200–206.

Bemak, F. (2000). Transforming the role of the counselor to provide leadership in educational reform through collaboration. *Professional School Counseling, 3,* 323–313.

Brigman, G., Mullis, F., Webb, L. & White, J.F. (2005). *School counselor consultation* (2nd ed.). Wiley.

Clemens, E. (2007). Developmental counseling and therapy as a model for school counselor consultation with teachers. *Professional School Counseling, 10*(4), 352–359.

Council for Accreditation of Counseling and Related Educational Programs. (2016). *2016 standards for accreditation.* Author.

Dickinson, K., & Parsons, R. (2019). *The school counselor as consultant: Expanding impact from intervention to prevention.* Cognella.

Kampwirth, T. J., & Powers, K. M. (2012). *Collaborative consultation in the schools: Effective practices for students with learning and behavior problems* (4th ed.). Pearson.

Kurpius, D. J. (1985). Consultation theory and process: An integrated model. *The Personnel and Guidance Journal, 56,* 335–338.

Parsons, R. D. (1996). *The skilled consultant.* Allyn & Bacon.

Parsons, R. D., & Kahn W. (2005). *The school counselor as consultant.* Brooks/Cole.

Schmidt, J. J. (2014). *Counseling in schools: Comprehensive programs of responsive services for all students* (6th ed.). Pearson.

Stone, C., & Dahir, C. (2016). *The transformed school counselor.* Cengage.

PART 3

SPECIAL CONSIDERATIONS

CHAPTER 8

ASSISTING THOSE WITH EDUCATIONAL CHALLENGES

I am moved by the way they embrace and navigate the challenges they have been dealt. I only hope I can be of some support.

—Maria S., Elementary school counselor

Each of the students with whom a school counselor works has strengths and talents, some of which have not yet been discovered. Each student also encounters unique and personal challenges as they navigate school and the road toward academic, career, and social/emotional development. There are some students, however, for whom the challenges may be greater than most and outside that which may be identified as normative. For these students, their growth will call for some extra support and guidance, and while this support will come from many directions and many different individuals, the school counselor is central to the coordination and advocacy of this support.

The current chapter will review the role of the school counselor in assisting those students who have been identified as having special or diverse needs and as such facing challenges beyond that experienced by most students.

Upon completion of this chapter readers will be able to do the following:

1. Describe the role and function of a multidisciplinary team (MDT).
2. Explain the role that school counselors can play in service of the MDT and the implementation of intervention strategies.
3. Identify ways in which a school counselor provides support and service to students with disabilities and other diverse learners, their teachers, and their parents/caretakers.

SCHOOL COUNSELORS: CALLED TO SERVICE

The role of the school counselor has evolved dramatically since its inception (Burnham & Jackson, 2000). Many of these changes we have seen in the processes and procedures employed in our schools, as well as the role and responsibilities of the school counselor that have been stimulated by legislative changes designed to better meet the challenges of an evolving society through school reform (Gysbers & Henderson, 2001; Paisley & McMahon, 2001). Baker and Gerler (2008) suggested that legislative changes designed to help marginalized students have played an important part in defining the role of the school counselor as an agent for social justice.

The school setting can be a difficult place for all children. However, for those with special or diverse needs, the challenges they face are often quite different than those addressed by their peers. These diverse learners may experience victimization by peers, social rejection and isolation, additional transitions throughout their schooling, and hurdles to their maximum achievement. The types of hurdles and challenges experienced can find their roots within the policies, attitudes, and behaviors of students and school personnel alike. It is in their role as an advocate for students and agents of systemic change that the school counselor can provide a very needed service to those with special needs (ASCA, 2020).

In addition to providing comprehensive programs designed to enhance the academic, career, and personal/social development of all students, school counselors serve as advocates for those with unique needs. School counselors advocate for and provide equal access and success by serving as collaborators, consultants, and change agents to bring about positive change in the entire school (Holcomb-McCoy, 2007; Pelsma & Krieshok, 2003).

It has been suggested that school counselors will not only provide the same programs and services offered to all students to those with special needs but will also engage in providing in-service training to faculty on issues such as multiculturally sensitive education about disabilities, civil rights, and current legislation, as well as be the contact point to assist families in negotiating the education system (Erford, 2003). School counselors are charged with "recognizing individual and group differences ... [and] are advocates for the equitable treatment of all students in school and in the community" (ASCA, 2018). Exercise 8.1 invites you to discover a deeper understanding of who diverse learners may be and what their needs may encompass.

Exercise 8.1: Who Are Diverse Learners and What Are Their Needs?

Directions: Interview a practicing school counselor and ask the questions that follow. You may want to ask school counselors who are at different levels (elementary, middle, high school) or are from different geographical areas. Additionally, discussing your findings with classmates may provide a broader perspective as to who are the diverse learners and what are their needs.

1. Who are the diverse learners in your school?
2. What do you perceive to be the challenges for these students in the classroom and out of the classroom?
3. How do you support these students?
4. What is your role in MDT (IEP, RTI, etc.) meetings for these students?
5. How do you modify your counseling curriculum for these students?
6. How do you advocate for these students (academic, social, college, and career)?
7. What challenges does the virtual world pose to the counselor and students?

STUDENTS WITH DISABILITIES

Diverse learners who have disabilities have federal and state laws directing public educational agencies on how to support these individuals. Since laws were first passed resulting in the free appropriate public education for all students (FAPE; U.S. Department of Education, 2010), schools have been charged with designing programs for students with special needs due to their disabilities. The ASCA's position paper, "The School Counselor and Students With Disabilities," notes that school counselors are called to help all students realize their potential and "meet or exceed academic standards with consideration for both the strengths and challenges resulting for disabilities and other special needs" (ASCA, 2016, p. 77). In their roles as advocates, coordinators, and school leaders, school counselors facilitate and encourage family involvement in their child's education; coordinate and collaborate with educational colleagues in the development, implementation, and assessment of service; and stand as advocates for students with special needs so that they receive every service possible on their road to success.

As noted in the ASCA (2016) position paper, school counselors contribute to the development of students with special needs by doing the following:

- Providing school counseling curriculum lessons, individual and/or group counseling to students with special needs within the scope of the school counseling program
- Providing short-term, goal-focused counseling in instances where it is appropriate to include these strategies as a part of the IEP or 504 plan
- Encouraging family involvement in the educational process
- Consulting and collaborating with staff and families to understand the special needs of a student and understanding the adaptations and modifications needed to assist the student
- Advocating for students with special needs in the school and the community
- Contributing to the school's multidisciplinary team within the scope and practice of the school counseling program

- Identifying students who may need to be assessed to determine special education or 504 plan eligibility
- Collaborating with other related student support professionals (e.g. school psychologists, physical therapists, occupational therapists, special education staff, and speech and language pathologists) in the delivery of services
- Assisting with developing academic, transition and postsecondary plans for students with IEPs and 504 plans as appropriate (p. 77)

IDEA AND THE COUNSELOR'S ROLE

The Individual With Disabilities Education Improvement Act (IDEA) of 2004 was significant in moving students with disabilities into the general education curriculum. School counselors are now charged with addressing the developmental needs of all students, including many with learning disabilities, speech/language delays, sensory impairments, and other health challenges (ASCA, 2019; Mauro, 2014).

As part of IDEA, schools are required to develop teams to create a specific individualized education program (IEP) as a means of providing students with special needs who are identified as eligible for receiving special education services appropriate for public education (Council for Exceptional Children [CEC], 2005). The IEP plans reflect the input from the parent(s) or legal guardian(s) of the child with a disability, at least one regular general education teacher, at least one special education teacher, a representative of the local education agency (LEA; e.g. school principal), individuals invited at the discretion of the parent or the agency with special knowledge regarding the child, and the child with a disability. School counselors can be quite valuable at these meetings, as their training in active listening, clarifying, and paraphrasing can prove helpful and beneficial in leading to goal setting.

Consulting, Collaborating, and Advocating

Because school counselors are trained in group dynamics and consultation processes, they are often included as a facilitator for team meetings and other educational planning committees (Milsom, 2007). Beyond facilitating such planning groups, the school counselor provides consultative support for the classroom teacher both in terms of assisting with early identification of students with a disability and offering suggestions for modification of learning tasks and environment to maximize student achievement (Hinnant et al., 2009; Nichter & Edmonson, 2005).

School counselors play an important role in coordinating and collaborating with parents and guardians about the programs and services that schools can offer their special needs students, and they can work with administrators to find appropriate programs for special needs students in accordance with federal and state laws. Case Illustration 8.1 provides an example of how the school counselor may support the student, parent, and teacher.

CASE ILLUSTRATION 8.1: OSCAR

Oscar was really having trouble asking for help and participating in class. The goals in Oscar's IEP were for reading and writing; however, because Oscar wouldn't say when he needed help or didn't understand, he was falling further behind. He just seemed to withdraw when he was stuck. The special education teacher working with him was frustrated and went to the school counselor for help.

After listening to the special education teacher, the school counselor checked in with the general classroom teacher and Oscar's parents to see how work was going in their settings. Discovering that the problem was universal, a team meeting was called in order to brainstorm strategies to help Oscar. At the meeting, Oscar's parents spoke of his love for art; in fact, Oscar preferred to draw or paint than do anything else. The classroom teacher also noted that Oscar was very close to one of the other class members, who he always hung around with at recess.

The school counselor suggested the following plan, including a strategy for each meeting participant:

> Parents: Parents directed to provide extra check-ins while Oscar was doing his homework and use a question guide provided by the special education teacher. Additionally, information on a community art class in which to enroll Oscar to utilize his strength and interest in art was provided, with the thought that the use of his strength would make him more comfortable to participate and ask questions.
>
> Classroom teacher: The classroom teacher should encourage participation, use forced choice tools, such as thumbs up/thumbs down, and have everyone write an answer on an individual whiteboard.
>
> Special education teacher: Special education teacher should encourage Oscar to ask for support, reinforce his asking with tokens to be used at the end of the lesson time to work with clay or draw.
>
> School counselor: School counselor will work individually with Oscar to role-play what and how to ask for support and invite him and his good buddy to share time in the counselor's office practicing expression of feelings with the use of games and role-play.

Multidisciplinary Team Member

A multidisciplinary team is a group of individuals from multiple disciplines who meet to pursue a common goal, such as evaluating a student for placement in special education or creating IEP for a student. Multidisciplinary teams are sometimes referred to as *child study teams* or *student support teams*, among other terms. The professional collaboration of a multidisciplinary team helps ensure that their work regarding students is as comprehensive and as unbiased as possible.

While the team serves many functions, one is to gather data to inform the team about students' abilities. These data come from various sources and through a variety of means, including the following:

- Medical history, educational performance, etc.
- Formal assessments, such as intelligence tests or tests of visual or aural acuity
- Informal assessments, such as samples of classroom work and observations of social behavior
- A baseline of performance to guide the development of an IEP and determine the effectiveness of subsequent education

Such data collection intends to be able to assess the areas of strengths and weaknesses in the student to create an educational program in which the student will be successful (U.S. Department of Education, 2006a). The specific data sought reflects the nature of the suspected disability. Thus, a child with behavioral, impulse control issues and demonstrating poor peer interactions, while excelling in academics, would most likely have data collected on the context and situational factors associated with the behavior of concern and not on intellectual capabilities. Conversely, a student who is struggling with reading, while demonstrating appropriate social behaviors in class and with peers, would be assessed for cognitive and academic ability to examine the learning difficulties. In this case, behavioral or social interaction assessment would not be needed.

While some of the data collection techniques (e.g. individual intelligence testing or personality measures) would be completed by the school psychologist and outside of the role, function, and competency of a school counselor, gathering data through interview and behavioral observation is something for which the counselor could provide leadership. School counselors can gather information through interviewing and observations. Interview data can be collected from parents, teachers, and staff who interact with the student. In addition to these data, observational data is also essential and mandated by IDEA (U.S. Department of Education, 2006a). To document the child's academic performance and behavior in the area or areas of difficulty, the child must be observed in their learning environment. The MDT must either "(A) use information obtained from an observation in routine classroom instruction and monitoring of the child's performance that was done before the child was referred for an evaluation, or (B) have at least one member of the [MDT] conduct an observation of the child's academic performance in the regular classroom after the child has been referred for an evaluation and parental consent is obtained" (U.S. Department of Education, 2006b). School counselors are quite adept at observing behavior and the elements in the environment that may have an effect on behavior such as teacher–student interactions and internal and external distractions and thus positions them to collect these data (ASCA, 2019).

Another value of the school counselor, when included on the MDT, comes from the fact that the school counselor is trained in both the theory and research highlighting the factors and processes that can inhibit or facilitate a student's personal, social, and emotional development and academic performance. The school counselor brings a whole-child perspective to the team, one that highlights the student's strengths and challenges as they attempt to function in the academic, social, and personal arenas.

Once the team completes its data collection they will compile the data into a multidisciplinary evaluation report (MDE). This report will serve as the foundation for the developing strategies that not only assist teachers working with the student but also assist the student and parents/caretakers to understand both the strengths of the student and the areas that will be addressed and strengthened. Case Illustration 8.2 provides a glimpse of how a school counselor can be beneficial to the MDT meetings.

CASE ILLUSTRATION 8.2: WHAT DOES THAT MEAN?

Ms. Toby, the middle school counselor, knew it was helpful to the parents to be at these team meetings. Parents had thanked her when she explained how things would go ahead of time and when she walked them out afterward, checking to see what they felt and thought and offering to speak with them any time they had questions. She was so glad she was in attendance at this meeting because she could see the parents were getting increasingly upset as the classroom teacher repeatedly brought up what their child could not do and they kept asking, "But, what does that mean?!"

Ms. Toby took the opportunity to join the conversation when the teacher paused to take a breath. She thanked the teacher for bringing up the areas for which they would like to help the student and steered the conversation to the student's strengths and what had worked well thus far. She described the new strategies that would be used, and when any new vocabulary words or acronyms were used, she explained what they meant.

When the meeting ended and Ms. Toby walked the parents down the hall, they thanked her for her help in understanding what was going on. They went on to say that it was very hard and emotional to be in a meeting when everyone is speaking about things you haven't heard of and didn't expect and all you want is for your child to do well and be happy. Ms. Toby assured them that she was glad she could be helpful and that was what school counselors did!

COUNSELOR SERVING THE STUDENT

One result of the MDE may be the inclusion of the school counselor's service as support for the identified student's academic, socioemotional, and career development. The counselor may work directly, one-on-one, with the student, or engage the student in a small group counseling process that targets the issues and challenges identified for that student. It is also possible that the counselor, in responding to the report, may provide developmental classroom lessons that will be of benefit not just to the identified student but to all within that class. Lessons targeting areas such as self-management, social skill development, stress management, and emotional regulation can be both remedial for those needing such remediation as well as preventive and developmental in nature for students not identified as having a disability. In addition to providing such direct programming to students, the school counselor in their role as consultant can work with the teachers to develop, implement, and assess strategies that will be employed by the teacher with his classroom. Strategies for teacher employment might include the use of modified assignments that allow for frequent breaks or the use of a token-economy reinforcement system, or even the adjustment of seating arrangements to provide all students with that context that is supportive of their learning styles. The strategies used by the school counselor for supporting students with disabilities can also be used to support other diverse learners.

WORKING WITH OTHER DIVERSE LEARNERS

As you read in Chapter 6, strategies and interventions used by the school counselor may be delivered in many tiers. Utilizing the multitiered system of support (MTSS) model, school counselors support all students, including those needing more support such as diverse learners. There are many students who may be considered as having diverse needs, and being aware of the populations and needs in your school will be of the upmost importance.

There are policies and laws that provide further support for some diverse learners. For example, ELs have the right to supplemental instruction, and their parents may have access to a translator and interpreter under the U.S. Department of Education's Office of Civil Rights (2020). Students who are identified as gifted may have their educational programming covered under special education, and students who are homeless have rights under the McKinney-Vento Act (National Center for Homeless Education, n.d.), such as the right to remain in the school of origin and receive transportation to and from that school.

There are many other students who have diverse needs that will require support from the school counselor, including students in foster care, students who are refugees, LGBTQ youth, and students with incarcerated parents. While this is not an exhaustive list, school counselors will serve their students well to be cognizant of the diverse needs and barriers that arise. It is important to remember that through advocacy and leadership, school counselors work to promote equitable treatment to and programming for all students.

School counselors can ethically and effectively provide equitable service doing such things as "maintaining their own professional knowledge and skills for working in a diverse work setting [and] creating an environment that encourages any student or group to feel comfortable to come forward with problems" (ASCA, 2018). While these will help support students' personal and career development, school counselors can support academic growth by "promoting access to all academic courses and learning paths for college and career for all students" (ASCA, 2018).

A TAKE-AWAY

The school counselor's primary responsibility is to provide a developmental school counseling program for all students. School counselors also provide related services to students with diverse needs as appropriate on a case-by-case basis. Providing support for students with disabilities, the school counselor may serve as part of the data collection team (i.e., MDT) and can provide input to the student's MDT team regarding issues germane to the student, especially when the team makes decisions about the provision of counseling services.

The counselor's knowledge and skills are of value not only in providing direct service to students with disabilities and other diverse learners, but also as a meeting facilitator and coordinator for teacher and parent input into the educational planning of students with special needs.

KEYSTONES

- Students with special needs often experience victimization by peers, social rejection and isolation, additional transitions throughout their schooling, and hurdles to their maximum achievement.
- School counselors acting as advocate for students and agents of systemic change can provide a very needed service to those with special needs.
- School counselors serve as valuable contributors to the data collection process, at once assessing the student's strengths and areas of challenge.
- School counselors contribute to the development of students with special needs by providing school counseling curriculum lessons and individual and/or group counseling to students with special needs within the scope of the school counseling program.
- School counselors are central to the encouragement and engagement of families in the educational process.
- School counselors assist in the education of students with special needs by consulting and collaborating with staff and families to understand the special needs of a student and understanding the adaptations and modifications needed to assist the student.

ADDITIONAL RESOURCES

Print

Marshak, L. E., Dandeneau, C .J., Prezant, F. P., & L'Amoreaux, N. A. (2010). *The school counselor's guide to helping students with disabilities.* Jossey-Bass.

Turnbull, A., Turnbull H., Erwin, E., Soodak, L., & Shogren K. (2015). *Families, professionals, and exceptionality: Positive outcomes through partnerships and trust.* Pearson.

Web

504 Plans, Free Appropriate Public Education for Students With Disabilities: Requirements Under Section 504 of The Rehabilitation Act of 1973: http://www2.ed.gov/about/offices/list/ocr/docs/edlite-FAPE504.html

National Dissemination Center for Children With Disabilities (NICHCY): http://www.nichcy.org

U.S. Department of Education: Education for Homeless Children & Youths (EHCY) programs: https://nche.ed.gov/wp-content/uploads/2018/12/ehcy_profile.pdf

REFERENCES

American School Counselor Association. (2016). *The school counselor and students with disabilities.* https://www.schoolcounselor.org/asca/media/asca/PositionStatements/PS_Disabilities.pdf

American School Counselor Association. (2018). *The school counselor and equity for all students.* https://www.schoolcounselor.org/asca/media/asca/PositionStatements/PS_Equity.pdf

American School Counselor Association. (2019). *The ASCA national model: A framework for school counseling programs* (4th ed.). Author.

American School Counselor Association. (2020). *Students with special needs specialist.* https://www.schoolcounselor.org/school-counselors/professional-development/asca-u-specialist-trainings/students-with-special-needs-specialist

Baker, S. B., & Gerler, E. R., Jr. (2008). *School counseling for the twenty-first century* (5th ed.). Pearson.

Burnham, J. J., & Jackson, C. M. (2000). School counselor roles: Discrepancies between actual practice and existing models. *Professional School Counseling, 4,* 41–49.

Council for Exceptional Children. (2005). *What's new in the new IDEA 2004: Frequently asked questions and answers.* Author.

Erford, B. T. (2003). *Transforming the school counseling profession.* Prentice-Hall.

Gysbers, N., & Henderson, P. (2001). Comprehensive guidance and counseling programs: A rich history and bright future. *Professional School Counseling, 4,* 246–257.

Holcomb-McCoy, C. (2007). *School counseling to close the achievement gap.* Corwin.

Hinnant, J., O'Brien, M., & Ghazarian, S. (2009). The longitudinal relations of teacher expectations to achievement in the early school years. *Journal of Educational Psychology, 101*(3), 662–670.

Mauro, T. (2014). Court throws out "mental retardation." *USA Today*. http://www.usatoday.com/story/opinion/2014/06/01/hall-florida-mental-retardation-intellectual-disability-supreme-court-column/9848687/

Milsom, A. (2007). Interventions to assist students with disabilities through school transitions. *Professional School Counseling Journal, 10*(3), 273–278.

National Center for Homeless Education. (n.d.). *The McKinney-Vento Homeless Assistance Act*. https://nche.ed.gov/mckinney-vento/

Nichter, M., & Edmonson, S. L. (2005). Counseling services for special education students. *Journal of Professional Counseling, Practice, Theory, & Research, 33*(2), 50–62.

Paisley, P., O., & McMahon, H. G. (2001). School counseling for the 21st century: Challenges and opportunities. *Professional School Counseling, 5*, 106–110.

Pelsma, D., & Krieshok, T. (2003). School counseling. In M. A. Richard & W. G. Emener (Eds.), *I'm a people person: A guide to human service professions* (pp. 187–197). C. C. Thomas.

U.S. Department of Education. (2006a). *Building the legacy: IDEA 2004*. https://sites.ed.gov/idea/building-the-legacy-idea-2004/

U.S. Department of Education. (2006b). IDEA. http://idea.ed.gov/

U.S. Department of Education. (2010). *Free Appropriate Public Education for Students With Disabilities: Requirements under section 504 of the Rehabilitation Act of 1973*. https://www2.ed.gov/about/offices/list/ocr/docs/edlite-FAPE504.html

U.S. Department of Education, Office of Civil Rights. (2020). *Schools' civil rights obligations to English learner students and limited English proficient parents*. https://www2.ed.gov/about/offices/list/ocr/ellresources.html

CHAPTER 9

ADDRESSING THREATS TO SOCIOEMOTIONAL DEVELOPMENT

I find it hard, sometimes, to get my head around the fact that so many of my students are dealing with really heavy emotional and social issues. They just seem too young to be so burdened.

—Tamara, High school counselor

It is hard to get one's head wrapped around the idea that our students may be living on the street or in cars, navigating violent households, locked into patterns of substance abuse, or coping with overwhelming anxieties and depression—but such is the life for many of today's students. The students presented at the counselor's door continue to present with normative developmental crises, such as adjusting to friendship demands, normative anxiety about separating from home, discomfort with adjusting to a new setting with new demands, and learning to organize and manage time and tasks. But counselors are now working with students whose issues are beyond normative. For some, the issues are significantly more complicated, more severe, and thus not only detrimental to their academic success but harmful to their well-being. School counselors are charged not only with the support of student academic success but also their socioemotional development (ASCA, 2019).

The current chapter will discuss a number of issues confronting the socioemotional development of students and the role and function the school counselor can serve in facilitating their development. Upon completing this chapter, readers will be able to do the following:

1. Describe the role school counselors play in service of all students' socioemotional development.
2. Describe the goals of socioemotional learning programs.
3. Provide examples of Tier I, II, and III counselor services targeting social anxiety, bullying, and stress.
4. Explain the steps to be taken in the case of students at risk for suicide.

CONCERNING STATISTICS

The issues confronting our students, and as an extension the school counselor, have increased in severity and complexity. Whereas failure to complete homework, for example, remains an issue addressed by teachers and counselors, the following facts place failure to do homework in a different category or level of concern for some of our students and require a different approach to resolve.

Drawing on data gathered by the U.S. Department of Education's EDFacts Initiative, the National Center for Homeless Education (2020) reported 1,354,363 unaccompanied homeless youth were identified in the 2016–2017 school year, and in January 2013, American communities counted 46,924 unaccompanied homeless youth living in shelters or on the street. Additionally, 40,727 of the identified population were transition-aged youth (48.6% unsheltered) and 6,197 were under the age of 18 (59.3% unsheltered). For these students, completing homework may have not been the first thing on their priority lists.

In looking at these statistics, as well as those found in Table 9.1 depicting the incidence of behavioral and emotional difficulties experienced by school-aged children and youth, it becomes very clear that the role of the school counselor in support of the social and emotional development of students is essential, not only for their academic success but for their overall well-being.

Table 9.1 Mental Health Challenges in U.S. Children

CHALLENGE	STATISTICS	SOURCE
Behavior problems	7.4% of children aged 3-17 years (approximately 4.5 million) have a diagnosed behavior problem. For children aged 3-17 years with behavior problems, more than 1 in 3 also have anxiety (36.6%) and about 1 in 5 also have depression (20.3%).	Ghandour et al. (2019).
Anxiety	7.1% of children aged 3-17 years (approximately 4.4 million) have diagnosed anxiety. For children aged 3-17 years with anxiety, more than 1 in 3 also have behavior problems (37.9%) and about 1 in 3 also have depression (32.3%).	Ghandour et al. (2019).
	Ever having been diagnosed with anxiety increased from 5.5% in 2007 to 6.4% in 2011-2012.	Bitsko et al. (2018).
Depression	3.2% of children aged 3-17 years (approximately 1.9 million) have diagnosed depression. Having another disorder is most common in children with depression: About 3 in 4 children aged 3-17 years with depression also have anxiety (73.8%), and almost 1 in 2 have behavior problems (47.2%).	Ghandour et al. (2019).
	Diagnoses of either anxiety or depression among children aged 6-17 years increased from 5.4% in 2003 to 8% in 2007, and to 8.4% in 2011-2012.	Bitsko et al. (2018).

The need and value of school counselors given these data are further highlighted by the fact that according to the Centers for Disease Control and Prevention (CDC, 2013) most students needing mental health support failed to receive it. In a study by Kaffenberger and Seligmant (2007), only one in five of the students in their sample were receiving necessary mental health services. Further, Atkins et al. (2010) noted that for school-aged children receiving behavioral and mental health services, 70–80 received those at school. It is clear that more than ever the school counselor's services, both as intervention and prevention, are becoming more and more central to what they are called to do.

THE SCHOOL COUNSELOR IN SERVICE OF SOCIOEMOTIONAL HEALTH

School counselors, while called to facilitate their students' academic achievement, understand the interrelatedness of a student's academic achievement and the elements of their emotional health and well-being. School counselors employ counseling curriculum, small-group counseling, and individual student planning, all to improve students' socioemotional well-being and remove social/emotional issues that may become barriers to their academic success.

Counselors play an important role in facilitating students' socioemotional development. Counselors provide programs and services that help students gain the knowledge, attitudes, and skills necessary for understanding and regulating their emotions, for feeling and demonstrating empathy, and for maintaining healthy, positive friendships. This process is what has been identified as social emotional learning (Collaborative for Academic, Social, and Emotional Learning [CASEL], 2019). It is a process that targets five main competencies: self-awareness, self-management, social-awareness, relationship building, and responsible decision-making skills (CASEL, 2013; Durlak et al., 2015; Maras et al., 2015).

In providing a curriculum-based program, counselors will often turn to programs that have been empirically tested for effectiveness. One such program, Student Success Skills, is a skills-based program designed to be implemented in a regular classroom and targets five specific lessons. Students are taught to (a) set goals and monitor progress; (b) build a caring, supportive, and encouraging environment; (c) develop and practice memory and cognitive skills; (d) develop anxiety- calming and emotional management skills; and (e) develop health optimism. Students are taught stress-reduction techniques that include mindfulness strategies such as muscle relaxation. While used as a Tier I, schoolwide program, it can be modified to be delivered as a Tier II service for students needing additional support, such as in a small counseling group. Numerous empirical studies have demonstrated the positive impact this program has on increasing students' socioemotional skills, cognitive factors, and academic achievement (e.g. Bowers et al., 2015; Lemberger et al., 2015).

In addition to providing schoolwide development programs, school counselors are also charged with identifying, intervening, and when possible preventing factors and conditions that act as barriers to their students' academic achievement and socioemotional development. School counselors play a very important in supporting those students during time of socioemotional crisis.

It is also important to note that school counselors are not psychotherapists, clinical psychologists, or mental health counselors. When a student's issues are chronic, or the results of trauma and/or abuse are deeply rooted in their personality and development, a school counselor intervenes through referral to those with specialized training, as school is not the appropriate setting for therapy. There are those in the community who have the unique knowledge and skill necessary to diagnose and treat significant socioemotional disorders (e.g. substance abuse, clinical depression, bipolar disorder, etc.), and the counselor's responsibility is to be aware of these resources and employ as needed.

While school counselors are not therapists, they do and can provide services that are supportive and therapeutic. School counselors, for example, provide direct service to students struggling in the areas of emotional and social functioning, services that are intentionally based on counseling theory and empirical research (ASCA, 2017; Dimmitt et al., 2007; Zyromski & Mariani, 2016). Counselors will most often provide counseling in an attempt to mitigate the negative effects of some aspect of the student's life. Quite often this process may only entail a meeting or two. For some issues, typically those of a normative developmental nature (e.g. relationship issues, initial transitional anxiety, or situational stress response), a school counselor may meet with the student over the course of several weeks (e.g. 4–8), or when the issues are more involved, meet and support the student throughout an entire academic year.

In addition to direct service to individual students, school counselors can, according to ASCA (2017), play a role in the facilitation of social/emotional development by doing the following:

- Collaborating with classroom teachers to provide the school counseling curriculum to all students through direct instruction, team teaching, or providing lesson plans for learning activities or units in classrooms aimed at social/emotional development
- Understanding the nature and range of human characteristics specific to child and adolescent development
- Identifying and employing appropriate appraisal methods for individual and group interventions that support K–12 students' social/emotional development
- Using assessment in the context of appropriate statistics and research methodology, follow-up assessment, and measurement methods to implement appropriate program planning for social/emotional development
- Selecting and implementing technology in a school counseling program to facilitate K–12 students' social/emotional development
- Serving as a referral source for students when social/emotional issues become too great to be dealt with solely by the school counselor, including crisis interventions

It is important for the school counselor to consider the environments, or systems, in which the students live when planning prevention and intervention strategies. Although the school counselor can support students in the school, the homes and communities in which students live and interact daily can greatly impact socioemotional development and may need to be included in the intervention. Case Illustration 9.1 describes how a school counselor may consider these systems when deciding on interventions.

CASE ILLUSTRATION 9.1: HE DOESN'T WANT TO COME TO SCHOOL

Mr. Gomez looked at the attendance chart and saw that Manny was out of school again. He had been meaning to meet with him, as he did with all the new students on his school counseling case load, but he hadn't gotten around to it yet. He knew the move from Mexico had been tough on Manny, and beginning high school in a new place was hard for anyone. Mr. Gomez decided to call home to try to connect with Manny's mother, who he knew was home with a newborn.

After speaking with Manny's mother, Mr. Gomez knew he had some work to do. Manny's mother had reported that Manny didn't want to come to school, that the students were mean and the teachers didn't care. She went on to say that Manny's father needed help with his migrant farming job and Manny would be better helping family than in a place of hate.

Knowing that relationships and connections were vital to positive socioemotional development, Mr. Gomez went into action. In the short term, Mr. Gomez would be able to make some connections that would hopefully help Manny and his family understand the new norms of education and the culture of their new community. He called the community-based organization that supported migrant families and requested a connection for the parents and for Manny. He then set up a buddy, or peer partner, who would be a support to Manny in school during class and lunch periods. He then called Manny's mother again and asked for a meeting so he could go over the plans he was putting into place.

Mr. Gomez knew that family support for Manny's education was going to be very important, and he realized the community agencies would be valuable for Manny and his parents. He also realized the school climate did not feel safe to Manny, and quite possibly did not feel safe to other students. He requested a team meeting with the other support personnel to discuss what could be done to create a positive and welcoming learning environment for all students.

Awareness of the challenges that your students may encounter will be of utmost importance, and considering how their home and social environments, as well as the norms of the community in which they live, may impact their socioemotional growth will be beneficial in addressing the issues in the most effective way.

CHALLENGES TO OUR STUDENTS' SOCIOEMOTIONAL WELL-BEING

School counselors will encounter students presenting with a wide range of challenges to their socioemotional development and functioning. In many cases, these challenges reflect momentary situational issues that often are resolved by themselves over time. This could be the situation of the two seventh-grade students who are "no longer besties." Others may require more ongoing support and the development of a student's insights and coping behaviors, while with others much more insidious problems will require treatments consisting of in-depth, intensive, or medication-assisted therapies, thus placing the school counselor in a position of referral agent.

For those situations that can be addressed and resolved within the school setting, school counselors need to be familiar with the research around factors involved in these situations, as well as the best -practice approaches to be employed. In most situations, counselors providing direct one-on-one or small -group interventions (Tier III) will call on theories and approaches that offer brief approaches to counseling (e.g. Adlerian therapy, solution-focused, and reality therapy). Other strategies often used in more extensive counseling are now also modified for delivery by school counselors (e.g. cognitive behavioral approaches). The value of the school counselor in providing intervention and prevention services in support of student social development and well-being can be seen in the following brief review of a sampling of issues confronting our students.

Social Relationships

School is not only a place for academic growth and development, but it is also a time to develop and hone one's social skills. Whether it is in meeting new peers or learning to work cooperatively with others, a student's social skills and comfort level can be put to test.

Anxiety when confronting a new social situation or demand is not unexpected, nor necessarily is it a matter of concern. Most of such anxiety is transient. For some students, however, the sense of social anxiety, isolation, and loneliness is more than normative or transient and becomes an issue for school counselor service.

In working directly with students experiencing social anxiety (Tier III), cognitive behavioral approaches appear to be quite efficacious (Herzig Anderson et al., 2012). Counselors can employ such intervention in face-to-face direct service with a student or as small-group interventions such as that described in the Skills for Academic and Social Success program (Ryan & Masia Warner, 2012). Counselors have also engaged creative, systemic changes to encourage social engagement and reduce social isolation. As a Tier I example, Griffin et al. (2017) describe the positive impact of simply placing two "buddy" benches in the school playgrounds. The students were told that if you are alone (a) sit at the buddy bench, and (b) if someone invites you to play with them, say yes or "no, thank you." And, if you see someone who is alone at the bench, (a) join them and invite them to play, talk, or walk with you, and (b) if they say no, say "Okay, maybe next time," and walk away. Such a relatively simple systemic change can have very broad-based preventive value.

Bullying and Victimization

One area of concern that has received a lot of attention is in the area of bullying and victimization. According to the National Center for Educational Statistics (2016), more than one out of every five (20.8%) students report being bullied. The potential for devastating impact of such bullying becomes clear when one considers that those who are victimized by bullying have been reported to have 2.2 times greater likelihood of suicidal ideation and 2.6 times more likelihood of attempting suicide than students not facing victimization (Gini & Espelagem, 2014).

The need for school counselors to act as agents of systemic change is apparent when data reveals that schoolwide bullying prevention programs such as the Olweus Bullying Prevention programs (Olweus et al., 2007) and the NoTrap! program (Menesini et al., 2012) significantly reduce the amount of bullying occurring schoolwide (Gaffney et al., 2019).

Trauma and Stress

While trauma is not by definition normative, the reality of today's student is that they live in a time of trauma and the effects of stress and trauma do not stop at the school door. Our children and youth are not insulated from trauma; in fact, they are at the highest risk of exposure to potentially traumatic events by adolescence (McLaughlin et al., 2013).

Students who have experienced some form of trauma may give evidence of emotional dysregulation, including emotional lability, anhedonia, flat or numbed affect, explosive or sudden anger, and incongruous or inappropriate affect (D'Andrea et al., 2012). Further, their inability to regulate emotions may give form to withdrawal, aggression, oppositional behavior, high-risk sexual behavior, self-mutilation, eating disorders, and substance abuse (Muehlenkamp et al., 2012; Weiss et al., 2012).

School counselors need to understand the nature of trauma and be able to provide support and referral when needed for those students experiencing debilitating stress and trauma response. School counselors can also provide leadership in providing psychoeducational programming that serves as preventive services for those at risk (Tier II) and for primary prevention for the general student body (Tier I).

One approach that has been reported as effective in helping adolescents learn techniques for coping with symptoms of trauma is the LIFT (Life Improvement for Teens) program (Jaycox et al., 2019). This program is delivered by school counselors within a psychoeducation curriculum and facilitates students' development of resiliency when faced with challenging experiences. Other strategies, such as the teaching of mindfulness, relaxation techniques, and cognitive coping strategies, have been used by school counselors both as interventions for students experiencing significant stress and trauma response and schoolwide as preventive programs (Murray et al., 2013; Sibinga et al., 2016).

Suicidal Ideation

Crisis is a term applied to a situation that is overwhelming an individual's ability to cope. Crisis is an experience in which the person's normal adaptive functions are no longer sufficient. Sadly, for some students the feeling of crisis results in their contemplation of suicide. Suicide ideation and suicide attempts are a reality. According to the CDC (2017) suicide is the second leading cause of death for those between the ages of 10–24.

The fact that students who engage in suicidal ideation and self-harm behaviors need more intervention than can be offered within the school does not mean that the school counselor does not have a role to play. It is critical that the school counselors understand how to assess a student's level of crisis and, along with others within the school, be able to ensure the student's safety until additional services can be provided. Granello and Granello (2007) offered an acronym, SLAP, to depict the steps a school counselor can take in assessing the level of immediacy and lethality of a student's suicide plan.

> **S: Specificity** of the plan. The more specific and detailed the plan is, the greater the concern and need for action.
>
> **L: Lethality** of the means for carrying out the suicide plan. Means of self-injury that are immediate (i.e., guns, driving off a cliff or into another vehicle, or jumping off a bridge) are deemed more lethal than means that take time to enact (i.e., drug overdose).
>
> **A: Availability** of the means for carrying out the suicide plan. If the plans call for the use of a gun, but the student doesn't have access to a weapon, then the immediacy of the plan is lower than should the student be in possession of a gun.
>
> **P: Proximity** to help. Is there time and means of discovering and rescuing the student? If a student's parents are out of town that would place the student at higher risk.

Regardless of the assessment of immediacy and lethality, school counselors need to take all suggestions of suicidal ideation as serious and needing immediate response. At a Tier III level of service, counselors need to (a) keep the student safe; (b) affirm their care and deep concern for the student; (c) contact the student's caregivers; (d) assist with the student's engagement with community-based service; and (e) provide support and follow-up care upon the student's return to school (Capuzzi, 2009; Granello & Granello, 2007).

When it comes to crisis and suicide prevention, school counselors need to engage the entire school community (Tier I and Tier II) in increasing both awareness of risks and procedures to follow. The school counselor, as leader, advocate, and coordinator, can inform all members of the school community (students, teachers, parents, administrators, and staff) about the warning signs of suicidal ideation and the procedures to follow if concerned about a student.

This section discussed a sampling of challenges students contend with and for which school counselors need to provide service. Exercise 9.1 invites you to explore the socioemotional challenges most frequently observed in a school setting of your choosing, as well as the school counselor's response to these challenges.

Exercise 9.1: Socioemotional Challenges and Responses

Directions: Interview a school worker (e.g. school counselor, school nurse, school psychologist, school social worker, principal) who would be familiar with the socioemotional challenges in the age group you are interested in working with.

After you have an idea of what the challenges are (e.g. bullying, peer pressure), find out what is being done for prevention of and/or intervention for these challenges. What role does the school counselor have in these strategies? Now consider what you might do if you were the school counselor and you encountered these challenges.

Although there are challenges that may seem more obvious or prevalent, school counselors will want to remain vigilant to any challenge that threatens to negatively impact the socioemotional development of a student. While extreme behaviors signal an immediate need for intervention (e.g. suicidal ideation, withdrawal), anything that impacts a student's self-worth or ability to bounce back from a situation signals the need for support. Consider the importance of taking the time to understand the thoughts and feelings of a student no matter the issue, as in Case Illustration 9.2.

CASE ILLUSTRATION 9.2: IT'S ONLY A TALENT SHOW

Amanda stood quietly at the entrance of the counseling office, so quietly I didn't notice her until I looked up to see what time it was. When she realized I had seen her she explained she didn't want to bother me and probably shouldn't even be at my door. I welcomed her into the office and asked if her teacher knew she had come to see me. She nodded her affirmation and again expressed doubt that she should have come. I offered to listen and waited for her to speak.

Amanda explained that she had been so excited to be included in the try-outs for the talent show. The audition was with a group of girls she so desperately wanted to be friends with, and this was her chance to be connected with the girls. Yesterday at the try-outs, right before their group's audition, the girls told her they decided it would be better not to have her try out with them. Devastated, Amanda told the music teacher about the decision of the group, only to be told, "It's only a talent show." She had received the same reaction from her parents last evening when she told them, and then again from her teacher when she asked to come to the counseling office.

She asked me if she shouldn't feel hurt, that perhaps she was overreacting and it really was better that she wasn't included—that perhaps she wasn't worthy of those friendships she desired or even to be in the talent show. We talked for a while and decided that we would meet over the next few weeks to explore her feelings, thoughts, and strengths and appropriate ways to cope with hurt and disappointment.

Amanda left with a smile on her face, and as she exited the office she let me know that before we had talked she was thinking she might just be a freak and should just be as quiet and invisible as possible. I reaffirmed that I was so happy that she chose to talk about what was bothering her, and I was reminded how fragile the development of middle school students still was, and no issue was ever too small or unimportant to talk about and address. And, oh yes, I would be moving forward with some much -needed information on socioemotional development with the teaching staff, and perhaps a parent training.

A TAKE-AWAY

School counselors are charged not only with the support of student academic success but also their socioemotional development (ASCA, 2019). This charge brings them into contact and service with students who are navigating normative life challenges, from adjusting to changing friendships to coping with increased independence. In many of these situations the counselor is called to provide a brief support and perhaps individual counseling.

The realities faced by many of our students, however, are causing much more than normative disruption to their emotional and social development. Whether it is the deleterious effects of social anxiety or the impact of bullying and victimization, some students are literally fighting for their survival and are thus less concerned about academic achievement. Today's school counselor will engage in one-on-one and small -group counseling, providing remediation and, when needed, referral for these students. In addition to such direct services, school counselors, acting as agents of systemic change, advocate for schoolwide prevention programming, targeting the development of student knowledge, attitudes, and skills necessary for understanding and regulating their emotions, demonstrating empathy, and maintaining healthy positive friendships.

KEYSTONES

- School counselors are charged not only with the support of student academic success but also their socioemotional development (ASCA, 2019).
- National statistics show the degree to which our youth are experiencing socio-emotional challenges that not only interfere with their academic achievement but also their well-being.
- School counselors employ counseling curriculum, small -group counseling, and individual student planning, all to improve students' socioemotional well-being and remove socioemotional issues that may become barriers to their academic success.
- Counselors operating from a social -emotional learning framework provide programs and services that help students gain the knowledge, attitudes, and skills necessary for understanding and regulating their emotions and feelings, demonstrating empathy, and maintaining healthy positive friendships.
- While school counselors are not therapists, they do and can provide services that are supportive and therapeutic.
- In working directly with students experiencing social anxiety (Tier III) school counselors can employ cognitive behavioral approaches as well as small -group strategies such as that described in the Skills for Academic and Social Success program (Ryan & Masia Warner, 2012).
- The need for school counselors acting as agents of systemic change is apparent when data reveals that schoolwide bullying prevention programs such as the Olweus Bullying Prevention programs (Olweus, et al., 2007), and the NoTrap! program (Menesini et al., 2012) can be effective in reducing the incidence of bullying and victimization, resulting in a more positive, supportive school climate.
- School counselors provide support and referral when needed for those students experiencing debilitating stress and trauma response, and offer psychoeducational programming that serves as preventive services for those at risk (Tier II) and as primary prevention for the general student body (Tier I).
- School counselors accept the reality of suicidal ideation among students and take steps to assess the presence of such ideation and its level of immediacy and lethality.
- School counselors, as leaders, advocates, and coordinators, inform all members of the school community (students, teachers, parents, administrators, and staff) about the warning signs of suicidal ideation and the procedures to follow if concerned about a student.

ADDITIONAL RESOURCES

Print

Capuzzi, D. (2009). Suicide prevention in the schools: *Guidelines for middle and high school settings* (2nd ed.). American Counseling Association.

O'Neil, K. A., Brodman, D. M., Cohen, J. S., Edmunds, J. M., & Kendall, P. C. (2012). Childhood anxiety disorders: The Coping Cat program. In E. Szigethy, J. R. Weisz, & R. L. Findling (Eds.), *Cognitive-behavior therapy for children and adolescents* (pp. 227–261). American Psychiatric Publishing.

Parsons, R. D., Dickinson, K. L., & Asempapa, B. (2021). *Intervention and prevention strategies that work! Empirically supported approaches to multitiered school counseling services.* Cognella.

Web

ASCA on Air, Social/emotional learning: https://videos.schoolcounselor.org/category/sel-library

Student Success Skills: https://studentsuccessskills.com

Autogenic Meditation, A video presentation, autogenic guided meditation to reduce panic and anxiety: https://www.youtube.com/watch?v=MFxlK1ZvOmA

REFERENCES

American School Counselor Association. (2014). *Mindsets and behaviors for student success: K–12 college- and career- readiness standards for every student.* Author.

American School Counselor Association. (2017). *The school counselor and social/emotional development.* https://www.schoolcounselor.org/asca/media/asca/PositionStatements/PS_SocialEmotional.pdf

American School Counselor Association. (2019). *ASCA national model: A framework for school counseling programs* (4th ed.). Author.

Atkins, M., Hoagwood, K. E., Kutash, K., & Seidman, E. (2010). Toward the integration of education and mental health in schools. *Administration and Policy in Mental Health, 37,* 40–47.

Bitsko, R. H., Holbrook, J. R., Ghandour, R. M., Blumberg, S. J., Visser. S. N., Perou. R., & Walkup, J. (2018). Epidemiology and impact of healthcare provider diagnosed anxiety and depression among US children. *Journal of Developmental and Behavioral Pediatrics, 39*(5), 395–403.

Bowers, H., Lemberger, M. E., Jones, M. H., & Rogers, J. E. (2015). The influence of repeated exposure to the student success skills program on middle school students' feelings of connectedness, behavioral and metacognitive skills, and reading achievement. *The Journal for Specialists in Group Work, 40,* 344–364.

Capuzzi, D. (2009). *Suicide prevention in the schools: Guidelines for middle and high school settings* (2nd ed.). American Counseling Association.

Centers for Disease Control and Prevention. (2010). *Mental health surveillance among children – United States, 2005-2011. https://www.cdc.gov/mmwr/preview/mmwrhtml/su6202a1.htm*

Centers for Disease Control and Prevention. (2017). *National vital statistics report.* https://www.cdc.gov/nchs/data/nvsr/nvsr68/nvsr68_06-508.pdf

Collaborative for Academic, Social, and Emotional Learning. (2017). *What is SEL?* http://www.casel.org/what-is-sel/

Collaborative for Academic, Social, and Emotional Learning. (2013). *CASEL school kit: A guide for implementing schoolwide academic, social, and emotional learning.* Author.

Collaborative for Academic, Social, and Emotional Learning. (2015). *2015 CASEL guide: Effective social and emotional learning programs.* http://casel.org/guide/

D'Andrea, W., Ford, J., Stolbach, B., & Spinazzola, J. (2012). Understanding interpersonal trauma in children: Why we need a developmentally appropriate trauma diagnosis. *American Journal of Orthopsychiatry, 82*(2), 187–200.

Dimmitt, C., Carey, J., & Hatch, T. (2007). *Evidence-based school counseling: Making a difference with data-driven practices.* Corwin.

Durlak, J. A., Domitrovich, C. E., Weissberg, R. P., & Gullotta, T. P. (Eds.). (2015). *Handbook of social and emotional learning: Research and practice.* Guilford.

Durlak, J. A., Weissberg, R. P., Dymnicki, A. B., Taylor, R. D., & Schellinger, K. B. (2011). The impact of enhancing students' social and emotional learning: A meta-analysis of school-based universal interventions. *Child Development, 82*(1), 405–432.

Gaffney, H., Farrington, D. P., & Ttofi, M. M. (2019). Examining the effectiveness of school-bullying intervention programs globally: A meta-analysis. *International Journal of Bullying Prevention, 1,* 14–31.

Ghandour, R. M., Sherman L. J., Vladutiu C. J., Ali M. M., Lynch S. E., Bitsko R. H., & Blumberg S. J. (2019). Prevalence and treatment of depression, anxiety, and conduct problems in U.S. children. *The Journal of Pediatrics, 206*(3), 256–267.

Gini, G., & Espelage D. L. (2014). Peer victimization, cyberbullying, and suicide risk in children and adolescents. *The Journal of the American Medical Association, 312*(5), 545–546.

Granello, D. H., & Granello, P. F. (2007). *Suicide: An essential guide for helping professionals and educators.* Pearson.

Griffin, A. A., Caldarella, P., Sabey, C. V., & Heath, M. A. (2017). The effects of a buddy bench on elementary students' solitary behavior during recess. *International Electronic Journal of Elementary Education, 10*(1), 27–36.

Herzig Anderson, K., Colognori, D., Fox, J.K., Stewart, C. E., & Masia Warner, C. (2012). School based anxiety treatments for children and adolescents. *Child and Adolescent Psychiatric Clinics of North America, 21,* 655–658.

Jaycox, L. H., Ayer, L., Vona, P., Hehman, C., Stein, B. D., Mahmud, A., Woolley, M., Meza, E., Thornton, E., & Venkatesh, B. (2019). Development and preliminary evaluation of a self-guided, internet-based tool for coping with stress and trauma: Life Improvement for Teens (LIFT). *Psychological Services, 16*(1), 85–94. https://doi.org/10.1037/ser0000277

Kaffenberger, C., & Seligman, L. (2007). Helping students with mental and emotional disorders. In B. T. Erford (Ed.) *Transforming the school counseling profession* (2nd ed.) (pp. 351–383). Pearson.

Lemberger, M. E., Selig, J. P., Bowers, H., & Rogers, J. E. (2015). Effects of the student success skills program on executive functioning skills, feelings of connectedness, and academic achievement in a predominantly Hispanic, low-income middle school district. *Journal of Counseling & Development, 93*, 25–37.

Maras, M. A., Thompson, A. M., Lewis, C, Thornburg, K., & Hawks, J. (2015). Developing a tiered response model for social-emotional learning through interdisciplinary collaboration. *Journal of Educational and Psychological Consultation, 25*(2–3), 198–223.

McLaughlin, K. A., Koenen, K. C., Hill, E. D., Petukhova, M., Sampson, N. A., Zaslavsky, A. M., & Kessler, R. C. (2013). Trauma exposure and posttraumatic stress disorder in a national sample of adolescents. *Journal of the American Academy of Child & Adolescent Psychiatry, 52*, 815–830.

Menesini, E., Nocentini, A., & Palladino, B. E. (2012). Empowering students against bullying and cyberbullying: Evaluation of an Italian peer-led model. *International Journal of Conflict and Violence, 6*(2), 314–320.

Muehlenkamp, J. J., Peat, C. M., Claes, L., & Smits, D. (2012). Self-injury and disordered eating: Expressing emotion dysregulation through the body. *Suicide and Life-Threatening Behavior, 42*, 416–425.

Murray, L. K., Cohen, J. A., & Mannarino, A. P. (2013). Trauma-focused cognitive behavioral therapy for youth who experience continuous traumatic exposure. *Peace and Conflict: Journal of Peace Psychology, 19*(2), 180–195. https://doi.org/10.1037/a0032533

National Center for Educational Statistics. (2016). Indicators of school crime and safety: 2016. https://nces.ed.gov/pubsearch/pubsinfo.asp?pubid=2017064#:~:text=Indicators%20of%20School%20Crime%20and%20Safety%3A%202016%3A%20Description%3A,of%20students%2C%20teachers%2C%20principals%2C%20and%20the%20general%20

National Center for Homeless Education. (2020). *National overview.* http://profiles.nche.seiservices.com/ConsolidatedStateProfile.aspx

Olweus, D., Limber, S. P., Flerx, V., Mullin, N., Riese, J., & Snyder, M. (2007). *Olweus bullying prevention program: Schoolwide guide.* Hazelden.

Ryan, J. L., & Masia Warner, C. (2012). Treating adolescents with social anxiety disorders in schools. *Child and Adolescent Psychiatric Clinics of North America, 21*, 105–118.

Sibinga, E. M., Webb, L., Ghazarian, S. R., & Ellen, J. M.(2016). School-based mindfulness instruction: An RCT. *Pediatrics, 137*(1) 1–8.

Weiss, N. H., Tull, M. T., Viana, A. G., Anestis, M. D., & Gratz, K. L. (2012). Impulsive behaviors as an emotion regulation strategy: Examining associations between PTSD, emotion dysregulation, and impulsive behaviors among substance-dependent inpatients. *Journal of Anxiety Disorders, 26*, 453–458.

Zyromski, B., & Mariani, M. A. (2016). *Facilitating evidence-based, data-driven school counseling: A manual for practice.* Corwin.

CHAPTER 10

CONNECTING WITH PARENTS/CARETAKERS

It's not always easy to get, but parent involvement in their child's educational journey is invaluable.

—Keana H., Middle school counselor

The value of parent/caretaker involvement in our schools, which was voiced by Keana H., the middle school counselor quoted at the introduction of this chapter, has been supported by the research. Research has consistently demonstrated family involvement to be associated with student achievement in school (Bryan & Henry, 2012; Burkhardt, 2004; Epstein, 2004). The ASCA (2016) cites research that demonstrates that school–family–community partnerships have increased the successful academic, career, and social/emotional development of all students.

The school–family partnership is an important factor to student success. "School counselors have an essential and unique role in promoting, facilitating, and advocating for collaboration with parents/guardians and community stakeholders" (ASCA, 2016, p. 67). The current chapter reviews the importance and value of school and family partnerships and ways to overcome many of the challenges that must be confronted for these partnerships to be formed and be effective.

After completing this chapter readers will be able to do the following:

1. Describe the value of engaging parents/caretakers in the educational process.
2. Identify ways in which school counselors can provide leadership in connecting school, family, and community.
3. Describe ways in which parents/caretakers can participate in support and extension of the work of the school counselor.
4. Identify the types of factors that may inhibit or stand as roadblocks to a parent or parents' involvement with the school counselor and the school.

PARENTS/CARETAKERS: VALUABLE ALLIES

The value of parents/caretakers as allies to our educational endeavors is not only intuitively appealing but is supported by over 40 years of research (Hornby & Lafaele, 2011). Whether parents are participating at home (helping with homework, etc.) or at school (attending parent workshops, conferences, etc.), parental involvement has been shown to have a positive impact on children's academic and personal/social well-being (Hornby & Lafaele, 2011). Family involvement benefits both the student and the school as it increases student achievement and attendance, promotes career development, enhances school climate, and fosters student resilience (Epstein & Sheldon, 2006).

Through engaging parents, school counselors can not only help increase parents' knowledge and skills about child development and educational processes, but help prepare them to assist in their child's academic and socioemotional development. One area in which parental engagement appears very helpful in facilitating their children's achievement is in providing involvement that reflects academic socialization (Hill & Tyson, 2009). School counselors can help encourage parents to communicate their valuing of education and their strategies for learning, as well as assist their children in connecting what they are learning to their interests and future goals. This academic socialization can position a student to maximize achievement.

SCHOOL COUNSELOR AS POINT OF CONTACT

School counselors enhance the collaboration of school–family–community stakeholders by being the catalyst through which these collaborations occur (Bryan & Henry, 2012). Epstein (2010) suggested that school counselors organize parent-to-parent forums, teach or arrange workshops on topics of interest to parents, teach parents how to communicate with the school and how to interpret school communications such as progress reports or testing reports, and provide opportunities for parents to volunteer at school. Not only can the school counselor be a valuable resource for parents, but a partnership with the parents can support and extend the effective and efficient delivery of school counseling program services (Taylor & Adelman, 2000). Students succeed at higher levels when the external conditions in which they live and the interpersonal relationships occurring between home, school, and community are all working in concert (Epstein et al., 2002). Exercise 10.1 invites you to apply these general findings to the lived experience of a counselor in your area.

Exercise 10.1: Connecting in Partnership

Directions: The needs of students change across their development, from elementary through graduation of high school. Interview counselors from elementary, middle, and high school and gather information regarding each of the following questions:

1. What means or strategies do you employ to keep your parents informed about the services and programs you provide?
2. Do you engage in a need assessment? If you do, does it include data from parents and students?
3. In what ways do you invite parents to participate or contribute to the school counseling program and its activities and services?

"A key to increase student achievement and to ensure more equitable practices in schools is to increase parent and community involvement" (Bryan & Holcomb-McCoy, 2007, p. 66). While Exercise 10.1 invited you to gather data from the field highlighting targets for parent/caretaker involvement, the following identifies some of the ways school counselors can foster these essential connections of school, family, and community. Perhaps those you interviewed employ some of the following strategies and targets.

Establishing Personalized Communication Networks

School counselors are valuable resources in the establishment of personal, productive, communication patterns throughout the school and between home, school and community (Lewis & Borunda, 2006). Since many parents had a very different experience with "guidance counselors," it is important for school counselors to not only introduce but also explain the scope of the counseling programs and services provided. Parents may have several questions about their child's education program and yet may wonder if it is appropriate to ask, or even whom to ask. School counselors need to connect and build that communication network. Case Illustration 10.1 provides one example of a counselor reaching out at the beginning of the school year to demonstrate availability and interest in connecting with parents.

CASE ILLUSTRATION 10.1: THE CHILDREN CALL ME MRS. E. (I.E., CAROL ECKINGTON)

A Little About Me:

I was born and raised right here, a real local, and in fact I went to this same middle school. But wow, have things changed since then.

I graduated from Central University with a Bachelor of Science degree in psychology. I worked for three years as a clinical intake specialist at the community mental health center. Eight years ago, I returned to get my master's degree in school counseling and have since acquired additional training for my license as a professional licensed counselor.

I have had the pleasure of working here at J. R. Middle School since getting my master's, and I truly can say I love coming to work each day.

Our Counseling Program

The counseling department (that's me, Mr. Sorinson, and Ms. Rodrigues) employs a comprehensive model of counseling services, one that reflects the principles of the model program outlined by our professional organization, the American School Counselor Association. We provide services for all students as a way of promoting their academic, career, and socioemotional development while at the same time offering programs and services for those students who are having a bit of a rough time. We are excited because we have a lot of great programs and services planned for this year. Our action plan is attached to this sheet and describes the goals, objectives, planned services, and measures we will employ to assess effectiveness. If you see something that we are missing, holler!

You and Me (We)

As I mentioned, school has certainly changed from my years as a middle schooler, and so has the role and function of the school counselor. We are fortunate to be able to not only provide intervention services but also programs aimed at fostering development. We are able to advocate for the children in service of moving the entire school community to the fulfillment of our mission.

In taking on this task it has become clear that your involvement is critical. We believe that it is vitally important for us to develop a connection, open our communication, and actively collaborate with you, the parent/guardian. We can provide support to your child and also to you through consultation, workshops, and support groups.

I invite you to reach out, even if it is just to say hi. Following you will find my contact information, both phone number and email, and of course my door is always open. (Oops, sometimes not, when I'm with students—so maybe calling to set a time to meet is best.)

I have listed a couple of the questions parents have asked in the past. You will see that some of the concerns you may have are not so unusual, so please don't hesitate to contact me. We would collaborate with your child's teacher(s) when appropriate.

- How is my child doing in school?
- What are my child's strengths and weaknesses?
- Are there any areas of concern or delayed development?
- What are my child's goals for this year?
- What are some suggestions for action at home?
- What programs are available to help my child to do better?
- Does my child get along well with adults?
- Does my child get along well with their peers?
- What can I do to improve discipline at home?
- Are there ways I can improve communication with my child?
- What can I expect after a change in the family (death, divorce, illness, financial status, moving)?
- What resources are available at school to help my child make friends?
- Can you direct us to what type of professional resources are available outside of school?
- What do I need to do to prepare my child for transitioning into high school?
- What do I do? My child is _____ (sad, not sleeping, not eating, overeating, has temper tantrums, etc.).
- What do I do if I don't like my child's friends?
- Should I restrict my child's access to the internet? To video games?

We Are Going to ROAR
As Leopold (our Lion mascot) would say, let's ROAR! That is what we intend to do. With your help, we will achieve our goal of providing your child with a truly growth-filled year, one of enjoyment, one of wonder, one of development.

School counselors employ a variety of strategies to connect and engage parents, including developing newsletters (both hard copy and digital) and counselor's blogs or web pages. These are employed both as a means of informing parents and sharing information, as well as identifying needs and interests and seeking feedback. Case Illustration 10.2 provides an example of a monthly newsletter created for the parents of an elementary school.

CASE ILLUSTRATION 10.2: SCHOOL COUNSELOR NEWSLETTER

School Counselor Newsletter

How can we keep our children's attention?

Hello Parents of Tiger Elementary,

At this point during your child's online learning experience you may be noticing how difficult it can be to keep your child focused on their school work. Unfortunately, the average attention span of a child is much different then the average attention span of an adult. Due to this we need to find ways to help our children keep their attention focused for the longest period of time possible. This newsletter hopes to identify how long a child's attention span can last and ways you, as parents, can help keep their attention focused for their longest periods of times. I hope you enjoy!

-Mr. Roesch

Thought of the Day:

If I am unable to stay motivated and keep my attention on one task for more then 20 minutes, how long will my child be able to stay motivated and keep their attention on one task?

Differences in Attention Span

Yes, every individual has differences in their attention-span abilities from birth, but let's just think about the differences between the average attention span of an adult and a child:

1. Think about how long you can stay focused on one specific task without needing to sway your attention to something else.
2. Think about how long your child can stay focused on one specific task until they need to sway their attention to something else.

An Adult's Attention Span

A common notion around maintaining concentration for adults is that you should take a small break every 45 minutes according to: https://skeptics.stackexchange.com/questions/8560/how-long-is-it-possible-to-maintain-

A Child's Attention Span

By using the image on the next page, we will say the minimum length for a child's attention span is about **10-15 minutes.**

So, why should we treat our child's ability to stay focused on one task as the same as an adult's ability to keep focused?

AGE	ATTENTION SPAN
2	4 - 10 min
3	6 - 15 min
4	8 - 20 min
5	10 - 25 min
6	12 - 30 min
7	14 - 35 min
8	16 - 40 min
9	18 - 45 min
10	20 - 50 min

Mr. Roesch's tips to get the most out of your child's attention span

- **Constantly switch the tasks your child is working on** Being able to switch one's attention from one hard task to another keeps them focused on those tasks without getting to a point where their focus begins to drift into space (due to mental exhaustion from focusing on one task for too long) rather than the task in front of them.
- **Give your children "Mental Breaks"** In order to prevent your child from consistently having their attention drift into space, give them mental breaks by letting them do fun or physical activities.
- **Find out your child's teacher's strategy to gain the undivided attention of their class** Many teachers use different strategies within their classrooms to get their class's attention in comparison to other teachers, so it is important to use the same attention grabber as your child's teacher so you do not confuse them.
- **Make the tasks interesting and enjoyable to your child** Every child has their own specific interest, so try to make the tasks that are boring and unenjoyable to your child relate to the specific topics or themes that interests your child. Keeping tasks more enjoyable makes individuals want to focus and work on it longer.

A **resource on various teaching strategies** your child's teacher may use to gain their class-room's attention:

http://www.kellybear.com/TeacherArticles/TeacherTip54.html

A **resource on tips** for teachers on **how to get children's attention** that could be useful for parents, and **generalized to the home atmosphere**:

https://www.scholastic.com/teachers/articles/teaching-content/teacher-tips-getting-childrens-attention/

A **resource** on how to help kids with their **attention and focus specifically for parents**:

https://www.care.com/c/stories/5152/10-tips-for-getting-kids-to-pay-attention/

Need Help?

If you have any questions on how to help your child through this difficult time please contact me.

This is an unordinary time for everyone, especially those families dealing with young children. I may not have an answer to all of your needs, but I am here to listen during this tough time.

Suggestions?

If you have any suggestions on another topic one of my news-letters can cover, please email me.

All suggestions are greatly appreciated!

While not all families have access to the internet, thus creating a need for hard copies to be sent or mailed home, others with such access may benefit from the counselor's creation of a web page. As with hard copy materials, the web page can be used to communicate information about deadlines, activities, and resources, as well as seek feedback and needs identification. Finally, when resources permit, a school counselor can create and devote a space as a parent resource room (Bemak, 2000). This resource room or center is open to parents/caretakers and houses materials such as brochures, videos, CDs, and so on that target areas of child development and parenting. As a welcoming place, the center would facilitate parent-to-parent engagement as they become informed about the things the school, and more specifically the counseling department, are doing.

Inviting Participation

Recognizing the richness of the resources that can be found among the parent population and the community, school counselors will establish a means for seeking and engaging parents and community volunteers. Volunteers can serve in many capacities, sharing their time and their talents.

In addition to providing another "pair of hands" when helping with presentations and community service activities, parents can participate in career and college days, and parents and community leaders can serve as members of an advisory board for the counseling department (ASCA, 2019). Their knowledge of what is happening outside the school and how this can impact student development and achievement within the school is truly a valuable resource. Their insights can help shape the type of services offered by the school counselor.

An area in which parental involvement is crucial and to which a school counselor brings leadership and advocacy skills is in the development of support for those students who are diverse learners. Those diverse learners who are identified as "English learners (EL) are students who speak languages other than English at home and who qualify to receive instructional support services, such as English as a second language (ESL), bilingual education, or language immersion programs" (Trainor et al., 2016, p. 147). Parent knowledge of student background and experiences provide pertinent information during curriculum and intervention planning sessions (Chu & Flores, 2011). Parents provide valuable information, including the student's prior education, native language, cultural norms, and literacy levels.

School counselors advocate for the students by assuring that parents and guardians are present in the meetings and that they have an active role in the decision-making process (ASCA, 2012). Also, when professional interpreters are needed, school counselors, serving as advocates, can screen professional interpreters to ensure they have received appropriate training and demonstrate cultural awareness (Paone et al., 2010).

Other diverse learners, such as those students who receive special education, benefit greatly when there is a partnership between school and home. Parents are part of the team meetings for planning educational goals for their child, and beyond that the school counselor can invite their participation in parent groups and workshops to provide support and strategies to help at home.

Helpers: Extending Intervention and Prevention Services

The interventions employed by the school counselor can oftentimes be increased in potency by engaging parents in program applications at home. A simple example of a counselor's enlistment of a parent as an extension to the intervention program employed at school occurs when parents apply the same behavioral reinforcement system being used at school to reward the same targeted behaviors at home. Counselors will also often invite parents to use the skills and preventive strategies taught to their children. For example, the principles and practices of (a) mindfulness, (b) conflict resolution, and (c) socioemotional learning taught to students for application in school can be augmented by helping parents understand these strategies and employ aspects of these programs in the home environment. This engagement of parents not only affirms their importance as collaborators in support of the school counselor's work but also highlights their central role and value to their child's socioemotional development.

Engaging parents in developing a supportive, even therapeutic, home environment for those students needing ongoing support may require the school counselor to provide parent education. Child development has accelerated as issues confronted by today's students, even when part of normal development, are being presented at earlier ages. Parents have questions and concerns about numerous issues and challenges in their child's life and the best way that they can be of support. Helping parents understand the nature of the issues experienced by their child and the best ways they, as parents, can provide support is a valuable service offered by school counselors.

Exercise 10.2: I'd Like to Know

Directions: Parenting can be challenging and may need to be different for each child depending on individual strengths and needs. School counselors can be a valuable resource to parents in learning about normative development and offering strategies to help with academic and social behaviors.

Speak with a parent of a child in an elementary, middle, or high school. You may want to speak to more than one parent to see if answers to the following questions are different between parents or different between grade levels of the child. After you have responses, consider what preventions/interventions you can do for Tier I, such as parent training, career and college events for parents and students, and classroom lessons on peer pressure, and for Tier II, preventions such as mindfulness or study skills groups for students.

1. What issues concern you regarding your child in academics? In the social domain? In personal development?
2. What topics would be helpful to have more information?
3. What could the school do that would be helpful?
4. How would you like to be involved in your child's education?
5. Are there any barriers to your involvement?

ADDRESSING BARRIERS TO PARENTAL ENGAGEMENT

In seeking to engage parents in a school–home collaboration, school counselors are aware that some parents experience unique barriers to such involvement. In addition to barriers related to ethnicity, culture, and language, some parents may be hindered by their level of education, financial circumstances, and even their psychological resources (Hornby & Lafaele, 2011). Other factors, such as being a single parent, having limited transportation, or having work hours that conflict with school hours and typical counselor availability, can all interfere with parents' interest and ability to engage with the school and the school counselor.

School counselors are aware of these factors, and as such build positive partnerships with all parents, adjusting types of programs and services as well as hours and means of engaging, in ways that reflect their sensitivity to the demands that parents are attempting to balance. The following exercise (10.3) invites you to investigate one school counselor's experience with barriers blocking parental collaboration and the steps they take to reduce these barriers.

Exercise 10.3: Increasing Parental Involvement

Directions: The number and variety of factors that can stand as barriers to parental involvement in the services of the school and school counselor are unique to every school and every population. Interview a school counselor and gather data around the following:

1. In what specific way do you invite parental involvement in the formation, delivery, or assessment of your programs and services?
2. What are the top factors that seem to prevent interested parents from actually becoming involved (e.g. scheduling problems, language difficulties, misunderstandings, etc.)?
3. What, if anything, have you done to increase parental knowledge of the school counseling program and increase their input and participation in the formation and delivery of your program?

A TAKE-AWAY

With parental involvement having a documented positive effect on children's academic achievement, parent–teacher relationships, teacher morale, school climate, school attendance, and parental confidence (Bower & Griffin, 2011; Cripps & Zyromski, 2009; Hill & Tyson, 2009; Hornby & Lafaele, 2011), it is important for school counselors to take the initiative to facilitate parental involvement at their schools. School counselors make natural partners or leaders in establishing school–family–community partnerships (Walker, 2010). School counselors are called to serve as the catalyst for the development of such partnerships by developing collaborative family–school programs and by working to involve all caregivers in children's learning and development (ASCA, 2019).

KEYSTONES

- The ASCA (2016) cites research that demonstrates that school–family–community partnerships have increased the successful academic, career, and socioemotional development of all students.
- Family involvement benefits both the student and the school as it increases student achievement and attendance, promotes career development, enhances school climate, and fosters student resilience.
- School counselors have an essential and unique role in promoting, facilitating, and advocating for collaboration with parents/guardians and community stakeholders.
- School counselors are valuable resources in the establishment of personal and productive communication patterns throughout the school and between home, school and community.
- In addition to providing another "pair of hands" when helping with presentations and community service activities, parents can participate in career and college days, and parents and community leaders can serve as members of an advisory board for the counseling department.
- The interventions employed by the school counselor can oftentimes be increased in potency by engaging parents in program applications at home.
- School counselors are aware of factors that hinder parent involvement, and as such adjust the types of programs and services, as well as hours and means of engaging, in ways that reflect their sensitivity to the demands that parents are attempting to balance.

ADDITIONAL RESOURCES

Print

Bryan, J., & Henry, L. (2012). A model for building school-family-community partnerships: Principles and process. *Journal of Counseling & Development*, *90*(4), 408–420.

Epstein, J. L., & Van Voorhis, F. L. (2010). School counselors' roles in developing partnerships with families and communities for student success. *Professional School Counseling*, *14*(1), 1–14.

Web

American School Counselor Association. (2016). *The school counselor and school-family-community partnerships*. https://www.schoolcounselor.org/asca/media/asca/Position-Statements/PS_Partnerships.pdf

Pinterest, Counselor Corner: https://www.pinterest.com/keshandthekids/counselors-corner-newsletter-topics/

Teachers Pay Teachers, Counselor newsletter templates: https://www.teacherspayteachers.com/Browse/Search:school%20counselor%20newsletters

REFERENCES

American School Counselor Association. (2016). *The school counselor and school–family–community partnerships.* https://www.schoolcounselor.org/asca/media/asca/Position-Statements/PS_Partnerships.pdf

American School Counselor Association. (2019). *The ASCA national model: A framework for school counseling programs* (4th ed.). Author.

Baker, A. J. L. (2001). Improving parent involvement programs and practices: A qualitative study of parent perceptions. In S. Redding & L. G. Thomas (Eds.), *The community of the school* (pp. 127–153). Academic Development Institute.

Bemak, F. (2000). Transforming the role of the counselor to provide leadership in educational reform through collaboration. *Professional School Counseling, 3,* 323–331.

Bower, H., & Griffin, D. (2011). Can the Epstein model of parental involvement work in a high-minority, high-poverty elementary school? A case study. *Professional School Counseling, 15*(2), 77–87.

Bryan, J., & Henry, L. (2012). A model for building school-family-community partnerships: Principles and process. *Journal of Counseling & Development, 90*(4), 408–420.

Bryan, J., & Holcomb-McCoy, C. (2007). An examination of school counselor involvement in school–family–community partnerships. Professional School Counseling, 19(5), 441-454.

Chu, S., & Flores, S. (2011). Assessment of English language learners with learning disabilities. *The Clearing House, 84*(6), 244–248. https://doi.org/10.1080/00098655.2011.590550.

Colbert, R. D. (1996). The counselor's role in advancing school and family partnerships. *School Counselor, 44*(2), 100–104.

Cripps, K., & Zyromski, B. (2009). Adolescents' psychological well-being and perceived parental involvement: Implications for parental involvement in middle schools. *Research in Middle-Level Education Online, 33*(4), 1–13.

Epstein, J. L. (1995). School/family/community partnerships. *Phi Delta Kappan, 76,* 701–712.

Epstein, J. L. (1987). Toward a theory of family–school connections: Teacher practices and parent involvement. In K. Hurrelman, F. Kaufmann, & F. Losel (Eds.), *Social intervention: Potential and constraints* (pp. 121–136). DeGruyter.

Epstein, J. L., & Sanders, M. G. (2006). Prospects for change: Preparing educators for school, family, and community partnerships. *Peabody Journal of Education, 87,* 81–120.

Epstein, J. L., Sanders, M. G., Simon, B. S., Salinas, K. C., Jansorn, N. R., & Van Voorhis, F. L. (2002). *School, family, and community partnerships: Your handbook for action* (2nd ed.) (pp. 9-62). Corwin.

Epstein, J. L. V. (2010). School counselors' roles in developing partnerships with families and communities for student success. *Professional School Counseling, 14*(1), 1.

Hill, N. E., & Craft, S. A. (2003). Parent–school involvement and school performance: Mediated pathways among socioeconomically comparable African-American and Euro-American families. *Journal of Educational Psychology, 95*(1), 74–83.

Hill, N. E., & Tyson, D. (2009). Parental involvement in middle school: A meta-analytic assessment of the strategies that promote achievement. *Developmental Psychology, 45*(3), 740–763.

Hornby, G., & Lafaele, R. (2011). Barriers to parental involvement in education: an explanatory model. *Educational Review, 63*(1), 37–52.

Lewis, R., & Borunda, R. (2006). Lived stories: Participatory leadership in school counseling. *Journal of Counseling and Development, 84*, 406–413.

Paone, T. R., Malott, K. M., & Maddux, C. (2010). School counselor collaboration with language interpreters: Results of a national survey. *Journal of School Counseling, 8*(13). http://jsc.montana.edu/articles/v8n13.pdf

Taylor, L., & Adelman, H. S. (2000). Connecting schools, families, and communities. *Professional School Counseling, 3*, 298-307.

Trainor, A., Murray, A., & Kim, H. (2016). English learners with disabilities in high school: Population characteristics, transition programs, and postschool outcomes. *Remedial and Special Education, 37*(3), 146–158.

Walker, J. M. T. S. (2010). Why do parents become involved in their children's education? Implications for school counselors. *Professional School Counseling, 14*(1), 27.

IMAGE CREDITS

CHAPTER 11

FOSTERING WELLNESS

An ounce of prevention is worth a pound of cure.

—Benjamin Franklin

The axiom attributed to Benjamin Franklin that *an ounce of prevention is worth a pound of cure* is not only as true today as it was in his time, but it has a special meaning when placed within the context of a comprehensive school counseling program. While school counselors play an essential role in providing support and essential interventions for students who are struggling in their academic, career, and socioemotional development, they are also positioned to affect the healthy development of all students through their engagement with preventive programming and developmental guidance curriculum.

The current chapter discusses the role of school counselors in fostering the healthy development and wellness of their students and the acquisition of the knowledge, dispositions, and skills necessary to navigate life's stressors. Upon the completion of this chapter the reader will be able to do the following:

1. Describe the sociocultural stressors encountered by students in the 21st century.
2. Explain what is meant by "wellness."
3. Describe the role of the school counselor in the facilitation of wellness.
4. Describe targets for preventive programming.

CERTAINLY NOT IMMUNE

Where to begin?

Research depicts life in the 21st century as one that is fast-paced, rapidly changing, and filled with new and often threatening challenges. Whether it is the experience of a new strain of virus, community shootings and violence, an expansion of the drug epidemic, or the stress of employment and economics in an age of transition, individuals today are experiencing stress and trauma at very high levels (Beilock & Carr, 2005; Holcomb-McCoy, 2005; Pedro-Carroll, 2001; Villalba & Borders, 2005). The American Psychological Association's annual survey "Stress in America" (2017) reported that as many as 63% of Americans are stressed about the future of the nation, money, work, political climate, violence, and crime.

Our students are not naturally inoculated from these stressors, nor the additional ones they encounter while attempting to successfully navigate the academic and social pressures experienced as part of their developmental stage and their role as a student. Since challenges to wellness can have lifelong ramifications on a person's physical health and emotional stability, it is in the best interest of children to teach them about wellness at an early age (Towey & Fleming, 2003).

It is a misconception that all stress is bad. Stress is a normal part of everyday life. But we know that stress that is very prolonged or very intense can be harmful and particularly so when experienced early in life, where it can impact the individual in the moment and have lasting effects into adult life (Santor et al., 2000). Given these realities, the need to assist our students in acquiring the knowledge and skills necessary to (a) avoid unneeded and unhealthy stress; (b) employ strategies for managing stress; and (c) develop resiliency is clear. The school counselor, through a comprehensive school counseling program that not only employs intervention services but also provides schoolwide prevention programs, can be central to assisting students in their development of resiliency and wellness.

WELLNESS

Wellness has been defined as "a way of life oriented toward optimal health and well-being, in which body, mind, and spirit are integrated by the individual to live life more fully with the human and natural community" (Meyers et al., 2000, p. 252). Essentially, wellness entails how individuals live their life physically and emotionally and the factors that positively or negatively impact their lives. Ideally, it is "the optimum state of health and well-being that each individual is capable of achieving" (Myers et al., 2000, p. 252).

For the school counselor, it is important to address students' overall life satisfaction in areas such as friendship, family, and self-concept, as well as motivation toward achieving goals, since it has been found that there is a moderate positive correlation between life satisfaction, goal achievement, and wellness (Briggs et al., 2010) for this age group. Students' wellness is impacted by the quality and quantity of their health behaviors such as sleep, diet, and physical inactivity, as well as societal factors, including the strength of family bonding, violence, poverty, social inequalities, family changes, the educational experience, and environmental degradation (Eckersley, 2011; Holcomb-McCoy, 2005; Villalba & Borders, 2005). While many of these factors may be outside of the influence of the school counselor, school counselors can and do provide programs that support good physical and mental health practices and teach skills of self-care, rational problem solving, social interaction, and emotional regulation, which are proactive and preventive. Without including preventive strategies in the school counseling program, the school counselor would likely be dealing with crises exclusively and "Band-Aiding" the student experience. Making prevention and wellness strategies a central part of the school counseling program, the school counselor will have more time to address a variety of other tasks, and most importantly will be providing skills that will act as lifelong protective factors to the students.

SCHOOL COUNSELING: WELLNESS-BASED

In numerous ways, the field of counseling and specifically school counseling has historical roots in wellness (Myers, 1992; Street, 1994). While much of the initial wellness efforts targeted students' nutrition and physical health (U.S. Department of Education, 2001), the focus has expanded to the development and implementation of programs that address the psycho-emotional factors essential for wellness (Myers & Sweeney, 2005b, 2005c, 2005d).

The ASCA has highlighted the value of preventive programming in our schools. ASCA's (2015) position is that "school counselors recognize and respond to the need for mental health and behavioral prevention, early intervention and crisis services that promote psychosocial wellness and development for all students" (p. 71). The ASCA (2019) national model outlines components of a comprehensive school counseling program that is not only comprehensive in scope but also preventive in design and developmental in nature. As noted in an ASCA (2015) position statement, school counselors, in a preventive role, are responsible for the following:

- Delivering school counseling curriculum that proactively enhances awareness of mental health; promotes positive, healthy behaviors; and seeks to remove the stigma associated with mental health issues
- Providing school-based prevention, universal interventions, and targeted interventions for students with mental health and behavioral health concerns
- Educating teachers, administrators, parents/guardians, and community stakeholders about the mental health concerns of students, including recognition of the role environmental factors have in causing or exacerbating mental health issues and providing resources and information

As with all programs developed by school counselors, wellness programs emerge from needs assessment and data analysis. School counselors will often employ wellness assessment instruments to gain a quantitative picture of students' wellness levels (Rayle et al., 2007). For example, Myers and Sweeney (2005) have developed the five-factor wellness evaluation of lifestyle (5F-WEL), which is a 99-item assessment specifically designed to measure wellness and is available in versions for children, adolescents, and adults. Other instruments often employed to identify student needs and potential targets for wellness and preventive programming are presented in Table 11.1.

Table 11.1 Assessing Wellness

1.	The Devereux Student Strengths Assessment and four-item accompanying screener, the DESSA-Mini, are behavior rating scales for elementary school-age children (K–8), completed by parents and/or teachers. The DESSA measures child strengths across eight scales, including optimistic thinking, self-management, goal-directed behavior, self-awareness, social awareness, personal responsibility, decision-making, and relationship skills.
2.	The Social-Emotional Assets and Resilience Scale (SEARS) for K–12 include a screener, as well as 52- to 54-item Teacher (SEARS-T), Parent (SEARS-P), Child (SEARS-C), and Adolescent (SEARS-A) versions, and assesses student levels of responsibility, social competence, empathy, and self-regulation.
3.	The Social Skills Improvement System Rating Scales is a set of rating scales designed to assess children's social behavior and assist in the implementation of interventions, which is part of the whole system. The system includes rating scales for teachers and parents covering the Pre-K to 18 years age range, and self-report versions for students at the grade-school level and beyond.
4.	The Behavioral and Emotional Rating Scale (BERS) and the Preschool BERS (PreBERS) are strength-based socioemotional assessment instruments.

Adapted from: Denham (2016).

WELLNESS PROGRAMMING

School counselors are, by definition, promoters of wellness, with programs that not only serve individual students but impact the entire school climate (Villalba & Borders, 2005). School counselors play a central role in the promotion of wellness within their schools, and research supports the efficacy of their programs (e.g. Myers et al., 2011; Villalba & Myers, 2008).

Counselors have developed and implemented a wide variety of wellness and prevention programs (e.g. Bargiel-Matusiewicz & Wilczynska-Kwiatek, 2009; Chesser et al., 2009; Tuuri et al., 2009). Programs have been created to address issues such as self-esteem, conflict resolution, substance abuse prevention, stress management, emotional resiliency, and mindfulness. These programs can be provided to individual students as interventions or delivered using group counseling formats or classroom guidance curriculum. According to the ASCA (2019) national model, a comprehensive school counseling curriculum includes the delivery of developmental units through classroom guidance composed of interconnected lessons, grounded in an overall scope and deliberate in sequence. For example, in addressing issues around the development of personal relationships, the school counselor can prepare activities and discussion points related to supporting others who are struggling with social connection. Case Illustration 11.1 provides an example of how school counselors may plan on addressing student needs in the personal and socioemotional domains through Tier I interventions.

CASE ILLUSTRATION 11.1: IS IT TOO EARLY?

The school counselors in the Mountainview District meet once a month to discuss student need and provide peer supervision as needed. At the end of the school year the counselors review the referrals from the past year so that they can plan the developmental class lessons for the next school year.

At the May meeting, the high school counselors reported the majority of issues that year had been with students experiencing anxiety, mostly due to stressors they felt pending post-high school decisions. In response to this stress, they saw an increase of drug and alcohol use. Although the middle school counselors reported seeing pressure from their students, it manifested primarily from negative peer pressure. They too noticed an increase in student use of alcohol and marijuana. The elementary school also reported many referrals due to stress, mostly stemming from relational aggression, with upper elementary students reporting use of alcohol.

The school counselors were all on board for teaching lessons for coping skills and peer pressure at every level, with the elementary lessons being preventative and the middle and high school lessons focusing on maintaining those skills and applying them to different situations. There was some dissension regarding teaching about drugs and alcohol at the elementary level, however. There was a question about introducing information about drugs and alcohol before it was developmentally appropriate, and wouldn't that prompt some students to start using? Wouldn't it be too early for these lessons?

The elementary counselors advocated for those lessons to start before fifth grade when use was already reported. In order for these lessons to be preventive, they needed to occur before the behavior was an issue. It was decided that it would be appropriate to include basic information about drugs and alcohol when teaching about appropriate coping skills and responses to peer pressure in the elementary counseling lessons, and it was not too early to do so.

Or, perhaps a program collaboratively presented by the school counselor and school nurse will integrate information on well-balanced diets, exercise, and self-esteem.

While school counselors are often the school professionals who develop, implement and assesses the wellness programs, there are times when the nature of the topic or program being delivered may be best served by engaging another professional, such as a school nurse, social worker, or physical education teacher. In these cases, the school counselor will serve as coordinator and collaborator. Case Illustration 11.2 provides an example of how this could occur.

CASE ILLUSTRATION 11.2: DO I LOOK TOO FAT?

Ms. Washington hung up from her phone call with Madison's mother and reflected on what she had just heard. Madison, a third-grade girl in school, was coming home having not eaten her lunch and had begun asking her mother each day if she looked too fat. Madison was tall for her age, and her weight was appropriate at the moment, but would not be if she didn't eat. Madison's mother couldn't believe her daughter would be concerned with her weight and how her clothes fit at only eight years old. She said this seemed to have started a few weeks ago when the health report card came home giving the BMI (body mass index) score, which for Madison was in the appropriate percentile.

Knowing that eating disorders could develop even at any age and could have long-term impact on boys and girls, she consulted with the health teacher and the nurse. They decided as a Tier I preventative measure that the health teacher would incorporate a nutrition unit into the third-grade curriculum and the nurse would join Ms. Washington to present a three-week unit of classroom lessons titled "Healthy Me!" This would focus on what body mass index meant, how the body changes in elementary and middle school, and how a proper diet can help the brain and body grow in a healthy way.

Considering Madison to be at risk for a negative self-image, Ms. Washington also invited Madison to be part of a Tier II small counseling group to discuss personal strengths and coping strategies.

Regardless of the specific focus, when providing wellness and preventive curriculum, school counselors ensure that students understand the meaning of wellness, engage in assessment of their current state of wellness, identify areas for improvement, and learn and employ strategies for growth (Myers et al., 2000).

RESILIENCY

One area receiving increased attention by mental health professionals, including school counselors, is the development and maintenance of personal resiliency. Resiliency is the ability to overcome challenges of all kinds—trauma, tragedy, and personal crises. Resiliency refers to one's ability to bounce back from disruptive experiences and difficult situations. It is a skill set involving thoughts and behaviors, which all can be learned and are thus a prime target for school counselor preventive programming.

It is not possible to protect our children, our students, from all the ups, downs, traumas, and setbacks of life. We cannot prevent adversity or undue stress, but school counselors can and do provide students with the tools necessary to be resilient and navigate these difficult situations. A program that has received much acclaim and empirical support, and one that can be employed within our schools, is the University of Pennsylvania's Resiliency Program. This program, as a school-based program, has been found to improve factors related to students' resilience and well-being (e.g. Cutuli et al., 2006; Reivich & Shattem, 2002).

The PRP is a cognitive behavioral group intervention program applicable for classroom delivery. The program is designed to help students think more rationally, realistically, and flexibly about the problems they encounter. The curriculum teaches social problem-solving skills and rational approaches to the interpretation of life experiences. Students are taught to identify their inaccurate and dysfunctional thoughts about experiences and challenge these thoughts while considering more rational, reasonable alternatives. The curriculum also teaches students strategies for solving problems and coping with difficult situations, including assertiveness skills, social problem solving, conflict negotiation skills, and relaxation techniques.

The program has been designed for employment within the classroom using a format of either twelve 90-minute lessons or 18 to 2460-minute lessons. The delivery schedule is adjusted according to a school's structure and schedule. The curriculum employs many pedagogical strategies, including role-plays, short stories, and illustrations/cartoons—all to illustrate the core concepts. Students practice their newly acquired skills and share their experiences.

A TAKE-AWAY

Today's students are increasingly confronted with difficult life events and circumstances that can strain their ability to cope and function. While school counselors provide intervention and remedial support for those students who are struggling with life's challenges, they also recognize the need for and value of helping all students develop the knowledge and skills necessary to grow in wellness and resiliency.

School counselors, in recognition of the importance of early intervention and prevention, provide programs that promote psychosocial wellness and foster development for all students. Counselors design and implement programs that are comprehensive in scope, preventive in design, and developmental in nature and are delivered to individual students, to small groups, and schoolwide.

KEYSTONES

- School counselors not only provide intervention and support for students who are struggling in their academic, career, and socioemotional development, they also provide programs that facilitate the healthy development of all students.

- Because challenges to wellness can have lifelong ramifications, it is in the best interest of children to teach them about wellness at an early age.
- School counselors provide programs that help students acquire the knowledge and skills necessary to (a) avoid unneeded and unhealthy stress, (b) employ strategies for managing stress, and (c) develop resiliency.
- ASCA's (2015) position is that "school counselors recognize and respond to the need for mental health and behavioral prevention, early intervention and crisis services that promote psychosocial wellness and development for all students" (p.71).
- Programs have been created to address issues such as self-esteem, conflict resolution, substance abuse prevention, stress management, emotional resiliency, and mindfulness. These programs are provided to individual students as interventions as well as delivered using group counseling formats and classroom guidance curriculum.
- One area of focus for school counselors is the development of students' resiliency, which is the ability to bounce back from disruptive experiences and difficult situations.
- Developing resiliency requires the teaching of rational thinking and skills of solving problems and coping with difficult situations, including assertiveness skills, social problem -solving, conflict negotiation skills, and relaxation techniques.

ADDITIONAL RESOURCES

Print

Dickinson, K. L., & Parsons, R. D. (2018). *A student's guide to managing stress.* Cognella.

Myers, J. E., & Villalba, J. A. (2007). Starting early: Helping kids understand and choose wellness behaviors. In M. Gentile (Ed.), *Wellness for life: A Multidisciplinary Approach to Choosing and Sustaining a Happy & Healthy Lifestyle.* American Occupational Therapy Association.

Reivich, K., & Shatte, A. (2003). *The resilience factor: 7 keys to finding your inner strength and overcoming life's hurdles.* Broadway Books.

Web

Healthy school action tools: https://www.mihealthtools.org/hsat/

Project School Wellness 101: https://www.projectschoolwellness.com/school-wellness-101/

University of Pennsylvania resiliency program: https://prezi.com/coyglhdijbod/penn-resiliency-program/

REFERENCES

American School Counselor Association. (2019). *ASCA National Model: A framework for school counseling programs*(4th ed.). Alexandria, VA: Author.

American Psychological Association. (2017). *Stress in America: The state of our nation.* https://www.apa.org/news/press/releases/stress/2017/state-nation.pdf

American School Counseling Association. (2015). *The school counselor and student mental health.* https://www.schoolcounselor.org/asca/media/asca/PositionStatements/PS_StudentMentalHealth.pdf

Bargiel-Matusiewicz, K., & Wilcynska-Kwiatek, A. (2009). Youth health promotion. *International Journal on Disability and Human Development*, 8, 187–190.

Beilock, S. L., & Carr, T. H. (2005). When high-powered people fail: Working memory and "choking under pressure" in math. *Psychological Science, 16*, 101–105.

Chesser, A., Hawley, S. R., & St. Romain, T. (2009). Community-based participatory research in developing an obesity intervention in a rural county. *Journal of Community Health Nursing, 26*, 35–43.

Cutuli, J. J., Chaplin, T. M., Gillham, J. E., Reivich, K. J., & Seligman, M. E. P. (2006). Preventing co-occurring depression symptoms in adolescents with conduct problems: The Penn Resiliency program. *New York Academy of Sciences, 1094*, 282–286.

Denham, S. (2016). *Tools to assess social and emotional learning in schools*. Edutopia. https://www.edutopia.org/blog/tools-assess-sel-in-schools-susanne-a-denham

Dodge, K. A. (1986). A Social Information Processing Model of Social Competence in Children. In M. Perlmutter (Ed.), *Minnesota Symposia on Child Psychology* (pp. 77–125).

Eckersley, R. (2011). A new narrative of young people's health and well-being. *Journal of Youth Studies*, 5(5), 627–638.

Holcomb-McCoy, C. (2005). Wellness and children: Research implications. In J. E. Myers & T. J. Sweeney (Eds.), *Counseling for wellness: Theory, research, and practice* (pp. 59–66). American Counseling Association.

Myers, J., & Sweeney, T. J. (2005a). Introduction. In J. E. Myers & T. J. Sweeney (Eds.), *Counseling for wellness* (pp. 1–4). American Counseling Association.

Myers, J., & Sweeney, T. J. (2005b). The wheel of wellness. In J. E. Myers & T. J. Sweeney (Eds.), *Counseling for wellness* (pp. 7–14). American Counseling Association.

Myers, J., & Sweeney, T. J. (2005c). The indivisible self: An evidence-based model of wellness. In J. E. Myers & T. J. Sweeney (Eds.), *Counseling for wellness* (pp. 29–42). American Counseling Association.

Myers, J., & Sweeney, T. J. (2005d). The indivisible self: An evidence-based model of wellness. *The Journal of Individual Psychology, 61*, 270–279.

Myers, J. E., Sweeney, T. J., & Witmer, J. M. (2000). The wheel of wellness counseling for wellness: A holistic model for treatment planning. *Journal of Counseling and Development, 78*, 251–266.

Myers, J., Willse, J. T., & Villalba, J. A. (2011). Promoting self-esteem in adolescents: The influence of wellness factors. *Journal of Counseling and Development, 89*, 28–36.

Pedro-Carroll, J. (2001). The promotion of wellness in children and families. *American Psychologist, 56,* 993–1104.

Rayle, A. D., Moorhead, H. J. H., Green, J., Griffin, C. A., & Ozimek, B. (2007). Adolescent girl-to-girl bullying: Wellness-based interventions for school counselors. *Journal of School Counseling, 5.* http://www.jsc.montana.edu/articles/v5n6.pdf

Reivich, K. & Shatté, A. (2002). *The resilience factor.* Broadway Books.

Santor, D. A., Messervey, D., & Kusumakar, V. (2000). Measuring peer pressure, popularity, and conformity in adolescent boys and girls: Predicting school performance, sexual attitudes, and substance abuse. *Journal of Youth and Adolescence, 29,* 163–182.

Seligman, M. (2018): PERMA and the building blocks of well-being, *The Journal of Positive Psychology, 13(4), 333–335.* https://doi.org/10.1080/17439760.2018.1437466

Street, S. (1994). The school counselor practice wellness. *School Counselor, 41,* 171–179.

Myers, J. E., & Sweeney, T. J. (2005). *Five factor wellness inventory: Adult, teenage, and elementary school versions.* Menlo Park, CA: Mind Garden, Inc.

Towey, K., & Fleming, M. (2003). *Healthy youth 2010: Supporting the 21 critical adolescent objectives.* American Medical Association.

Tuuri, G., Zonovec, M., Silverman, L., Geaghan, J., Solmon, M., Holston, D., Guarino, A., Roy, H., & Murphy, E. (2009). Smart Bodies school wellness program increased children's knowledge of healthy nutrition practices and self-efficacy to consume fruit and vegetables. *Appetite, 52,* 445–451.

U.S. Department of Education (2001). *Title I: Improving the academic achievement of the disadvantaged.* http://www2.ed.gov/policy/elsec/leg/esea02/pg1.html

Villalba, J. A. (2007). Incorporating wellness into group work in elementary schools. *The Journal for Specialists in Group Work, 32,* 31–40.

Villalba, J. A., & Borders, L. A. (2005). Wellness applications in schools. In J. E. Myers & T. J. Sweeney (Eds.), *Counseling for wellness: Theory, research, and practice* (pp. 227–234). American Counseling Association.

Villalba, J. A., & Myers, J. E. (2008). Effectiveness of wellness-based classroom guidance in elementary school settings: A pilot study. *Journal of School Counseling,* 6(9), 1–30.

PART 4

COUNSELING IN ACTION

CHAPTER 12

THE JOURNEY BEGINS

Pre-K to Middle School

Their energy, their excitement, and their innocence is such a joy to experience.
—Linda K, School counselor pre-K to fourth grade

From their first day of school, students in elementary grade levels embark on a journey that year after year will result in the acquisition of increased knowledge and the development of new skills and growth in self-concept and feelings of competence and confidence. The early years of their school experience are critical in that they provide the foundation for all that follows.

Elementary school counselors have the opportunity to facilitate students' development of social skills and positive peer relationships, school skills such as organization and time management, as well as growth in self-acceptance and independence. Elementary school counselors also provide leadership in the early identification and removal of any barriers to academic achievement and socioemotional development. The role of elementary school counselors as they support and facilitate all students' success in academic, personal, social, and career development cannot be overstated.

The current chapter reviews the unique challenges and opportunities encountered by those serving as elementary school counselors. Upon completion of this chapter, readers will be able to do the following:

1. Describe the developmental challenges facing students in elementary school.
2. Describe the role and function of an elementary school counselor.
3. Identify the components of a comprehensive elementary school counseling program.

DEVELOPMENTAL NEEDS AND CHALLENGES

The time of elementary school is one in which numerous changes in a student's physical, cognitive, social, and emotional development occur. With entry into formal schooling, children are moved to a world that includes a host of new adults, new settings, new tasks and task demands, as well as a new set of rules and peer connections. Elementary-aged students are not only growing in academic knowledge and skills but are also developing their decision-making and communication skills and establishing attitudes about self, peers, and school (ASCA, 2019). Elementary school years set the tone for developing the knowledge, attitudes, and skills necessary for children to become healthy, competent, and confident learners.

Success in school requires much more than cognitive abilities and the capability of mastering specific academic content. Success in school requires that students possess (a) self-regulation skills, including learning to focus, reducing distractions, engaging in activities to improve memory, and managing emotions; (b) social skills, including communicating appropriately with school staff and peers and resolving conflict with peers, both individually and as a team; (c) self-management skills, such as impulse control, stress management, self-motivation, organization, and time management; and (d) responsible decision-making skills, including problem solving and goal setting (Brigman & Campbell, 2003; Zins et al., 2004). The elementary school counselor has the expertise to design and implement programs that foster the development of all students' ability to grow in each of these areas, thus supporting all students' success in school.

ELEMENTARY SCHOOL COUNSELOR

The specific role and function of an elementary school counselor, as well as the focus of the services provided, are tailored to the needs of all stakeholders, the mission of the school and district, and any specific constraints that are presented. But even with this as a caveat and the reality of widespread diversity in what elementary school counselors do, all elementary school counselors, with their training in child development, group dynamics, and intervention and prevention skills, serve the students' academic, socioemotional, and career needs. Their training as professional educators with a mental health perspective enables them to understand and respond to the challenges encountered by today's students.

Elementary school counselors support students through their developmental challenges by providing education, prevention, and intervention activities (ASCA, 2019). Through their comprehensive counseling programs, elementary school counselors provide students with a variety of services, including academic support, goal setting, career awareness, education/understanding of self, peer relationships, problem solving, and conflict resolution, and so on.

While being trained to employ direct, one-to-one counseling services, and possessing the skills necessary for engaging even the youngest of their students in a helping, working alliance, elementary school counselors do not work in isolation of all others serving their students. Elementary school counselors, with their leadership abilities and their ecological view of the school and its impact on the students, collaboratively engage teachers, administrators, and parents in the design and implementation of intervention and prevention programs. This collaboration is especially valuable in assisting school counselors in their efforts to identify students at risk of academic and social/emotional difficulty and to remove barriers to student healthy development and academic success. Through an early intervention and prevention approach to academic, personal, and social barriers in school, school counselors can promote well-being and a healthy love of learning that will carry over into the next phases of school.

PROGRAMMING FOR STUDENT NEEDS

As previously noted, the programs developed and implemented by the elementary school counselor will reflect the unique mission of the school and the specific needs of its stakeholders. Even with this uniqueness in mind, it can be stated that the elementary school counselor, regardless of their setting, is called to design, develop, implement, and evaluate programs and services that are comprehensive, developmental, and system -wide. The programs developed by elementary school counselors are data -driven and result -based and reflect ASCA's (2019) national standards in the academic, career, and personal/ social domains.

Using data collected through a variety of sources, such as teaching observations, attendance and discipline records, and academic reports, elementary school counselors will design programs to address the needs revealed by these data. In addition to targeting those with special challenges, the elementary school counselor engages in activities that take them into the classroom to provide responsive services and developmental counseling lessons. While recognizing the need for remediation and intervention, elementary school counselors provide programs for all students in an attempt to preventively help develop the knowledge, skills, and attitudes necessary to succeed in school and secure a solid foundation in those skills throughout life.

As noted in Table 12.1, the services provided by elementary school counselors in a comprehensive program not only vary in terms of mode of delivery (direct and indirect), but also in the recipients of the services offered (i.e., student, parents, teachers, administrators).

Table 12.1 Services in a Comprehensive Counseling Program

RECIPIENT	NATURE OF SERVICE
Direct service to student	Instruction: Teaching the school counseling curriculum to students focused through the lens of selected student standards from the ASCA mind-sets and behaviors for student success. Appraisal and advisement: Assessing student abilities, interests, and achievements to help them make decisions about their future. Counseling: Providing professional assistance and support to a student or small group of students during times of transition, heightened stress, critical change, or other situations impeding student success. Crisis interventions
Direct service to parents	Communication/networking (school newsletter/counselor blog, doughnuts with special someone, etc.) Interpretation of assessment results One-on-one parent conferencing Parent/teacher conferences Parent education and presentations (bullying prevention, homework help, etc.)
Direct service to administrators/Schoolwide	Child study/IEP teams Schoolwide needs assessments Student data and results (school improvement plan, etc.) Student recognition programs (PBIS, etc.) Schoolwide prevention programming (e.g. antibullying, PBIS, school climate)
Indirect service to students (Note: All direct services to teachers, parents, administrators are indirectly assisting students.)	Consultation: Share strategies supporting student achievement with parents, teachers, other educators, and community organizations. Collaboration: Work with other educators, parents, and the community to support student achievement. Referrals: Helping students and families access community resources for additional assistance and information.

Adapted from: ASCA (2019).

A SAMPLE COMPREHENSIVE COUNSELING PROGRAM

To suggest that an elementary school counselor has much to do and often little time in which to do it may be an understatement. In addition to holding individual and group counseling sessions, responding to unexpected emergencies and crises, the elementary school counselor provides a developmental curriculum and helps to coordinate services in support of the students.

Table 12.2 provides a sample of one elementary school counselor's planned monthly calendar. The items listed each month reflect responsive activities, providing intervention and prevention programming, as well as those that call on the counselor's leadership ability as they provide collaboration and coordination services in support of the individual student and schoolwide Tier I services. What it does not show is the reality of each day, a day that is always filled with the unexpected. Exercise 12. 1invites you to get a firsthand look at a counselor's day and the expanse of planned and unplanned activities as well as the need for counselor flexibility.

Table 12.2 A Sample of One Elementary School Counselor's Planned Calendar

MONTH	AREAS	RESPONSIVE SERVICES (INTERVENTION AND PREVENTION)	SYSTEM SUPPORT (INCLUDING TEAM MEETINGS)	TIER I SERVICE/ CURRICULUM
August	Academic	Screenings	Input for ER, re-evals, IEP, and 504 evaluations/ referrals Participate in MTSS/MDT meetings Review new student files	New Student and Kindergarten orientation classes and schedules New -parent orientation "Welcome back from the counselor" classroom visits
	Career	Look to our future (monthly career presentations and activities)		
	Personal/ social	Individual counseling as needed Group counseling as needed Assisting with kindergarten students	Coordinate PBIS Recognition of pro-social behaviors	New Student Orientation and tours: Team building Positive person/kindness and caring program
September	Academic	Academic screenings Parent/teacher/ student conferences	Input for ER, re-evals, IEP, and 504 evaluations/referrals Participate in MDT meetings Review new student files and progress Participate with external referral agencies and develop support program	Developmental counseling lessons (all grades) Being and doing your best/skills for success
	Career	Look to our future		Begin planning for Career Day
	Personal/ social	Individual counseling as needed Group counseling as needed Lunch bunch	Coordinate PBIS Recognition of pro-social behaviors	Positive person/kindness and caring The three R's (respectful, responsible, and ready to learn)

October	Academic	Screenings Parent/teacher/student conferences	Input for ER, re-evals, IEP, and 504 evaluations/referrals Participate in MDT meetings Follow up on new students	Developmental counseling lessons: Respect
	Career	Look to our future	Oversee career highlight	Vo-Tech tours
	Personal/social	Individual counseling as needed Group counseling as needed IEP support groups Lunch bunch	Recognition of pro-social behaviors	The three R's (respectful, responsible, and ready to learn)
November	Academic	Screenings Parent/teacher/student conferences	Input for ER, re-evals, IEP, and 504 evaluations/referrals Participate in MDT meetings Review new student files	
	Career	Look to our future	Oversee career highlight	Career: Look who is coming to our school
	Personal/social	Individual counseling as needed Group counseling as needed Lunch bunch IEP support groups	Recognition of pro-social behaviors	Developmental counseling lessons: Goal setting The three R's (respectful, responsible, and ready to learn)
January	Academic	Screenings Parent/teacher/student conferences Early intervention Transition planning meetings	Input for ER, re-evals, input for ER, RR, IEP, and 504 evaluations/referrals Participate in MDT/MTSS meetings Review new student files	
	Career	Look to our future	Oversee career highlight	Continue Career Day plans
	Personal/social	Individual counseling as needed Group counseling as needed Lunch bunch IEP support groups	Recognition of pro-social behaviors	Developmental counseling lessons: Making small steps toward our goals The three R's (respectful, responsible, and ready to learn) Assembly on mindfulness (prior to state assessments)

(Continued)

Table 12.2 *(Continued)*

March	Academic	Screenings Parent/teacher/student conferences	Input for ER, re-evals, IEP, and 504 evaluations/referrals Participate in MDT meetings Review new student files PSSA Getting Ready Assembly Be Smart program	
	Career	Look to our future	Project Wisdom	Finalize Career Day plans
	Personal/social	Individual counseling as needed Group counseling as needed Lunch bunch IEP support groups	Recognition of pro-social behaviors	Guidance lessons: No reason to fear, test anxiety The three R's (respectful, responsible, and ready to learn) Moving from preschool tours/meetings
May	Academic	Screenings Parent/teacher/student conferences IEP transition conferences	Input for ER, re-evals, IEP, and 504 evaluations/referrals Participate in MDT meetings Coordinate Be Smart program	Fifth-grade to sixth-grade transition tours
	Career	Look to our future	Oversee career highlight	Pick two and learn
	Personal/social	Individual counseling as needed Group counseling as needed IEP support groups Lunch Bunch	Recognition of pro-social behaviors	Developmental counseling lessons: Friendship The three R's (respectful, responsible, and ready to learn)
June	Academic	Screenings Parent/teacher/student conferences	Participate in MDT meetings Participate in child study/MTSS meetings Coordinate Be Smart program	Celebration assembly for graduates and recognition for pro-social behaviors (PBIS)
	Career	Look to our future	Oversee career highlight	Career Day
	Personal/social	Terminating individual counseling Terminating group counseling Lunch bunch		Year-end outcomes assessment and report Setting goals for next year

Exercise 12.1: Not Always as Smooth as Planned

Directions: While elementary school counselors are great at planning and may spend a lot of their summer preparation time doing just that, they are also aware that what is planned does not always go off without a hitch. Interview three elementary school counselors and have them respond to the following. If possible, interview elementary school counselors who work in different geographic areas (states, regions, urban, rural, etc.).

1. Do you typically prepare an annual calendar and/or a monthly listing of the activities you hope to initiate?
2. Do you have some form of calendar or plan for each day?
3. What are the typical "unplanned" requests for your service or demands on your time that you encounter in any one day?
4. What has been the most disruptive event or situation to your normal planning that you have encountered over your career.
5. Given your experience with planning, what is your suggestion for a counselor just starting their career?

In providing direct services, school counselors (a) develop the core curriculum that is integrated schoolwide at all levels, (b) assist students in individual planning, (c) provide responsive services that include crisis assistance and counseling, and (d) provide indirect services on behalf of students that can include referrals to outside agencies as well as collaboration/consultation with educators and administrators. Delivery is the area elementary school counselors have the opportunity for direct impact with the students, and this, along with consultation and collaboration, which indirectly impact students, is where most of the working hours of the school day would be spent. However, because of other duties associated with the role of the counselor, this is not always the case.

LIFE AS AN ELEMENTARY SCHOOL COUNSELOR (VOICES FROM THOSE WHO SERVE)

As we close out the chapter we thought it would be of value to share the lived experience of the elementary school counselor through the voices of those who serve each day. There are many ups and downs that come with the job. The brief sampling provided here does not do justice to the richness of the professional experience one has as an elementary school counselor. It is highly suggested that you visit an elementary school and talk with a school counselor about the gifts and challenges of being an elementary school counselor.

The Joy of an Assembly (Rachael K., First- to Fourth-Grade School Counselor)

At the end of the year, we have an "awards" assembly. It is always such a joy to see the children being recognized for their hard work. But this year it was particularly heartwarming and affirming. Alicia was one of my fourth-grade students. She was new to our school and presented with extreme social anxiety. She found every way and means to hide in class, at recess, wherever and whenever she was in contact with peers. At the beginning of the year, she would get physically ill if she had to go to the cafeteria for lunch, so we often ate together in my office. She is a very bright, musically gifted student, and I employed a lot of cognitive behavioral strategies to eventually increase her social involvement with her peers. The bottom line to my story is that I sat at this year-end assembly with the entire school community present and here was Alicia, the *host*, the Miss of Ceremonies, leading the entire process. She opened the assembly with a solo presentation on her cello that truly brought tears to my eyes. These moments remind me of why I know it is a gift to be an elementary school counselor.

Tough to Leave Work at Work (Raul, Fifth-year Elementary School Counselor, 5 Years)

This is my fifth year at S. T. Elementary School, and I wish I could tell you I am getting hardened to my experience. I am not. S. T. Elementary is located in a very poor, urban community, which is one of the highest nationally in terms of crime, drug abuse, and violence. The children in our schools often remind me of those seen from war-torn countries. They come to school often wearing the same clothes for days, they are often in need of a shower, and it is clear that their only meals, or at least their only nutritional meals, will be delivered here at school. Yes, the community is rough, the best of families are struggling, and at times students are truly "challenging." But our students are children. They have dreams (still), they smile and giggle, they show surprise when they get the answer, and once you connect they are an endless source of unconditional love.

It's been five years and I have not been hardened to the realities of this community. At times I wish I were as it would hurt less. But I know that if I were I would not experience the life connections I have with my students and me with them. I can't leave the job at work, but I know that I must find ways to renew myself and keep well so that I can be my best for them.

Five years and I hope it never ends.

Guess Who I Saw? (Virginia, Elementary School Counselor, 24 Years)

Ask any school counselor if they had one student who had been both an absolute thorn in their side and the biggest joy they ever encountered, and I'll bet my lunch money that they did. For me, after 24 years, I've got a couple.

Russell is among the top of the list. Simply stating his name is all I would need to say to have those who taught him and they would respond with a head shake and a wide grin. I work with students pre K to eighth grade, and for all of his nine years at R. L. D. Elementary School, Russell and I were a pair.

Russell was a student who walked to a different beat. He was always seeing things a little differently. Even from first grade he would always challenge (politely) the why of classroom or school requirements. He would pose questions or make observations that would knock you off your feet with the level of insight and creativity. And while being the bane of his teachers, he was one of the most loved students in his class. Russell was and remains a unique individual.

While it was obvious that he is a very bright individual, his grades were barely passing. Each year our team would gather to figure out how we would pull Russell to the end line (while maintaining our sanity). Well, we did! He successfully transitioned to high school, and as is the case with all that we do, life moved on and I lost contact with Russell's progress.

That was 14 ago.

I was cleaning up (actually straightening) my office as an end-of-school ritual, and who do I see in the doorway? A 6'3" handsome young man, appearing as if he just stepped out of a fashion magazine, and yet still with the impish grin and curious look in his eye. Before I had a chance to say hello, he was giving me a huge bear hug. Russell.

We sat and we talked, and he shared that he was finishing up a doctorate in clinical psychology. I cannot share everything that we discussed, simply because I cry each time I think about it. He tried to help me see how important my belief in him and my consistent and persistent presence in his life was to his development.

As he was leaving, following another heart-felt thanks and a hug, he showed me the dedication to be included in his dissertation, and there along with his other mentors and loved ones was the name of this old elementary school counselor. Really humbling.

A TAKE-AWAY

The elementary school years are times in which a child can begin to develop feelings of competence and industry. They will learn to navigate social groups and social conflicts. They will have opportunities to challenge their abilities and develop confidence as learners. But the elementary school years can present barriers to a child's academic and socioemotional development.

It is at these times when both normative challenges and more atypical barriers are present that the school counselor becomes such a valued resource to the students, their teachers, and their parents. Through the development and implementation of a comprehensive developmental school counseling program, elementary school counselors help all students acquire the knowledge, skills, and attitudes necessary to succeed in the areas of academic, career, and personal/social development.

KEYSTONES

- Elementary school counselors have the opportunity to facilitate students' development of social skills and positive peer relationships, school skills such as organization and time management, as well as growth in self-acceptance and independence.
- Success in school requires that students possess (a) self-regulation skills, including learning to focus, reducing distractions, engaging in activities to improve memory, and managing emotions; (b) social skills, including communicating appropriately with school staff and peers and resolving conflict with peers, both individually and as a team; (c) self-management skills, such as impulse control, stress management, self-motivation, organization, and time management; and (d) responsible decision-making skills, including problem- solving and goal- setting.
- Elementary school counselors, with their leadership abilities and their ecological view of the school and its impact on the students, collaboratively engage teachers, administrators, and parents in the design and implementation of intervention and prevention programs.
- Using data collected through a variety of sources, such as teaching observations, attendance and discipline records, and academic reports, elementary school counselors will design comprehensive counseling programs to address the needs revealed by these data.
- Elementary school counselors provide direct services such as (a) developing the core curriculum that is integrated schoolwide at all levels, (b) assisting students in individual planning, and (c) providing responsive services that include crisis assistance and counseling. They also provide indirect services through referral and collaboration.

ADDITIONAL RESOURCES

Print

Chen-Hayes, S. F., Ockerman, M. S., & Mason, E. C. (2013). *101 solutions for school counselors and leaders in challenging times*. Corwin.

Hatch, P. (2013). *The use of data in school counseling: Hatching results for students. Programs and the Profession*. Corwin.

Web

75 free counseling resources: https://confidentcounselors.com/2018/03/04/freeschoolcounselingresources/

Elementary School Counseling Resources: http://www.elementaryschoolcounseling.org/resources.html

School Counseling Lessons for Elementary Students: https://onlinecounselingprograms.com/resources/school-counselor-toolkit/student-development/elementary/

REFERENCES

American School Counselor Association. (2019). *The essential role of elementary school counselors* https://www.schoolcounselor.org/getmedia/1691fcb1-2dbf-49fc-9629-278610ae-deaa/Why-Elem.pdf

Brigman, G., & Campbell, C. (2003). Helping students improve academic achievement and school success behavior. *Professional School Counseling, 7*, 91–98.

Zins, J., Weissberg, R., Wang, M., & Walberg, H. (Eds.). (2004). *Building academic success on social and emotional learning: What does the research say?* Teachers College Press.

CHAPTER 13

MIDDLE SCHOOL

A Time of Change

When I said goodbye for the summer, they were children ... here we are in September, and wow have they changed!

—Elisha, Middle school counselor

They were changed, indeed. For those in early adolescence (ages 10–14), much can and will change over a few months. Ask any teacher, counselor, or parent and you will get similar reactions; the middle school student is one going through massive changes across their physical, emotional, social, and cognitive domains. They are changes that can be stressful to the student and those who care about them. They are changes that call for counselor support.

This period of development, early adolescence, has been identified as a period of *sturm und drang* (storm and stress). The developmental changes experienced during this period may be the most intense transformations in the human life cycle. These changes can have a significant impact on a variety of developmental outcomes, including academic achievement, self-concept development, and achievement motivation.

Middle school counselors understand the developmental characteristics of early adolescents and the difficulty posed by entry and transition through the middle school years. The comprehensive counseling programs developed and implemented by the middle school counselor provide intervention support for those in need and preventive programs to facilitate this development for all students.

The current chapter reviews the nature of changes encountered by the middle school student and the way middle school counselors can facilitate healthy development and academic success. After completing this chapter, readers will be able to do the following:

1. Describe the changes experienced by the preadolescent and the challenges they can pose.

2. Identify targets for service that may be unique to those serving as middle school counselors.
3. Describe goals for schoolwide, Tier I programming that are particularly useful for the middle school student.

UNIQUE CHALLENGES FOR STUDENT AND COUNSELOR

For any service to be effective, it must reflect the needs and characteristics of the population served. The comprehensive school counseling program developed and implemented by the middle school counselor will be tailored to the unique needs of the students navigating this early adolescent period of development. As is true for all school counseling programs, services will be provided on a one-to-one basis as well as by way of small group and in-class instruction. Additionally, as part of the comprehensive school counseling programs, the programs and services provided by the middle school counselor will help to remove barriers to all students' academic success, socioemotional development, and career development progress.

In addition to the scope of services typically provided by all school counselors, middle school counselors target specific areas of concern and develop services that will facilitate healthy development for all middle school students.

Physical/Biological Changes

As suggested by the quote that opened this chapter, when schools reopen each fall, middle school counselors are greeted by the presence of young men and women, who, only three months prior, were children. Changes in the middle school student's physical appearance are rapid and dramatic. As adults, we can observe these changes as beautiful, wonderful, and exciting. Sadly, we know that for many students, especially those who are early or late to develop by normative standards, these noticeable changes are less than welcome and sometimes painful. The individual differences in physical growth and change that one can observe among middle school students can be a source of anxiety. Feeling out of sync with peers can be a significant challenge to the preadolescent's developing self-concept. Students may be worried about these changes and how they are looked at by others, especially as it is so important for most students to fit in to their peer group. Some students may experience substantial drops in self-esteem as a result of these things.

The Counselor's Response

Middle school counselors understand that these changes happen with significant variance, variance that is typical. With their understanding of normative development and its variation, especially during these early years, middle school counselors can provide support and psychoeducational programs that can help students understand and feel more comfortable with individual differences and thus reduce student anxiety.

Changes in Cognitive Abilities

Middle school students are experiencing significant changes both in the structure of their brains and the nature of the way they think and process information. While they are beginning to think in terms of higher order, abstract, and if/then thinking, they often do not have the capacity to test the validity of their thinking or weigh the risk and benefits of their ideas and the decisions that may result.

Middle school counselors are familiar with increased anxiety experienced by their students, an anxiety that often stems from their faulty thinking. The middle school student is one who can genuinely be catastrophic in the way they interpret life challenges. Ask any middle school counselor about the "drama" their students present daily, and you will get numerous illustrations of students taking a social conflict or rejection as the ultimate proof of their lack of value and the reality that they will never have friends. The feelings that result from this distorted thinking is real and sad. The experience and the faulty conclusions are the natural consequences of the yet-fully developed brain and the yet-to-be mastered abstract thinking.

The Counselor's Response

Middle school counselors are all too familiar with the negative thinking patterns of middle school students and the resulting disruption to their emotional well-being. These negative, distorted thoughts can become intrusive and take a toll on a student's mood, attention to tasks, working memory, and academic performance (Putwain et al., 2010; Vytal et al., 2012).

With direct one-to-one or small group counseling, the middle school counselor employs their knowledge and skills to provide the empathic support needed as well as the therapeutic confrontation and psycho-education required for healthy development. Their training in intervention strategies, such as a cognitive behavioral approach, proves invaluable at times of such student distress.

In addition to providing individual and small-group intervention, middle school counselors often employ schoolwide psychoeducational programs to help students understand their emotional reactions and develop strategies for emotional self-regulation. One type of schoolwide program that has been used is the Rational Emotive Education (REE) curriculum (Bernard, 2005) that teaches rational critical thinking skills and effective psychological problem-solving methods.

One of the saddest consequences of a student's distorted thinking is the creation of suicidal ideation. It is during this period and the period of adolescence that suicide becomes a significant health problem. The suicide rate for persons aged 10–14 nearly tripled from 2007 to 2017 (Curtin & Heron, 2019).

Not only do middle school counselors provide the support and referral necessary for students who struggle with such thoughts of self-harm, but they also play a role in engaging teachers and parents in preventive efforts. Middle school counselors provide consultation to parents and teachers, assisting in developing the knowledge and skill necessary for identifying children at risk and intervening as needed and appropriate.

Changes in Social Relationships

Transitioning from the social setting of elementary school into a social environment composed of many from other elementary schools and with new norms of social engagement makes navigating peer relationships a challenge for many in middle school. One specific area of concern for school counselors is the presence of bullying and peer violence.

Fighting increases during the middle school years, and more students are bullied in middle school than in either elementary or high school (Juvonen et al., 2004). A National Institute of Child Health and Human Development study found that bullying in schools occurred most frequently in Grades 6 through 8 (Nansel et al., 2001).

The Counselor's Response

While middle school counselors provide one-to-one counseling to those targeted by bullying as well as to those who bully, they also engage in schoolwide programming that targets the creation of safer school environments. Middle school counselors are central to not only raising the awareness of the school community to the existence of bullying and its devastating impact on those bullied, but are also key to the development and implementation of a schoolwide, comprehensive approach to the reduction of bullying. Many schools, with the leadership of the middle school counselor, have instituted whole school programs (see Table 13.1).

Table 13.1 Schoolwide Antibullying Programs

Cyber Bullying: A Prevention Curriculum for Grades 6-12. https://www.violencepreventionworks.org/public/document/cyber_bullying_6-12_scope.pdf	Cyber Bullying: A Prevention Curriculum for Grades 6-12 is a program that addresses attitudes and behaviors associated with cyberbullying. It consists of an eight-session curriculum.
"Don't Laugh at Me": Operation Respect. http://www.operationrespect.org	Don't Laugh at Me is a program designed for use with elementary and middle school youth to help address bullying, ridiculing, teasing, and harassing in today's schools.

(Continued)

Table 13.1 (*Continued*)

Olweus Bullying Prevention Program. http://www.clemson.edu/olweus/ http://www.violencepreventionworks.org/public/index.page	The Olweus Bullying Prevention Program (OBPP) is designed for students in elementary, middle, and junior high schools (students ages 5–15 years old). The program has been recognized by the U.S. Departments of Justice and Education as an effective program.
The Bully Free program. http://bully-free.com	The Bully Free program is a comprehensive schoolwide (and system-wide) antibullying program. The program also includes parent involvement, community involvement, and all the elements and components that must be present in effective antibullying programs.

Changing Self-Concept and Identity Formation

Perhaps the most significant area of change experienced during this development period is in the area of the development of self-concept and identity formation. This changing sense of self is impacted by a variety of interactive experiences, including school achievement, social relations with others, and development of career interests and choices, along with a great deal of exploration of different activities and roles. In addition to developing a sense of self, the middle school student will also attempt to find value in that sense of identity. Given the increasing role and force of peers during the middle school years, and their potential to impact another's sense and valuing of self, school counselors often turn their attention to programs that facilitate respectful, empathic interaction between students.

The Counselor's Response

It appears that this sense of value, this area of self-esteem, is particularly vulnerable during the middle school years, especially in the transition from elementary school (Eccles, 2004). Middle school counselors understand both the importance of this stage of identity formation as well as the fact that a student's sense of self and self-worth can be fragile. Some students may experience disruptive feelings of self-doubt and require individual and small-group support.

The middle school counselor understands that all students navigating this developmental period could benefit from programs that increase their sense of self-efficacy in the academic and social realms. Teaching students how to set small, reasonable goals; monitoring their progress; and celebrating their successes are but some of the skills taught by middle school counselor. Other programs such as On My Own Two Feet have been employed by middle school counselors in collaboration with the classroom teacher.

Changes in Academics and Achievement Motivation

The significant changes noted in the development of the middle school student come together to impact their engagement with their academics and their motivation to achieve. Research has indicated that intrinsic motivation to learn appears to decline during this period, and for many students their perception of their academic competence also declines (Wigfield et al., 2015). These data point to the fact that an essential target for middle school counseling programming is in the identification of students most at risk of becoming academically demotivated and working with family and teachers to intervene.

The Counselor's Response

A primary focus for a middle school counseling program is the development of students' interests, motivations, and skills necessary to succeed academically. To this end, middle school counselors provide individual, group, and classroom programs that help students identify specific interests to further their course selection and recognize their assets, as well as develop skills essential for managing and successfully addressing school demands. For example, middle school counselors provide group counseling sessions and classroom guidance lessons that include goal setting, organization, and time management, as well as career awareness. These, along with the development of personal qualities such as self-efficacy, persistence, and resiliency, have been shown to correlate with academic achievement positively (Polirstok, 2017).

Connecting With Families

While family engagement in the educational process of their children is always a needed and valued resource, research suggests it is especially important during middle school. Research highlights the value of family involvement in student achievement in school (Wood & Bauman, 2017).

The Counselor's Response

Middle school counselors are aware of the essential role families play in the development and education of the early adolescent. It is also a time when many parents may not feel they need to be as involved in their child's education. As such, middle school counselors assume the role of leader and coordinator in helping parents understand the importance of the school–family connection and developing that connection. The desire to increase family involvement reflects the values and position of the ASCA, as reflected in the ASCA (2019) national model. Middle school counselors engage in practices ranging from the creation of newsletters and blogs for information dissemination to the offering of parent orientation and information sessions and the development of advisory boards with parent representation. Each of these activities has as their goal the strengthening of the family–school bond.

MIDDLE SCHOOL COUNSELORS: MUCH TO DO

Middle school is a critical time in the development of our youth. There are numerous challenges to this development, and the school counselor plays a vital role in facilitating the academic success and psychosocial development of the middle school student. Through the provision of individual and group counseling, classroom instruction, and the coordination and collaboration with key players in the development and implementation of schoolwide prevention programming, middle school counselors attempt to remove barriers to the healthy development of their students. The extent of the services provided can be seen in one illustration of a middle school counselor's annual counselor (see Figure 13.1).

Figure 13.1 Sampling of middle school counselor's monthly planner

School: ____________________

School Year: ____________________

	INDIVIDUAL STUDENT PLANNING	**SCHOOL COUNSELING CURRICULUM**	**RESPONSIVE SERVICES *(PLANNED FOR EACH MONTH)***	**PROGRAM MANAGEMENT AND SYSTEM SUPPORT**
August	Awareness of academic and career training opportunities (e.g. academic and career magnet, accelerated courses and programs, tutorial and remedial programs) Academic course planning Interpretation of academic, career, and social-emotional assessment scores Participation in the development/monitoring of academic and behavior intervention plans (e.g. daily progress monitoring sheets, IEPs) Participation in the development of academic and behavior accommodation plans (e.g. Section 504 Plans, IEPs)	New Student Orientation Sixth grade Transition Camp Check-in with new students	Individual short-term counseling and support Small-group counseling Consultation Prevention services Crisis counseling and management Referral to school- and community-based services Referral to adult and peer helpers Dissemination of information	School counseling program needs assessment Student Services Team/ Advisory Development and distribution of school counseling program master calendar Administrator-Counselor School Counseling Program Collaborative Partnership Agreement Registration Council meeting (data review and program planning) Section 504 Student Lists

October	Academic course planning Interpretation of academic, career, and social-emotional assessment scores Participation in the development/monitoring of academic and behavior intervention plans (e.g. daily progress monitoring sheets, IEPs) Participation in the development of academic and behavior accommodation plans (e.g. Section 504 Plans, IEPs)	Bullying Prevention (e.g. Second Step, Olweus, Bully Busters) Sixth grade mindfulness lessons	See the list of responsive services above	Teaming for student success (e.g. MTSS/RTI/ IEP Section 504, grade level/ department meetings, district/community meetings) Academic and behavior support programs (e.g. tutoring, mentoring, peer counseling, college outreach) Coordinating school support programs/ services (registration and scheduling, testing and assessment) Professional development training (e.g. district school counselor meetings) School counseling program needs assessment
March	Awareness of academic and career training opportunities (e.g. academic and career magnet, accelerated courses and programs, tutorial and remedial programs) Academic course planning Interpretation of academic, career and social-emotional assessment scores Participation in the development/monitoring of academic and behavior intervention plans (e.g. daily progress monitoring sheets, IEPs) Participation in the development of academic and behavior accommodation plans (e.g. Section 504 Plans, IEPs) Career Academy Forum – Grade 8	Seventh grade - Human Growth and Development lessons Eighth grade – career awareness module	See the list of responsive services above	Teaming for student success (e.g. MTSS/RTI/ IEP, Section 504, grade level/ department meetings, district/community meetings) Academic and behavior support programs (e.g. tutoring, mentoring, peer counseling, college outreach) Coordinating school support programs/ services (registration and scheduling, testing and assessment) School counseling program needs assessment High school course registration – Grade 8 Academic and Career Academy Open House programs

(Continued)

May	Awareness of academic and career training opportunities (e.g. academic and career magnet, accelerated courses and programs, tutorial and remedial programs) Academic course planning Participation in the development/monitoring of academic and behavior intervention plans Participation in the development of academic and behavior accommodation plans for current and transitioning students (incoming sixth grade students, exiting eighth grade students) Interpretation of academic, career and social-emotional assessment scores	Eighth grade - Four-Year High School Plan	See the list of responsive services above	Teaming for student success (e.g. MTSS/RTI/ IEP, Section 504, grade level/department meetings, district/community meetings) Academic and behavior support programs (e.g. tutoring, mentoring, peer counseling, college outreach) Coordinating school support programs/services (registration and scheduling, testing and assessment) School counseling program needs assessment School Open House Assessments Career Day meeting (data review, program audit, results report, program, planning)

The activities listed in Figure 13.1 reflect a sampling of those that were "planned." Life as a middle school counselor *rarely* goes according to plans. There are daily crises and emergencies that will require counselor attention, and there are needs that will emerge that were unanticipated. The message to be received is that serving as a middle school counselor requires flexibility, adaptability, and resiliency. Exercise 13.1 invites you to interview, and, if possible, shadow a middle school counselor to gain a better and more realistic view of what it is like to be a middle school counselor.

Exercise 13.1: Not Always as Smooth as Planned

Directions: While middle school counselors are great at planning, they are also aware that what is planned does not always go off without a hitch. Interview three middle school counselors and ask them respond to the following. If possible, ask to shadow one or more of your interviewees during the school day.

1. Do you typically prepare an annual calendar and/or a monthly listing of the activities you hope to initiate?
2. Do you have some form of schedule or plan for each day?

3. What are the typical "unplanned" requests for your service or demands on your time that you encounter in any one day?
4. What has been the most disruptive event or situation to your typical planning that you have encountered over your career?
5. Given your experience with planning, what is your suggestion to a counselor just starting their career?

LIFE AS A MIDDLE SCHOOL COUNSELOR (VOICES FROM THOSE WHO SERVE)

Sharing the "lived" experiences of the middle school counselor through the voices of those who serve each day may bring the value and awesomeness of the vocation they have chosen. Some days are heartwarming and some are exhausting, but all are important in the lives of our students. It is highly suggested that you visit a middle school and talk with a school counselor about the gifts and challenges of being a middle school counselor.

Making Connections (na 'Khia W., Sixth Grade School Counselor)

Every year the first week of school finds the sixth graders trying to find their way around their new school and hurriedly working their new combination locks. They smile as I walk among them in the hallways as the connections have started to develop through our transition visits and orientation camp. They look so young but feel so much. They want to make it work on their own, show how mature they are, yet many need a good deal of support.

I make it a point to meet with each of my sixth grade students at the beginning of the school year to make sure they know I'm there to help with whatever is needed. Being able to remain their counselor for the three years they are here really seems to help. By the time I send them off to the high school I know them well and they know school counselors are there to help with any problems with friends, family, teachers, and their own personal journey. Some of my favorite moments are hearing my students at their eighth grade graduation event talk about how intimidated they were to start middle school and how ready they are to start high school because they learned so much about themselves and are looking forward to new challenges.

The Drama (Jordan P., Middle School Counselor)

Middle school dances may seem like a good opportunity for students to socially interact during a supervised event, but I have never seen so much drama when it comes to who is going to the dance with who and the apparent planning and scheming that is involved when considering if they should drink alcohol beforehand. There was one dance at which

I was chaperoning that we had to call an ambulance to take a student to have his stomach pumped from alcohol poisoning. I love working with middle school students, but their inability to problem -solve and make good decisions often causes dire consequences. It means I need to work harder to keep them from hurting themselves and others. Middle school students need more understanding, patience, and structure than students at any other developmental level. They may be exhausting at times, but they are worth it!

Growing Into Leaders (Jen T., Middle School Counselor, Student Council Advisor)

As the faculty advisor for the student council, I marvel at the way our students can grow into leadership roles. I am particularly pleased when after having worked with students who were using their social power for their own personal needs and satisfaction they have learned that using that power in a leadership role can help make positive changes in the system.

Vanessa had been one of the most popular students in her class for several years. The problem was that popularity stemmed from the control and power she gained by acts of relational aggression toward other girls who didn't have much, if any, social support. Working individually with Vanessa and helping her realize how her skills as a leader could be detrimental as she had been using them, and how those skills could make a positive difference, was rewarding for many, as Vanessa worked on student council and advocated for after -school clubs so that every student had the opportunity to be socially connected.

A TAKE-AWAY

Since middle school is truly a period marked by and as transition, the programs and services offered by middle counselors are geared to facilitating these transitions, reducing the stress of change, and facilitating the students' development of resiliency. One of the most crucial goals for middle school counselors is to provide a blend of challenge and support that promotes autonomy, decision-making skills, academic salience, and identity development among early adolescents. The middle school counselor is invested in creating a school environment where each student can find confidence in themselves and believe in their competence as learners.

KEYSTONES

- Students in middle school, as early adolescents, are entering a developmental period of rapid and dramatic change.
- Middle school counselors provide services targeted to the many changes occurring during this developmental period.

- Individual difference in rate and timing of the various changes is a key characteristic of this change and can be a major source of anxiety, especially for the students who develop earlier and later than their peers.
- While developing higher order, abstract, and if/then thinking, middle school students often do not have the capacity to test the validity of their thinking or weigh the risk and benefits of their ideas and the decisions that may result.
- The drama experienced by the middle school student and their emotional lability can be a reflection of their often irrational and distorted ways of processing data.
- Social inclusion becomes both a major task and concern for middle school students as they move from adult dependence to peer interdependence.
- Perhaps the most significant area of change experienced during this development period is in the area of the development of self-concept and identity formation; finding their own unique set of competencies and interests is key to middle school years.
- Family engagement in the educational process of their children is always a needed and valued resource, but research suggests it is especially important during middle school.

ADDITIONAL RESOURCES

Print

Cushman, K., & Rogers, L. (2009). *Fire in the middle school bathroom: Advice for teachers from middle schoolers*. New Press.

Handrich, T., & Schroeder, D. (2010). *The ultimate middle school counseling handbook*. Research Press.

Phifer, L., Crowder, A., Elsenraat, T., & Hull, T. (2017). *CBT toolbox for children and adolescents*. PESI.

Web

Character.Org provides resources/lessons for developing character: https://www.character.org/character-building-practices/

The Character Development and Leadership Curriculum: https://www.characterandleadership.com/curriculum-overview/

Loveisrespect.org provides a tool kit for helping students develop healthy relationships: http://www.loveisrespect.org/wp-content/uploads/2016/08/middle-school-educators-toolkit.pdf

Collaborative Career Development Resources: https://www.uft.org/files/attachments/guidance-collaborative-career-development.pdf

REFERENCES

American School Counselor Association. (2019). *The ASCA national model: A framework for school counseling programs* (4th ed.). Author.

Bernard, M. E. (2005). *Program achieve: A curriculum of lessons for teaching students to achieve and develop social-emotional-behavioral well being,* Vols. 1–6. (3rd ed.). Australian Scholarships Group.

Curtin, S. C. & Heron, M. (2019). *Death rates due to suicide and homicide among persons aged 10-24: United States, 2000–2017.* https://www.cdc.gov/nchs/data/databriefs/db352-h.pdf

Eccles, J. S. (2004). Schools, academic motivation, and stage-environment fit. In R. M. Lerner & L. D. Steinberg (Eds.), *Handbook of adolescent psychology* (2nd ed.) (pp. 125–153). Wiley.

Nansel, T. R., Overpeck, M., Pilla, R. S., Ruan, W. J., Simons-Morton, B., & Scheidt, P. (2001). Bullying behavior among U.S. youth: Prevalence and association with psychosocial adjustment. *Journal of the American Medical Association, 285*(16), 2094–2100.

Polirstok, S. (2017). Strategies to improve academic achievement in secondary school students: Perspectives on grit and mindset. *SAGE Open, 7*(4). https://journals.sagepub.com/doi/full/10.1177/2158244017745111

Putwain, D. W., Connors, L., & Symes, W. (2010). Do cognitive distortions mediate the test anxiety-examination performance relationship? *Educational Psychology, 30*(1), 11–26.

Vytal, K., Cornwell, B., Arkin, N., & Grillon, C. (2012). Describing the interplay between anxiety and cognition: From impaired performance under low cognitive load to reduced anxiety under high load. *Psychophysiology, 49*(6), 842–852.

Wood, L., & Bauman, E. (2017). *How family, school, and community engagement can improve student achievement and influence school reform.* Nellie Mae Education Foundation. https://www.nmefoundation.org/wp-content/uploads/2020/05/Final-Report-Family-Engagement-AIR.pdf

Wigfield, A., Eccles, J. S., Fredricks, J., Simpkins, Roeser, U., & Schiefele, S., Simpkins-Chaput, S. (2015). Development of achievement motivation, and engagement. In R. Lerner, M. Lamb, & C. Garcia Coll (Eds.), *Handbook of child psychology and developmental science,* Vol. 3 (7th ed.) (pp. 657–700). Wiley. https://doi.org/10.1002/9781118963418

CHAPTER 14

HIGH SCHOOL COUNSELOR

Assisting Students in Transition to Adulthood

Every day is an adventure.

—Michael, High school counselor

The phrase "every day is an adventure" could apply to the experience of all school counselors regardless of the age of the students they serve. For the high school counselor, the phrase has a particular meaning in that the high school student is in the process of engaging in an adventure into adulthood.

High school students are experiencing significant changes in their sense of identity, their need for autonomy, and their articulation of a future, one that will allow them to make an impact. The tasks confronted by the high school student have no one clear resolution, and that fluidity can create excessive stress on the student and the need for counselor support.

The current chapter reviews academic, social, emotional, and career challenges faced by those in high school and the way school counselors can facilitate healthy development and academic success. After completing this chapter, readers will be able to do the following:

1. Describe the developmental tasks that confront high school students as they transition out of the K–12 school system into adulthood.
2. Identify primary targets for high school counselor services.
3. Describe the unique challenges to the high school student's identification and planning of a post-high school career/vocational path.

NORMATIVE DEVELOPMENTAL CHALLENGES

The developmental changes that presented in middle school continue through a student's high school years. The high school student is on the fast track toward biological, psychological, and social maturity. They have not, however, arrived.

Students in high school are experiencing challenges as they attempt to come to a fuller understanding and acceptance of their changing bodies, learning how to respond in a healthy, responsible way to their emerging sexuality and refining their ability to engage in formal, abstract thinking. The high school years are also those that invite the adolescent to navigate the unique social challenges encountered as they move from dependency to autonomy and independence. It is a time when the demands of adulthood (e.g. economic independence) become apparent, even though the ability to address those demands is still in formation. The psycho-social and academic tasks to be accomplished during high school are significant, and many high school students, while feeling they can go it alone, need and benefit from the comprehensive counseling services developed and implemented by the school counselor.

THE UNIQUENESS OF "ME"

The changes encountered can and often do shake the adolescent's sense of identity. As a result, if one theme or core issue were to be identified as that which calls for adolescents' full attention it would be the establishment of a stable identity, one that will carry them into productive adult lives.

The question of self-identity and the recognition of their uniqueness is central to the high school student's transition into adulthood. The growth experienced during the middle and late adolescent period of development is centered on the development of social autonomy, development of vocational directions, and clarification of personal values, beliefs, and interests.

Adolescents are acutely aware that they are more than a mere extension of their parents. They are awakening to the reality of their uniqueness and separation from parents. This awareness, while certainly empowering, can be quite unsettling in the early stages, and for some a source of anxiety.

Throughout their high school experience, students will redefine their sources of personal strength and move toward self-reliance. This process of further developing their personal sense of identity positions them to establish emotional and psychological independence from their parents. High school students begin to find a sense of interdependence with those within their lives, redefining their relationships with parents, peers, and members of the community at large. The timing and form of this transition will be affected by the student's social/cultural context and expectations. The impact of this redefinition of relationships can range from pleasant and productive to quite confusing and even conflictual.

Casting off the cloak of childhood and the level of dependency implied, the high school student is both excited and anxious about their movement toward independence. It is a process that is not without its challenges.

The unfolding of the high school student's independence can stimulate conflict with adults in their lives (e.g. teachers, parents, counselors). Conflicts between parents and teens during this time of development often are the result of the high school student's attempts to develop a personal ideology.

Middle and later adolescence is a time when the student begins to assess and perhaps question parental values, and often values held within their culture or by society at large. This questioning, while a necessary step to their development and ownership of their values, can place the high school student in conflict with peers, family members, and other segments of society. Assisting the adolescent with the resolution of the intra- and interpersonal conflicts caused by this search for identity and meaning become a significant focus for the high school counselor's direct service.

The changes and transitions experienced by the high school student do not occur in a bubble. These changes are disruptive to the students themselves as well as others who function within their system. As such, the high school counselor plays a vital role in assisting parents (and teachers) with an understanding of the nature of adolescent development, as well as the development of strategies they can employ to support the adolescent in their growth. This service of the high school counselor can become a primary focus for many of the indirect services (e.g. in-service, newsletters, conferences) that they provide.

ROLE AND FUNCTION OF THE HIGH SCHOOL COUNSELOR

High school counselors are an integral part of the school system and the entire educational process. While it is obvious that the high school counselor is there to provide for the academic, psychosocial, emotional, and vocational needs of the students, they are also leaders engaging all of the stakeholders in the delivery of programs and services that are "comprehensive in scope, preventive in design and developmental in nature" (ASCA, 2019, p. 64).

Academics

The primary responsibility for high school counselors is to help students in their journey toward academic success. While academic achievement is a concern for all counselors, including those working at the elementary and middle school levels, counselors working with high school students place greater emphasis on facilitating students' self-direction and increased responsibility for their academic success.

High school counselors will assist students with the scheduling process, ensuring that students are selecting courses that are challenging and are those that will prepare them for achieving their post-high school goals. Planning the educational path to follow may start before the student's entry into high school and will become a focus of the high school counselor. High school counselors serve as an information source for students and their parents, helping them to understand the scope and sequence of the curriculum and the opportunities for course selections and specific career-focused experiences that will be available to students throughout their high school career. The counselor will continue to support the students' course selection choices, as well as provide individual and family conferences and information sessions as a way of eliciting family support.

Many high school counselors employ programs such as the four-year course planner in Naviance to assist students in developing, assessing, and modifying their educational and vocational plans throughout the high school experience.

Psychosocial Development

High school students often need direct one-on-one services and small-group counseling as they attempt to cope with stress, anxiety, and interpersonal conflicts. As is true for students in the lower grades, high school students turn to their counselor for assistance in adjusting to normative developmental challenges. It is not unusual to find a student dropping into the counselor's office upset about the ending of a special friendship, or an argument with parents over an issue of curfew, or a moment of anxiety thinking about their uncertain future. The upset, the stress, or distress experienced as a result of these events are real and, as most counselors understand, are part of the typical development terrain navigated by a high school student.

In addition to such normative challenges, today's students are being confronted by threats to their well-being not previously known or experienced by generations past. Today's students are faced with widespread community violence and trauma. Today's students have their self-concepts, their self-esteem under attack, often 24/7, through the various means of social media contact. The barrage of cyberbullying, for example, has been shown to not only increase feelings of victimization but can result in a sense of hopelessness, despair, and suicidal ideation and behavior. Mix in the epidemic of prescription and nonprescription drug abuse, and it is easy to see that the psychosocial health of our teens is under attack.

The high school counselor is invaluable in offering direct support in the form of one-to-one and small-group counseling for students whose ability to succeed academically is being thwarted by these threats to their socioemotional well-being. Additionally, given the widespread nature of these threats, today's high school counselors are providing wellness-based education and preventive programming to facilitate student development of the knowledge and skills necessary for all their students to address these threats.

Post-High School Planning

Children, almost at any age, are often asked the question, "What do you want to be when you grow up?" While such a question, in one form or another, may be posed to the preschool child or the elementary and middle school student, it takes on exceptional importance when asked of the high school student. This question has special meaning to those transitioning from high school into the roles and responsibilities of adulthood.

The high school student is challenged with identifying a career path, at least at a preliminary level. The answer to this question will reflect their vocational goals and post-high school direction. The task of selecting a vocational pathway is certainly not new to transitioning from high school to adult life. The question of the desired career path, which has been posed to generations past, is not as easily addressed or resolved for students of the 21st century. Jobs, careers, vocations that existed when students, currently in high school, started middle school may no longer be a viable option. Technology and mechanization have replaced many in the workforce and closed off specific career paths. Similarly, careers that were not even on the radar or only faintly hinted at when students began high school may be, by the end of their four years, the careers of the future. Times are changing and changing rapidly.

High school counselors are a vital contributor to student understanding and planning for the post-high school educational experience. Counselors provide their students with information regarding admission requirements for colleges and training programs and guide them in their use of this information in their own high school course selections. This part of a comprehensive counseling program appears especially valuable for under-resourced or first-generation college goers.

Assisting the high school student with vocational direction becomes central to a comprehensive counseling program in high schools. High school counselors are knowledgeable about paths toward careers and advise students regarding their education options during and after high school. In addition to providing data on the state of today's careers, high school counselors in the 21st century also assist students with developing the resiliency and adaptability that will be required for successfully navigating their career pathways over their employment years.

Table 14.1 presents a number of the typical duties enacted by the high school counselor in the service of assisting students in the envisioning and planning for their post-high school journey.

Table 14.1 Assisting Students With Future Plans

Counselors engage in the following in their efforts to support students with envisioning and planning for a post–high school future:

- Disseminate information on financial aid
- Provide scholarship information
- Supply school-to-career guidance
- Provide vocational interest and aptitude measures
- Interpret standardized test scores
- Provide information on college admission test preparation as well as offer supportive programs
- Link students to career mentors
- Coordinate parent conferences
- Facilitate college applications
- Complete letters of recommendations
- Provide student resources
- Maintain and collate records

(*Continued*)

Table 14.1 (*Continued*)

- Review course selections to align with future plans
- Provide teachers and parents information to support students' career exploration and post-secondary educational opportunities
- Plan and execute career days
- Serve as liaison with community resources–connecting internship experience, mentoring opportunities, and job tracking experiences.

PLANNED AND UNPLANNED

The varied roles and functions of a high school counselor are extensive. Table 14.2 provides a brief look at the types of planned activities included in one high school counselor's annual calendar. The listing fails to reflect all the additional roles and services offered by the high school counselor, such as providing individual and group counseling. This planned calendar does not reflect the interruptions, the unplanned emergencies and crises that present. Additionally, there is no room on the calendar that gives space to the numerous class conferences, college application duties, letters of recommendation, and responses to the needs of teachers and parents.

Table 14.2 Sampling of High School Counselor's Planned Activities

MONTH	ACTIVITIES PLANNED
August	• Schedule changes • Register new students • Foreign exchange registration • Update all 504 plans • Set up Rotary/Kiwanis visitation schedule • National Merit Scholarship coordination • School Is Cool supplies coordination • Back-to-School night • Update counseling website links
October	• Senior conferences • Curriculum guide preparation/departments • PSA-test administration • Out-of-state college fair • International baccalaureate (IB) classroom guidance, 11th grade college prep/ Naviance • Classroom guidance for 9–11th (transition, career/college prep) • Family Financial Aid Night • Letters of recommendations/college applications • Career planning/state requirements • Senior applications/ELA • Parent–teacher conferences

	• Suicide awareness presentation • Peace circles • ELA monitoring • D/F List: First-quarter grade monitoring • AVID class presentations: Naviance • STAT team
January	• Complete and finalize all registration material • Registration meeting with department • Begin registration process at middle and senior high school • Mid-year reports • Update IB registration forms and materials • ELA presentations • College applications • AP reminders • Community college field trip as part of the partnership program • Community project • Junior conferences
February	• Begin graduation march plans • Continue registration process (presentations and collection) • IB registration (ninth grade) • Classroom guidance (10th-grade college planning) • Gather freshman Academy nominations • IB parent night and registration process • Upcoming ninth-grade Parent Information Night • AP sign-up • Community project • Junior conferences
May	• Refine March order (with changes) • Graduation practice setup • Graduation and Convocation day setup • IEP and 504 transition meetings for eighth graders moving into high school • Cinco De Mayo: Celebrate culture and diversity • Scholarship breakfast celebration • 504 coordination with junior high • Naviance student survey (9th–12th) • Master schedule conflicts resolution (each counselor's caseload) • Class schedule for caseloads • End-of-year check-out for all grade levels • Schedule changes (for the upcoming year) • Graduation issues: Naviance • Community project report due: School board • AP testing • Convocation, graduation • Final transcript to colleges for seniors • Final transcript to NCAA clearinghouse for all college-bound athletes

Adapted from: Poudre school district, Colorado: https://phs.psdschools.org/node/3243

Listing only those services that are planned supports both the need and value of today's high school counselor. However, this is but the tip of the iceberg. That which is planned is only the surface of that which is performed, only a small part of the life of a school counselor. Exercise 14.1 invites you to reach out to a high school counselor and get a firsthand report of life as a high school counselor.

Exercise 14.1: Life as a High School Counselor

Directions: High school counselors have an array of responsibilities and duties that vary depending on the time of the school year. Interview one or more high school counselors and ask the following questions:

1. What do you like most about your position?
2. What is the most challenging part of your position, and what kind of changes would you need to make it less challenging?
3. Do your tasks differ over the school year? If so, how is the majority of your time spent in the fall months compared to the spring months?
4. What is your role with the faculty and staff?
5. What would be important to learn and experience as a high school counseling intern?
6. What would be helpful for a new high school counselor to know?

LIFE AS A HIGH SCHOOL COUNSELOR (VOICES FROM THOSE WHO SERVE)

The daily lives of high school counselors vary greatly, as in the case of all counselors. By sharing a few of the voices of high school counselors, we hope you can get a feel for the gifts and challenges that make their days at times fulfilling, exhausting, and of great value and meaning to our students.

Expanding Perspectives (Manny I., High School Counselor)

I could tell Maria was not happy with the course selection her parents had encouraged her to follow. It was a typical plan for students who would be working right out of high school, and Maria's family expected her to help with the family business. When I asked Maria to tell me about her goals she immediately said she would be working with her parents because that's the way it is. Speaking with her a bit longer, Maria expressed her desire for a different career path that would include education after high school, but there was no way to finance any further schooling, so she had never mentioned anything to her parents.

Fortunately, as a ninth-grade student there was time to change her course plan so that she had the classes needed to pursue her passion to help others as a nurse. However, the family needed a better understanding of Maria's passion and the different financial options for Maria to attend a nursing program. It was a successful meeting with Maria and her parents as we developed a plan for Maria to move forward with her goal, which included a change in course plans and applying for scholarships and financial aid when it was time to apply for a nursing program.

Healthy Options (Ebonnie V., High School Counselor)

Helping my students make good choices when their brains aren't fully developed is a top priority for me. With most of them driving and some experimenting with alcohol and drugs, we've set up assemblies and workshops promoting safety and are instituting mindfulness exercises during homeroom everyday as a positive coping strategy. These students are precious and their lives are just beginning—we want to support healthy development every way we can in the school environment. They think they are so grown up, but they have so much to learn!

An Ending and a Beginning (Clif B., High School Counselor)

Well, the challenges of the high school student and counselor are many, with the drama, academic pressure, postsecondary choices, identity development, healthy and unhealthy relationships—but there are wonderful aspects to being a high school counselor. To me, the greatest gift is watching each student, each with their own trials and triumphs, walk across the platform to receive their diploma. They have completed 12 or more years of school and marked a milestone in their lives as they approach the platform, while beginning a new part of their journey as they come off the platform. It's just awesome to experience that moment and know that in some small way, I may have helped to positively support that journey!

A TAKE-AWAY

High school students continue to experience development within the academic, socio-emotional, and career domains. This development is impacted by many facets, including pressures and expectations of the student, of family, and of society as the student moves to transition out of the K–12 school system. High school counselors are invaluable with supporting these students as they journey toward greater independence.

KEYSTONES

- High school students experience significant changes in their sense of identity, their need for autonomy, and their articulation of a future after high school.

- High school students begin to find a sense of interdependence with those within their lives, redefining their relationships with parents, peers, and members of the community at large.
- Adolescents are acutely aware that they are more than a mere extension of their parents. This awareness, while certainly empowering, can be quite unsettling is in the early stages, and for some a source of anxiety.
- High school counselors serve as an information source for students and their parents, helping them to understand the scope and sequence of the curriculum and the opportunities for course selections and specific career-focused experiences.
- High school students often need direct, one-on-one services and small-group counseling as they attempt to cope with stress, anxiety, and interpersonal conflicts.
- Today's students have their self-concepts, their self-esteem, under attack, often 24/7, through the various means of social media contact.
- The high school student is challenged with identifying a career path that will reflect their vocational goals and post-high school direction.
- Assisting the high school student with vocational direction becomes central to a high school counselor's comprehensive counseling program.

ADDITIONAL RESOURCES

Print

Hatch, T. (2019). *Hatching results for secondary school counseling.* Corwin.

Jensen, F. E., & Nutt, A. E. (2015). *The teenage brain.* New York, NY: HarperCollins.

Schab, L. M. (2008). *The Anxiety Workbook for Teens.* Instant Help Books.

Web

The Carl D. Perkins Vocational and Technical Education Act of 1998 permits funds to be used for career guidance and academic counseling for students participating in vocational education programs: https://www2.ed.gov/offices/OVAE/CTE/legis.html

The Education World Counseling Center is an online resource area for school counselors and covers academic development, career and college development, personal and social development, assessment, and counseling techniques: https://www.educationworld.com

REFERENCES

American School Counselor Association. (2019). *The ASCA national model: A framework for school counseling programs* (4th ed). Author.

Index

About the Authors

Richard D. Parsons, Ph.D. is a full professor in the Counselor Education Department at West Chester University. He has over 40 years of university teaching experience in counselor preparation programs. Before his university teaching, Dr. Parsons spent nine years as a school counselor in an inner-city high school. He has had a private clinical practice for over 40 years and serves as a consultant to educational institutions and mental health service organizations throughout the tri-state area of Pennsylvania, New Jersey and Delaware. He has been the recipient of many awards and honors, including the Pennsylvania Counselor of the Year Award.

Dr. Parsons has authored or co-authored over 80 professional articles and books. His most recent books include the co-authored texts *Counselor Wellness: Caring for Self to Care for Others* (Cognella Academic Publishing); *The School Counselor as Consultant: Expanding Impact from Intervention to Prevention* (Cognella Academic Publishing); *Intentional Counseling* (SAGE); and *Ethical Practices in the Human Services* (SAGE). Dr. Parsons also serves as coeditor for a 24-book series, *Counseling and Professional Identity*, published by SAGE Publications and as editor of a 10-book series entitled *The Cognella Series on Student Success*, published by Cognella Academic Publishing.

Karen L. Dickinson, Ph.D. is an associate professor in the Department of Counselor Education at West Chester University. She also serves as the graduate coordinator and assistant chairperson of the Department, having served as the school counseling program coordinator for several years. Dr. Dickinson has over 10 years of experience teaching at the university level in counseling preparation programs and spent over three decades in the K-12 educational system supporting students as a general education teacher, a special education teacher, and a school counselor.

Dr. Dickinson is the coauthor of *Counselor Wellness: Caring for Self to Care for Others* (Cognella Academic Publishing); *School Counselor as Consultant: Expanding Impact from Intervention to Prevention* (Cognella Academic Publishing); *A Student's Guide to Stress Management* (Cognella Academic Publishing), and *Ethical Practice: Beyond Knowing Ethics to Being Ethical* (SAGE). She is a contributing author for *Working with Students with Disabilities*, a text for school counselors, and ancillary author for *Field Experience: Transitioning from Student to Professional*, both for SAGE Publications. She has presented nationally and internationally on the topic of bullying and students with disabilities. Her other presentations and research focus on the school counselor as advocate and leader, and training the 21st-century school counselor to support diverse student populations.

CPSIA information can be obtained
at www.ICGtesting.com
Printed in the USA
LVHW062020280822
727000LV00008B/514